The Pleasure of Influence

The Pleasure of Influence

Conversations with
American Male Fiction Writers

Rob Trucks

NotaBell Books
An Imprint of Purdue University Press
West Lafayette, Indiana

Printed in the United States of America

Library of Congress Cataloging-in-Publication Data

Trucks, Rob, 1961–
   The pleasure of influence : conversations with eleven contemporary
American male fiction writers / Rob Trucks.
      p.   cm.
   ISBN 1-55753-253-2 (pbk.: alk. paper)
      1. American fiction—20th century—History and criticism—Theory, etc.
   2. American fiction—Male authors—History and criticism—Theory, etc.
   3. Authors, American—20th century—Interviews.   4. Male authors,
   American—Interviews.   5. Fiction—Authorship.   I. Title.

   PS379.T72 2002
   813′ .54099286–dc21

                                                          2002004464

For Karan

Acknowledgments

Thanks to the authors, their families and publishers, my family (both Alabama and New Jersey) as well as the editors and staff of the magazines in which these interviews first appeared: *Black Warrior Review*, *The Blue Moon Review*, *New Orleans Review*, *Indiana Review*, *Glimmer Train Stories*, *The Journal*, and *TriQuarterly*, particularly Mindy Wilson, Chris Chambers, Doug Lawson, Ralph Adamo, Susan Burmeister-Brown, Linda Swanson-Davies, Michelle Herman, and Susan Hahn.

Additional thanks to Will Blythe, Richard Giles, Steve Springer, C. J. Hicks, Elizabeth McCracken, Geoff Schmidt, Inman Majors, Valerie Vogrin, Colleen Tully, Tim Parrish, Michael Smith, Will Kimbrough, Jennifer Horne, Don Noble, Julie Gardner Flippo, Stella Connell, Amber Vogel, and Dorinda Oliver.

Contents

Introduction   xi

THOM JONES   1

RICK MOODY   21

STEVE ERICKSON   41

ROBERT OLEN BUTLER   65

GORDON LISH   89

STEPHEN DIXON   125

CHRIS OFFUTT   153

STEWART O'NAN   175

BARRY HANNAH   205

RUSSELL BANKS   233

CHARLES JOHNSON   257

Introduction

On certain autumn Saturday afternoons, select small towns in the South swell with numbers much greater than their daily populations. The village of Auburn, Alabama, for example, becomes the fifth-largest city in the state. Its resident population, excepting college students, falls short of twenty thousand citizens, yet on these afternoons, more than eighty thousand people fill Jordan-Hare Stadium to watch a football game.

You almost wonder how it can be done. It's like a snake consuming a rabbit. You can view it. You can watch it happen. And afterward you shake your head at the achieved impossibility of it all.

Some fans, in their fully equipped Winnebagos, advance on the town early enough in the week to capture the choicest parking spaces on campus. Others pull in just early enough to tailgate the morning of the game and enter the stadium shortly after the charcoal cools. A few stragglers dare to enter after the kickoff, but these people are viewed about as warmly as worshippers arriving at church after the opening hymn. Days early or minutes late, the eighty thousand congregating football fans take their seats on aluminum benches where they gaze upon a grass field occupied by twenty-two players, eleven per squad, at any given time.

Here, then, is the question: How many of those eighty thousand are watching the left guard as he pushes forward in an effort to release the fullback into the defensive backfield? As he rises to his full height, arms extended, in order to provide pass protection for his quarterback? As he circles around the center beside him in an attempt to lead the tailback in a sweep around the right end?

The answer: Out of eighty thousand fans on a southern Saturday autumn afternoon, between twenty and thirty people are watching the left guard. Everyone else is watching the misnamed skilled positions—the quarterback, the running back, the kick return specialist—whoever has the ball.

The left guard's girlfriend, should he have one, is watching his every move, even when he's on the sideline. This is called love. The left guard's parents are watching intently, as well. The offensive line coach definitely is watching the performance of the left guard, though his attention is divided evenly among the other offensive linemen. Beefy boys, perhaps still in high school, watch more dreamily than the left guard's girlfriend, wondering if perhaps they have what it takes to play on the line at this level of competition.

Out of eighty thousand gathered fans, the only other spectators concentrating on the play of that left guard are men who, at one time in their lives, also played left guard. Not only are these former linemen the only fans focused on the left guard's play, they are also the only spectators truly capable of judging his performance. No one knows better the skill, talent, and execution required at the position.

The same can be said for cabinetmakers, farmers, chefs, and lawyers.

The same can be said for stock car drivers, photographers, salesclerks, and teachers.

The same can be said for writers.

The literary interview is as close as a reader can come to knowing how a writer works. No game films are recorded. No highlight reels are shown on local newscasts the night a writer finishes a particularly fine chapter. The process of composition is an internal one. A real-time videotape of a novelist at work would interest precious few viewers. Not even the writer's love interest could bear to watch for more than a few minutes. The interview lets us discover how the thing is done. It is how we might learn about this seemingly impossible act of creation.

The literary writer is underappreciated. The writer's audience, more than likely, will fall well short of the left guard's. Few literary artists today reach even a peripheral audience of eighty thousand readers. Most are kept company by a spouse or partner, parents, perhaps a well-meaning editor or two, pulling for them to succeed. Their followers are often other writers.

Why should we care about the left guard who is watched, purposefully, by such a minuscule percentage of that massive gathered crowd? Why should we care about the views expressed by a writer whose works we have never read?

Because there's something to be said for a thing done well.

There is an appreciation, in all of us, for how a thing is done.

I am not a scholar, nor was it my intention to approach this project in a scholarly way. I am a reader and a writer who maintains, firmly, that writers are the best readers.

In 1985, while still in graduate school, I conducted my first interview, with the novelist Graeme Gibson. When we met, Gibson had published three books of fiction, as well as a collection of interviews entitled *Eleven Canadian Novelists*. That semester Gibson's spouse, Margaret Atwood, taught a course on southern Ontario fiction at the University of Alabama. There was, of course, a term paper requirement. I was never quite able to take in the purpose of the term paper. I found the idea perplexing—that one sustains an original idea by spending hours in the library searching out the opinions of others. I looked for a way out of the assignment and found it.

My interview with Graeme Gibson was called "The Twelfth Canadian Novelist." If I remember correctly, Margaret Atwood gave me an A minus for my effort. I thought I deserved better though, of course, I had to defer to her expertise. After all, she was, without question, more familiar with my subject than I was.

This interview project began ten years later with a short assignment from *Spin* magazine: a one hundred-word review of Thom Jones's *Cold Snap*. I think I was given two weeks to write it. I wanted to do a good job. I also was afraid of doing a bad job. Fear, for me, has always been a primary motivator. In those two weeks, I not only read *Cold Snap* twice, but Jones's first collection, *Pugilist at Rest*, twice as well. One hundred words in two weeks may not sound like much of a challenge, but trust me, it's harder than it sounds. Two hundred, five hundred, or even a thousand words would have been an easier assignment. How do you capture the essence of a book, of a writer like Thom Jones, in a mere one hundred words?

I had words and questions left over. I wanted to ask Thom Jones about boxing, The Doors, Vietnam, and the philosophers who people his fiction like family. Later that month, I was given the opportunity to meet and interview Thom Jones when he traveled through New York in support of *Cold Snap*. The man is a born storyteller, and our meeting, from my perspective, went well. The folks at the *Black Warrior Review* expressed an interest in publishing the result, and I was on my way. Of course, at that point, I didn't quite know where I was headed.

Rick Moody came a year later, and some time around the late fall of 1996, when I interviewed Steve Erickson, Robert Olen Butler, and Gordon Lish, the idea of a collection arose. I approached writers whose work interested me so much that I was willing to spend weeks, sometimes months, of concentrated time in preparation. Not every writer I approached consented to be interviewed. A couple of authors were passed over because face-to-face meetings proved impossible to arrange. It didn't take long to realize that the face-to-face interview yields a different tone than a phone or e-mail interview, and I wanted consistency within the format whenever possible.

When I was a teacher, on the first day of class, before I handed out any assignments and while my students squirmed to be let out early, I went over the elements of fiction to show them what to look for—to show them that literature is much more than plot. I wanted to teach them how to read—to teach them how to read as writers.

To prepare for an interview, I read, as a writer, every word of the author's work that I could lay my hands on. Then I asked about what interested me. Often that included questions I thought other readers and writers might ask were they given the opportunity. The mission, with each writer, was to discuss the writer's fiction and, more broadly, the writer's attitude toward the process of writing. Any time you sit with someone for an hour and a half or two hours (or longer) and ask the right questions about a subject as personal as career, livelihood, or calling, you're bound to learn something. The interview turns into a biography of sorts. Each writer has a more personal story to tell than can be found within any work of fiction. In these interviews, the oft-employed mask of character falls away.

Though I believe that these writers should be viewed individually, the assembly of these conversations into a collection invites the question, What do the writers have in common? Most have earned a substantial portion of their income from teaching. Gordon Lish, in fact, may be better known as a teacher and editor than as an author. Only Steve Erickson has escaped late-afternoon faculty meetings and committee assignments entirely. Several of the authors have tried their hand at the movies in one way or another. Russell Banks and Rick Moody garnered increased attention when films by noted directors, Atom Egoyan and Ang Lee, respectively, were adapted from their novels *The Sweet Hereafter* and *The Ice Storm*. Barry Hannah worked with Robert Altman in Hollywood for a time—the only writer, to my knowledge, to follow Faulkner's commute to California in order to write screenplays. Stewart O'Nan has written six screenplays, but considering the author's workaholic tendencies, that number will no doubt double in the next five years.

The range of the writers' publishing experience is great. Stephen Dixon has published more than twenty volumes of fiction, and Thom Jones has so far published three. Approximately half the writers—Offutt, Moody, Johnson, Erickson, and O'Nan—have published works of nonfiction. Russell Banks published a few books of poetry before his first story collection appeared, and Charles Johnson released two books of drawings before his first novel came out. I doubt that any of those interviewed would be pleased to find a thematic ordering inflicted on them, and accordingly, the conversations appear in the same sequence in which they were conducted.

During the course of this project, I called my mother and asked if she would photocopy my interview with Graeme Gibson because after several moves, I no longer possessed a copy of it myself. God bless the mothers who diligently store the efforts of their children. I read that interview with the benefit of ten years' worth of distance, and it wasn't bad work—an A minus, at least—but one particular thought of Gibson's stuck with me—that books have more to do with books than they do with life.

I'm sure that this thought has been expressed many times in a variety of ways, but it was the first time I had listened. It struck me that in order to portray life vividly and accurately, a writer might go not just to his or her own personal experience but to the literary efforts of others. As proof I can offer the influence of *The Catcher in the Rye* on Chris Offutt and Thom Jones, the inspiration provided by Michael Lesy's *Wisconsin Death Trip* for Stewart O'Nan's *Prayer for the Dying*, and the use of Camus's *The Stranger* as a model for Barry Hannah's *Ray*. Russell Banks's multilayered *Trailerpark*, which focuses on an entire community, recalls Sherwood Anderson's *Winesburg, Ohio*. One short story within *Trailerpark*, "Black Man and White Woman in Dark Green Rowboat," follows the situational story line of Dreiser's *American Tragedy*, and Banks relied on Hemingway's "Hills Like White Elephants" as a guide for the story's pacing. The examples, you will find, are numerous.

All of the writers in this collection are working with personal truths, particular to their experience, yet they operate within a defined referential tradition. The material is unmistakably their own, the way they tell the story is their own, but they are, as you will see in the interviews, always mindful of the work that preceded them.

The rationale behind the term paper assignment, the production of an original idea supported by the work of others, is much clearer to me now. It is part of the continuing call and response of literature. After most of these interviews, I have been compelled to return to the works of other writers: Nicholson Baker's *The Mezzanine* after interviewing Rick Moody, Cormac McCarthy's *Blood Meridian* after interviewing Gordon Lish, Thomas Bernhard's *The Loser* after Stephen Dixon, Lesy's *Wisconsin Death Trip* after Stewart O'Nan, and Ralph Ellison's *Invisible Man* following Charles Johnson.

The last conversation in this collection is with Charles Johnson, an interview conducted in April of 1998. Charles Johnson, as much as any writer in this collection, represents the power and appreciation of the literary tradition. He casually mentioned reading more than eighty books on magic for his first novel, *Faith and the Good Thing*. He spent six years reading sea stories in preparation for *Middle Passage*. He has read books and articles on Martin Luther King, Jr., and continues to do so well after he finished writing *Dreamer*.

I think of the light in Charles Johnson's eyes as he described a few short passages from that novel: how the rooming house set afire by Chaym Smith is the same rooming house where *Native Son*'s Bigger Thomas lived and how the landlady of that rooming house, Vera Thomas, is Bigger's older sister. In this there is a tribute, an homage, a tip of the hat to Richard Wright and his work, a thank-you for the tradition of literature that has come before us.

I think of the light in Charles Johnson's eyes, a representation of almost boyish glee in a man then three days shy of his fiftieth birthday, and know that the title of this collection, *The Pleasure of Influence*, is an accurate one. That pleasure is what the writers collected here and so many other writers share, with or without an audience.

A Conversation with Thom Jones

I interviewed Thom Jones in the early afternoon of a 1995 spring Sunday in his hotel room near Times Square in New York City. Jones was in town to give two readings to promote the publication of his second short story collection, *Cold Snap*. His first book, *The Pugilist at Rest,* was published when Jones was 48 years old. The collection was nominated for a National Book Award, and the attention it garnered made Jones a once-in-a-generation literary success story.

He had arrived in town the night before and gone out with friends to the West Village, so he had not been up long. (He says he's a big sleeper.) Jones wore jeans and a rumpled Forty-Niners T-shirt that looked like it had been slept in. He has overly dark hair and is of medium build, which might betray the mental image some readers may have of the boxing author.

We talked for about an hour before I started the tape recorder to signal the official beginning of the interview. Jones picked at his room service cheeseburger during the time we discussed baseball (he's a White Sox fan), his next writing project, the IRA [Irish Republican Army] and his admiration for them, and graduate writing programs, including the reading list that he's given to his students at the University of Iowa.

Jones speaks tangentially and, though I began taking notes early in the interview, the talk soon became much more conversational, taking sharp turns as Jones seems to find a story to tell in response to every question.

The apparent pessimism that ends this piece is not the overwhelming feeling one gets from spending time with Thom Jones. On the whole, the author comes across as gracious and polite. In fact, his manner is so close to gentle that if one struggled to create a boxing metaphor based on what he or she knows of this man, it would be that he seems, in some way, beaten, despite the fact that his publisher has flown him to New York in advance of the follow-up to the most successful literary debut in recent memory.

A number of critics and readers assume that most of your fiction is autobiographical. Assumptions have been made about you, like that you were in Vietnam. Where do these assumptions come from, and do you have a responsibility to correct them?

I was not in Vietnam. I was a boxer in the Marine Corps. It was a way to get out of hard work, and I'd been boxing since I was seven because my dad was a fighter. I was always in good shape. I liked to box and what not. I found that I could always get in with heavyweights when I was a lightweight and at least never get hurt because I was a good defensive fighter.

But I was in the Marines and there was a smoker coming up and I was in pretty decent shape for the Marine Corps but not in boxing shape, which is totally different, and I got in with this guy who was the middleweight champion of the First Division. But he was heavier than that. It was kind of an "anything goes" kind of thing, and I had been drinking even.

But I got in, though, and I found that it was hard to hold my hands up because I hadn't done it in a long time. My abs got very tired, and I was instantly exhausted after thirty seconds and he was just pounding the shit out of me, too. Just hammering me. I couldn't even see the punches coming. I think he was afraid of me because he knew I had a lot of experience and he went out there fighting like, Let's let it happen, and he knocked me down. Well, not quite down, more like out, on my feet. Like I was there and then I wasn't there.

Somehow I was still fighting though. And I managed to get a second wind. I relaxed and then I started fighting better. And survived. That's about what you could say, survived.

I had a headache, like in double vision, for a couple weeks after that. It just wouldn't go away and I felt really awful. I was pissing blood and I had a cracked rib, or two, and a broken eye socket. Punctured eardrum. I thought his gloves were loaded. I mean, I'd never been hit like that. But how can you know?

Then the next thing you knew I was in the nuthouse and I didn't know how I got there, what the hell was going on. I had like amnesia and they thought I was a schizophrenic, so ultimately I got discharged as such. And I kept having these crazy spells and I went back to Aurora, Illinois, and I was working in factories then and I was totally ashamed and depressed and all my buddies were going to Vietnam and I wanted to go.

So I wasn't in Vietnam, but I knew enough about Marines. I'd been in recon and I knew weapons and procedures and all that, and then my outfit got wiped out there and only one guy lived and I heard the story about how it happened. It was only then that I realized that fate had delivered me from something, and I got this kind of mystical feeling that there was something else for me to do with life. And I always wanted to be a writer and thought maybe that would be it.

You graduated from high school in Aurora and then you volunteered for the Marines?

No. I went to Northern Illinois University for a semester, and I fell in love with a girl and she broke my heart so I joined the Marines. Common enough thing to do.

How were your grades?

My grades? I was always very bright but my grades sucked. In fact, I got a D in English and that was why I had to leave Northern, because they'd let me in provisionally. Because I was in the lower third of my high school class. And I was always terrible at English so that I would become a writer . . .

But some guy in college said, You ought to read *Catcher in the Rye* because this guy complains even more than you do. So he gave me that book and I read it and I loved it, and that's when I had this idea that I could become a writer, even though it was the most impossible god-damn thing you could imagine. But even in those days, through read-ing Salinger, being an author was considered the ultimate thing. It's different now because of TV and media. But people read more then and being an author was wonderful because, and I heard Robert Stone say it, to be an author you have to know everything. I mean you can be a dentist or a doctor and you can know this or know that, but for a writer to write he must know and understand human beings. Like psychology and the souls of people.

The second writer who really got me was Dostoevsky. When I went into the Marines and got out as a so-called schizophrenic, I went to my hometown doctor and he realized that there was something more wrong with me, but that I wasn't schizophrenic. And he sent me to a neurologist, this White Russian who'd escaped the Stalinist purges, and got his medical degree in Germany, and we just liked each other im-mediately. He gave me *The Idiot* to read so I could understand what was the matter, because I was not having grand-mal fits. I was having these Dostoevsky-like fits, temporal lobe—although he had grand-mal seizures and then I, even, for a time, had them myself. But we began this relationship, the doctor and I, and I started taking these antidepressants when I was twenty years old. And the epilepsy has been a trial.

But when I wrote the story about Vietnam, I knew the story. I knew the Marine Corps and then I just listened to what these Marines told me. I never thought I'd write; I was just curious about how things went down in recon and it turns out they use recon, kind of like bait, just to draw some fire. Those guys were just asking for it. They weren't really intended to come home.

So there I would've been—dead. Some of them were so good it was impossible to kill them. They were really elite and I just didn't think they could ever be killed and yet they were.

A lot of the excitement surrounding Pugilist *had to do with more than the writing, I think—the idea that Thom Jones came out of nowhere, since it's very unusual to have your first story published when you're in your late forties. But you didn't come out of nowhere. Did you go back to school after the epilepsy diagnosis?*

Yeah, I stayed in Aurora and worked factory jobs and would go to college when I saved enough for a semester. And a friend there said I ought to write.

He went out to the University of Hawaii and said, Why don't you come here, you know. There's no out-of-state tuition; it's really cheap. So I applied and got in and went and I started writing myself while I was there.

So you read Catcher in the Rye *and then* The Idiot *and you liked the idea of being a writer, but you didn't actually start writing fiction until you went to Hawaii? Or were you putting out short stories after you got out of high school?*

I wrote my first short story after *The Idiot*. I understood Dostoevsky immediately. I mean, he's still a pretty heavy dude but somehow I understood it. And I was not used to sophisticated literature. But I read everything he wrote and it was all comprehensible. But I didn't understand *Madame Bovary* or anything like it until I was twenty-nine years old. But I did get into Dostoevsky because I could hear the whole thing.

So then I wrote a story, kind of a Norman Rockwell story, before I left for Hawaii. I showed it to my friend and he worked on it a little bit, cleaned it up, and I sent it to *The Atlantic Monthly* and they wanted it, but would I change some things? It was a very straight, very nice, conventional story. And I thought, Boy, this is easy. Is that all? But I couldn't do what they wanted me to do. I didn't have the skills to rewrite it.

But I was writing another story, which was "Wipeout." I remember I took a six-pack of beer and wrote it. That was basically written in one session and pretty much unchanged.

So the first draft of "Wipeout" is probably twenty-five years old?

It's the second story I ever wrote. The other one, the *Atlantic* one, I think I burned in a fit of Fuck this, I've been there. It's just as well.

So you went to the University of Hawaii about what time?

1966, 1967. Meanwhile, my wife had been at the Sorbonne. She was Jorgeson's girl, so she wrote to me and she knew that he'd been killed. And so I sent her some licorice, I think, in France. I mean how do you do that? Send something to France? But I pulled it off and we became pen pals because we both loved him very much and then, when she came back from France, she stopped in Chicago and I said, I'll meet you at the airport. I really liked her a lot, and so I stopped in Seattle on the way to Hawaii and spent four days with her and she had some other guy who she was sort of going with, but I could tell that I really liked her and I continued to write her when I was in Hawaii so she came to visit me during the spring and the other guy was gone and it was me.

And so I went to the University of Hawaii to finish and I wanted to be an ad writer. That was my plan. But I got into Iowa, and so we came to Iowa City in 1970. I had aid and we stayed there, and then my wife got in the French program. She got a really nice deal. They sent us to France in the middle of it. I had finished my degree by then and hers was like a very advanced degree, beyond a master's but it wasn't really a Ph.D. exactly. So we lived in southern France and Paris. We went all around Europe and into Africa and that was when I got this taste for world travel.

What about when you graduated from Iowa and you have the degree that pretty much says you know how to write? Were you able to continue writing in France and Africa?

Well, I wrote my second novel in France. I didn't speak French and there wasn't much to do.

When did you write the first one?

When I was a senior in college. Random House came very close to taking it. It was pretty good. It was another one of those deals where, If you fix this and take out some of the filthy language, we'll take it. It was a young adult book. It was about a dog. They shot him out of a cannon; he was a dog in the Russian circus. I used him a little bit in "Black Lights." And he had a brain injury, and he could think but he didn't reveal it. It was pretty good but it was one of those things where you have to be there.

Where is it now?

I do have that still, but it's never going to be touched, I'm sure.

Have people said, Show me what you've written, and you said, No, you really don't want to see this?

That's it. Because after "The Pugilist" they said, What else have you got? I did get calls. Like the day after it was published some of the best agents called me. The very day it came out. The *New Yorker* got a lot of calls; they'd never run a thing like this before. I think they were a little worried how it would go over. It was pretty extreme, but it went way better than you could've imagined.

So you had an agent when the story was published by the New Yorker?

Yes, I did have an agent.

But "Pugilist" was a slush pile find?

Yes, it was a slush pile find. That's how I got the agent.

What was your life like on the day you mailed the story?

Well, when I mailed the story to the *New Yorker*, I read in the *Writer's Marketplace* the things that Robert Gottlieb had put down. Don't write what you think we want, write what you like to read. Which is, you know, a cliché, but it's true, like most clichés. And I thought, Oh, I get it. Because I was writing and not getting anywhere.

I'd written "Rocket Man." That's the first story where I knew I was on the right track. I knew that I was gonna be all right. And suddenly I had a computer, too, and that was the best because I'm lazy and didn't like to type drafts on typewriters. I wrote "Rocket Man" and my friend

John Jackson, liked it very much and sent it to Richard Ford who's a friend of his and Richard said, Why don't you send it to Joyce Carol Oates? She likes boxing.

So off it went to the *Ontario Review*, and Joyce liked it a lot and she said rewrite it, so I rewrote it but it didn't get in. So I started sending her other stories and she was very cordial and what not, but none of them were quite right. But when I sent it to the *New Yorker* it was like—at that point I said to John, I can't write anything better than "Rocket Man," and John said, Thom, don't take it personal. These people are getting paid to reject stories. That's what they're paid to do. You have to write something that's so good they can't reject it. And when he said that, and what I had read about Gottlieb, it was like something had finally broken. It was like writing an ad. I thought, It's not me.

You know I used to turn red when I got a rejection slip. I would think, They're laughing, or Did you read that Thom Jones? Get a load of this. Isn't that stupid? Ha ha ha ha. Paranoid, embarrassed. But I thought, It's not about me. Just give them a story they can't reject. Well, I can do that. No problem. So I wrote "The Pugilist," and I knew they couldn't reject it.

How much of that paranoia comes from the graduate writing workshop? We talked before about the personal investment a student has to make to enter a writing program. Do you think the writing program itself contributed to making you identify so closely with the story? Would Thom Jones and "The Pugilist" have been so interconnected if you hadn't gone to a writing program?

I think when you go into a writing program you make a commitment to yourself that you're going to be a writer, that that's your business. A lot of times when you leave, then real life catches up and you're isolated and your friends aren't there anymore, and I think that's the great thing about Iowa. It's not that I've taught anybody anything, but it's that people are going to emerge as writers. Everybody there—I firmly believe this—they wouldn't be there if they didn't trust themselves at a deep level and were capable. I think they're all capable. But as in boxing, anybody who's got the build and condition can do it, but do they have the will to do it? How bad is the fire of desire?

With writing, it's the same deal. A lot of them leave Iowa and go, Oh, maybe I'll go to law school. I need to have some social status and money. I can't live like this anymore. So they opt out. And they're comfortable doing it or they didn't really ever have it.

For me, I felt there was nothing else I could do. I wasn't smart enough to go to medical school or whatever. So when I became a janitor, I was actually thinking, Writers die here. I couldn't get back into ad writing. I'd been too long pushing a broom. They'd say, Send me a portfolio and a résumé, and then when I came in they said, we looked at your résumé. How come you were a janitor? And I said, Well, I was trying to write a serious novel and I don't have to think at work and I can think about my stuff, you know. It's a mechanical job. And they didn't buy it.

The gaps are very hard to explain.

Yeah. It was like if I'd just gotten out of prison it would've been easier.

You talked earlier about shame. It seems like the fire of desire that you were talking about earlier—that the number one hurdle is shame. But what about family? If you have the ego or maybe even the selfishness to say, Screw the rest of the world; I know I'm supposed to be a writer, what do you do about family? Obviously your wife is very supportive.

Absolutely. She knew that I wanted to be a writer. It's a case of opposites in our marriage. I was working as a janitor. She stuck with me through the alcoholism, everything. But I think part of her attraction to me had to do with the fact that I was a free spirit, whereas she's much more conventional.

Does she have to have as much faith in your writing as you do in order to maintain that support?

No. She's just a very good, loyal person, friend, wife. She's exceptional and devoted.

Does she look at your fiction before it leaves the house?

No. In the beginning, yes. Sometimes I get her to proof something, but it's not really to her liking. The stuff I write is not.

"I Want to Live" is basically a true story about her mother and she did read that with a great sense of interest. And some of her friends in the neighborhood read it and said, Well, this perspective, this voice is not how a woman thinks. Sixty-one-year-old women don't think this way, and so on and so on.

And I said, That's true, but it had to come through the filter of me, and the cancer. I assume that the risk of it is that you can go too much over the edge by going too much "in your face." But I also felt that I could do it, so I wrote that story and people have criticized it—said that it sounds like an angry teenybopper or something, the voice. And I say, Well, you know, it did get into *Best American Short Stories*.

How sensitive are you to what critics have to say?

Well, I'm pretty sensitive to it. But if a critic is intelligent and writes something, I take it to heart. Ted Solotaroff wrote sort of a mixed review and I think he was exactly right on the money. I had no resentment at all because he's an intelligent writer. And I think he was a little bit struck by this instant fame. Like every five years a writer will do what I've done: come out of nowhere and be hot and so people get all kinds of feeling about that. Some people say welcome. . . .

And some get jealous. . . .

And some think, Who is this asshole?

Are you worried at all about the reception for Cold Snap? *That critics might have a chance to rethink their praise for* Pugilist?

I've gotten starred reviews already from *Publisher's* and *Kirkus*, so it looks good.

Were you worried? Second books are notorious for not living up to expectations.

I'd rather be a janitor than a critic. I'd rather be a janitor than almost anything. Sometimes I look back fondly on those days. But yeah, the second books tend to get slammed, but there was an evolution, I think. *Cold Snap* has a sweeter, nicer voice. I mean, life's treating you well. It's hard to be so angry and bitter. So it's a new thing.

Two of the stories have already made anthologies. From *The Pugilist*, they've anthologized several of those—"White Horse," "The Pugilist," "I Want to Live." "Black Lights" and "Wipeout" made honorable mention in *Best American*. "Rocket Man" got mentioned.

What do you have to fucking do? Write *Sgt. Pepper's Lonely Hearts Club Band*? When you buy a record album, one song's on the charts and the rest of them are so-so or lame. And that's okay. That's acceptable. With a story collection, the same thing happens. A couple of stories are going to be better than others.

I take it that you think that "Cold Snap" is the strongest story in the collection?

No, not at all.

Which story are you most proud of?

"Cold Snap" is something I just tossed off in a day. It was one of those easy ones. Sometimes I really struggle over stories. You know, I don't like any of my work when I'm done with it.

You don't like it or you don't go back to it?

Well, I just don't like to look back. I'm a very severe critic of my own work. It makes you a better rewriter, I think.

If you can't pick a favorite, is there a story in Cold Snap *that you wish you had back?*

No, that's the good thing. But "Rocketfire Red" isn't really a story; it's a voice.

But it's finished, right? It may not be a story, but it's a nice piece; you've done as much as you can with it, and it's finished and time to let it go. Is that the perspective?

I don't think any writer feels that the conception and the end result are quite the same, so you never really feel like you've pulled it off. I think a book like *Dispatches* or *Dog Soldiers*, which I think are virtually perfect, I mean, God, if I had only written one of those. But then you get into that deal where you're thinking, Well, I'm sure Robert Stone and Michael Herr aren't sitting around feeling satisfied. And if I write a perfect story someday, that won't do it for me either.

I want to go back. From the perspective of critics and readers, there is an autobiographical feel to a lot of your fiction. Can you pinpoint where that comes from? Is it because a number of characters, like Jorgeson and your mother-in-law, are based in real life? Should we feel like the material is autobiographical?

When I write a first-person story, I'm a method actor. I become that character. I became the character in "Pugilist," too. It's not me. At some level it's me. But the autobiography got out of control a bit in "Break on Through," and I never was very happy with that one. But people liked it.

That one seems to be more revealing, from what I know about you.

Yeah, I think it reveals some of the shame I felt in my life. But the people in the story, they're real people. Joyce Oates wanted to publish "Pugilist," but she thought I should cut the Schopenhauer and the Freud because they were too familiar. At that point, you know, you'd cut off your left arm to get into the *Ontario Review*.

But I couldn't do it. I just couldn't do that. But she said in the note, You've really established a voice here. Why don't you go ahead and write the whole novel? And I think her assumption was, of course, that I had been to Vietnam. Well, I had gone through my Vietnam possibilities because they were all hearsay. But the plan was to do that.

So Candida, my agent, says, Give me a hundred pages that I can approach a publisher with and we'll see. So I tried to write a Vietnam novel and I wrote "Black Lights" and "Break on Through," and that was what I had. I had this time off, six weeks vacation time, so I took that and started writing it, and in the meantime they were saying, What else have you got? and I thought, Oh God, nothing. Well, what should I send next? Well, "I Want to Live," I'll send that, see what happens.

Boom! First try, *Harper's* took it. Then, what else have you got? What else have you got? "A White Horse?" And I thought, That's something I wrote on a typewriter and I threw it away. And my wife said, Why'd you throw that story away? And I said, It stinks. It sucks. And she said, It's not that bad, guy saves a horse. It's pretty cool, and I said, Nah, nah, nah, it's no good. I'd have to type it all on the computer and all that.

And so I went out to the garage to get a Diet Coke and it was sitting there in the recycle pile. I'm glad she recycles. And I went out there and I thought, Shit. Okay goddamn it, I'm gonna do this. But fuck, it's gonna ruin the whole day. And I went back in and I just did it, no fucking around. This is it, one time. And so I did it, sent it to the *New Yorker*, and later I heard from them. They had been sitting on "The Pugilist" for a long time and they went, Well, who is this guy? Is he plagiarizing? You never know.

How many non-fiction pieces have you done? How many have been published?

They all backfired on me. They all backfired on me. I remember after I tried to do a piece on E. M. Cioran for *Esquire*, I wrote "Black Lights" in three days. I didn't even leave the house. And here was three months down the drain to make five thousand and I got almost twice that much for "Black Lights" in three days' time. Fiction's my game.

We were talking about critics before. I know in the Poets & Writers *piece you said, "I think I've done enough boxing stories for a while." There seems to be a consensus between yourself and the critics that it was great once but . . .*

What came first? Are you "boxed out" or are you sensitive about being known as "Thom Jones, the boxing writer?" The last two pieces in Cold Snap, obviously "Dynamite Hands" and the piece before that, "Pot Shack," seem to go back to those days.

Yeah, I've spent so much time in gyms. There are very interesting people that you run into there. I didn't quit boxing until I was forty-four. I mean, I was training fighters. Well, one in particular. That was where the story "Rocket Man" came out of. He kind of saved my ass when I was drinking. He won a light-heavyweight title in Washington State. Almost made it to Nationals but didn't.

Anyhow, that's a good point. That was in my mind. If I wrote a Vietnam novel, I'd be typed. But I find that when I write a *New Yorker* story, it's a certain kind of story. They lean that way. To make them work for the *New Yorker*, they're a certain kind of story. And it depends on the magazine.

But you don't sit down and write with a magazine in mind, do you?

Well, every story I write is with the *New Yorker* in mind because that's where I want to be.

You're that conscious of your reader when you sit down at the computer?

I'm conscious of that but I'm thinking I owe a lot to the *New Yorker*. They've been very good to me. And I owe a lot to *Playboy*. And I owe a great deal to *Harper's*. Those are people I really want to write prize-winning stories for. I want them to be proud and I respect their magazine.

What about influences other than literature? Obviously the Doors run through your fiction. Is that personal preference or because it fits the time period? Is it a Schopenhauer device, or is it more organic than that?

I've got the same five CDs in my player: *The Doors Live* double album, *L.A. Woman*, *Morrison Hotel*, Jimi Hendrix, though sometimes I pull that one out and put Creedence Clearwater Revival in. Now it's Crowded House. I like them. And the Doors access my subconscious mind. They make me bolder.

So you literally have the music on while you're writing?

Oh, absolutely. Whenever I get stuck, the guitar riff in "Light My Fire," on the double album—it's different than *The Best of the Doors*—I'll just punch that and I can soar. I can write anything. So I like the Doors. I never got sick of them. You think you'd get sick of them but I, for some reason, don't. And the funny thing is, I remember I heard "Light My Fire" when I was in Hawaii and I hated it. I think it was because of the fear. It was letting out repressed emotions.

Then let's talk about fear for a second. In "Break on Through," Tommy's told by his father that "Boxing is the science of controlling fear." What fears do you still have?

I've always been a very frightened person.

What are you scared of? Can you control your fears?

In some arenas of life I can, but my stepfather was a scary guy. I used to be afraid to be in the same room with him. And one day I got big enough to kick his ass. And I left home forever. That was the fear. I think a lot of men know that.

I was very bright so I was a couple grades ahead in school and I was small. I graduated from high school when I was barely seventeen. And I was small. I did all my growing when I joined the Marines. I grew like four inches in boot camp. But in boxing, I always felt very comfortable in the ring once I got past the fear. The ultimate fear in Aurora, Illinois, was a physical fight. It was a totally blue-collar, nasty place. But I didn't know. I thought the whole world was that way. And I thought, Why lift weights or any of that when the ultimate thing you're trying to do is defend yourself?

I was never a streetfighter, because once I learned how to fight you exude a kind of confidence and people just don't mess with you. Even now, in fact, since I've been here, I got into a screaming match down in the lobby with this guy because he was jacking me around.

And somebody popped into a cab in front of me. He had given the bellman a five and I thought, How much do you give them? He got in the cab and I knocked on the window and I said, You motherfucker. What the fuck is wrong with you? You stupid ass. He said, Just a minute, just a minute. I'm sorry. Would you like to share the cab with me? I'll take you uptown.

Well, that's a decent gesture.

Yeah, he was an English guy. And I said, You broke the queue. Get the fuck out of here. Bam! I was ready to go. I was ready to go. I just do that. But I was all stoked up with anxiety. I don't like coming on the road.

You don't seem to be particularly worried about the reaction to Cold Snap, *so what is the anxiety or fear now?*

Oh, the diabetes. Fear for my life. I'm very sick with it. I've got this contracture problem with my hand. It's called Duypenchase contraction. They're starting to turn into claws. Duypenchase was a French coachman, an alcoholic, and his hands froze because the tendons get these white tissue growths on them. White tissue, connective tissue. With me it's my little fingers, and they really hurt like hell.

This would be the narrator in "Dynamite Hands"?

Well, that's the irony because I didn't have it when I wrote that. But my hands have been broken many times. And I've got these lumps. Now suddenly I've had this pain in my shoulder where I can't lift it over my head.

I went to the doctor and he said, Oh, you've got Duypenchase and it goes to the shoulder, too. You're getting these lumps in your shoulder. And I said, What can you do about it? He gave me some anti-inflammatories which, naturally, I get a fucking rash from, and now I'm playing with this fucking rash, nasal sores, ulcers, like I've been snorting coke or something, and he said, I hope it'll cool the shoulder off because there really isn't much more we can do. And I hope it doesn't fry your kidneys. Like, It's up to you: Fry your kidneys or freeze your shoulder.

I'm a very brittle diabetic so it's progressing rapidly with me. Of course, I could be toasted other ways, like eyes or kidneys. And I feel like I've got to get this writing done. These things that I need to write. That's my fear.

And my daughter. I want her to have a father. You know, my father walked out. The worst thing you can do to somebody. And that sense of abandonment has always been my fear. So I want her to grow up. And I want to see it, at least until she gets everything good. I love her more than anything. And my wife. My family means a lot to me.

Let's talk about your family. I don't know that we actually finished the question: What was your life like when you mailed "Pugilist" to the New Yorker?

I was in Lacey, working as a janitor and writing weekends and mornings. Writing's harder work than work. But I thought, This is it. I just survived the alcohol thing, which almost killed me. And it took me a year to get to where I could even function.

You mailed "Pugilist" in the spring of 1992?

Sooner than that. They were holding on to it for almost a year. I got a call and they said, This is the *New Yorker*. We're going to buy your story. And I said, Well, how much do you get? And she said, It's a considerable amount of money. And I said, How much? And she said, Well, it's a considerable amount. And I realized she didn't want me asking any more about that. And she said, Well, you don't sound very thrilled. And I said, I'm very happy.

How's your life different now than it was on that day?

It's the same. It's like winning the lottery. Three days later you find that you're still you. I've had chances to become arrogant and to think I'm a great thing but, as far as I'm concerned, the ability to write is not any better than being good at fixing cars. Being a human being and trying to be decent, leave the world a better place and all that stuff, I believe in that.

This is my one Schopenhauer quote. Schopenhauer writes that "As a general rule, the longer a man's fame is likely to last, the longer it will be in coming for all excellent products require time for their development." That seems to fit because the late forties is a late start for a literary debut. Do you think his statement is true? Or do you hope it's true?

Well, Schopenhauer was a wonderful, good man. Freud called him one of the five greatest people who ever lived. He lived his life in obscurity. Nobody would buy his books. But Schopenhauer was a courageous person who did live the prescription more than anyone.

Early in his life he was a Jew-hater and a misogynist and possibly a repressed homosexual or something. But he also saw the futility of life. He wrote his great work when he was twenty-five. I can't find any flaws in it. It's kind of a Buddhist kind of deal. It's better that the world had never been, really, that it was as sterile as the moon, because whatever happens in life, it's gonna end up badly. I'm beginning to catch on to that now. But I always felt that way, even as a kid. So maybe it's not so much that he's right, but that we're friends. We're just friends. He influenced me and gave me great relief.

I think he had enough integrity and self-esteem that he knew he was a great man. His mother, Johanna, was a very popular novelist in her day, and one day in a fit of rage he said, Some day I'm going to be greater than you, and she just laughed in his face, but he was right.

So as long as you have the integrity and the self-esteem, then the fame is icing and not the cake?

What is fame?

It seems, if nothing else, that it would decrease your doubt.

It doesn't; it doesn't. I always feel that it could end anytime. I mean, basically writers fuck up when they go off the deep end—run off with a young girl and dump their wives or get into alcohol or something—and I don't do those things. But I do have the diabetes and the epilepsy. My health is just not . . .

My body used to be very strong and dependable and now, every day, it's Well, how will I feel in two hours? I might be lying on the damn floor. So I have to kind of baby myself.

So what's the outlook for your writing?

I realize that it is a great honor to be able to do what I'm doing and I want to make the best of it, and give my best. The writers that saved my life, I used to think, What a wonderful thing that they lived. God only knows what they had to go through to get it together. And nobody feels much pity for them. But the books lived. And they spoke to me. Sometimes they feel like they were written just for me. And I know that every reader feels this way but I thought, If I could someday do that, I would think that that would be the greatest thing you could be.

I used to tell my students that the most powerful literature for them will be the stories that hit them in their hearts and stay there.

I go for the heart. I write from the heart. I don't know what makes my voice different or original. I think it's just the willingness to hold nothing back, to say anything, and then have people say, Well, I've thought that. You know, when you're on the edge, if you push it too far—and I think this was my problem as a learning writer—is that I was just off in the deep end.

The other thing is that artistically, sometimes you're so fucking crazy. I know a lot of great writers, like Theodore Roethke, who held it together for a while and then, Boom! Hemingway, you know? Boom! And then they lose it. If you can get on the edge and stay there as long as possible . . .

A couple of story collections, you know, that's nothing. I want to write some novels, something good. You know, I can't ever extinguish that desire. At some point I die.

I mean, Dostoevsky was so debilitated, I don't know how the man made it. Shit, he had to be tough. That mock execution, then Siberia, then the war. I mean, what a tough motherfucker. But what a shock. I know how delicate people are, really, and fragile. To be lined up, I think, in the second wave to be shot and then they shot blanks at everybody. One guy went insane. And then Dostoevsky, off to Siberia he goes. And then *House of the Dead*. What a great book that was. I don't know how he did it. But he had to do it. Either you do it or you die.

And now we have a society that's full of polarities and rage and violence. America is so violent and people are out of touch with everything, and it doesn't slow down enough that you can ever make any sense out of it. But I'm plugged into it though. I understand it. I have rage and anger and all that. But there's no way to fix it. To me it seems that people are optimistic in America, but when you really consider how many things can go wrong and will go wrong, it's almost as though we're in Hell. If there weren't boxer dogs, then it would be Hell. But there are boxer dogs.

The last question is one of your own. It comes from "Pugilist": "Has man become any better since the time of Theogenes?"

No.

A Conversation with Rick Moody

In the spring of 1996, Rick Moody was thirty-four years old and had just published his third book. His first novel, *Garden State,* won the Pushcart Prize. His second novel, *The Ice Storm,* was being filmed by director Ang Lee, and stories from Moody's third book, *The Ring of Brightest Angels around Heaven,* had appeared in the *New Yorker, Esquire,* and *Harper's.* The eponymous novella, a story involving the sex and drug underworld of Lower Manhattan in the 1980s, was the first since Philip Roth's *Goodbye, Columbus* to be printed in its entirety by *The Paris Review.*

The press clippings for *The Ring of Brightest Angels around Heaven,* however, focused on Moody as an outsider, a one-time editorial assistant who was asked to leave New York publisher Farrar Straus because his literary opinions were out of step with management. Reviews of *Ring* carried such titles as "A Shock to the System," "Dropping Out," "Guttering Out," and "Lost Boys, Sad Girls," and the accompanying publicity photos suggested Moody as one of his latest characters, a hip city dweller with shaggy hair and dark sunglasses, walking the streets of New York in steel-toed boots. In person, the author was anything but the cynically tough figure depicted in his press photos, presenting, instead, a rather slump-shouldered, hands-in-pockets timidity.

This interview took place at Lupe's East L.A. Kitchen, a hole-in-the-wall Mexican restaurant on Manhattan's Sixth Avenue.

Tell me about "Primary Sources" and the reasons for including it in The Ring of Brightest Angels around Heaven. *A few reviewers assumed it was a story.*

I never pretended it was fiction at all. When I first got a good computer, I realized how easy it was to annotate. And I also had a job after I got out of publishing, working as a copy editor, and these two things combined to lead me to think about bibliographies as expressive items. So I set myself this task of trying to compose a bibliography that was like a poem or something. I mean, I would never claim to have a poetic gift, but I thought, Would it be possible to make a list of books that was, in itself, evocative? So I just went for it.

At first it had no annotation at all, but then I kind of felt like it needed more, so I just contextualized. But once I'd made the list, which is straight autobiography really, I started writing stories in earnest for a collection, and I finished a bunch, and I realized that "Primary Sources," in a way, informed the book. It was the bibliography for the book of short stories. So I just figured, What the hell.

What was your editor's reaction to its inclusion?

Everyone always liked that story.

You just called it a story.

Thing. Object. When it was published in the *New Yorker*, there was a vigorous debate about what it was. I mean, I think the European novel gives us an example of fiction that's essentially true that's still literature. I would say that "Primary Sources" is just literature. It belongs in the fiction and literature section of the bookstore, not the biography section.

Five years from now, if you write a "Primary Sources Two," will it be the same? Is "Primary Sources" more connected with you or more connected with Ring of Brightest Angels?

Well, it's interesting. I've thought about this actually and there's stuff on the list now that I wouldn't put on there if I did it today. I think that's sort of what's interesting about it.

As an exercise it would mutate routinely in future years, but I scorched that earth and I probably wouldn't do one again. Other people have done them, and a number of people I know use it as a teaching exercise, and I think that's a good idea. It gets people thinking about, to use a pretentious word, intertextuality and influence and stuff, and those are cool things to think about for writers.

Tell me about the Feelies. They get a dedication in Garden State, *and they're listed in "Primary Sources." Is there a personal connection with the band, or is music that much a part of your writing?*

It's more that music is a big part of what I do. I've always revered the Feelies and when I was writing *Garden State* I listened almost incessantly to this one record called *The Good Earth*. What I liked about it was it seemed like its ambition was to tell the truth about what it was like for someone in their twenties, sort of rattling around in the suburbs without particular ambitions to get any further than that. So it seemed to be true to me, sort of a true document. And that was what I aspired to do, in a way—add a sort of fictional analog to the record, with *Garden State*.

I actually tried to get the Feelies to give the book a blurb. I had a galley of *Garden State* sent to them, and then I attended what ended up to be one of their last concerts at Town Hall. Then I went backstage and I met them and it was great. They turned out to be really amiable and incredibly well-read and informed guys. I'd been told that they didn't read that much but they turned out to be smart as shit. One guy, Bill Million, starts talking to me about William Carlos Williams's *Paterson* and the tradition of labor unions in northern Jersey, and after that I just thought they were great guys.

So if Garden State *had to have a soundtrack, it would be the Feelies'* Good Earth?

Absolutely.

Friends of mine play a game where you pick a band, then pick the best album by that band. I've been lambasted by people who consider themselves "true" Feelies fans for not picking Crazy Rhythms. *A lot of Feelies fans think Peter Buck ruined the production on* The Good Earth, *but I think that album beats anything else they put out.*

I agree.

I've read that you listen to minimalist music while writing now.

Now I do listen to a lot of that and it has to do with lyrics. It's just a problem. Lyrics have the potential to distract me a little bit. So I'll listen to rock and roll when I write first drafts, but I never listen to it when I try to edit. Then I would play Lamont Young or John Cage or something like that.

So there's music in the background during the entire writing process?

Yeah, almost always.

But the music that's in the CD player has more to do with what draft you're working on than what story you're working on?

Yes.

Do you ever have one album or one CD that goes with the story, whether it's the first draft or the fourth draft?

Yeah, sort of. I know there are a couple of records that serve both functions with every draft. *Music for Airports* by Brian Eno is a record that I listened to excessively for many years, and I still do. I mean, I know every snap and crackle of the vinyl copy that I have. That record manages to affect me in a tonal way without being obtrusive, so I use it for everything.

You played in a band, didn't you?

A couple.

When you were at Brown?

That was the band I had for the longest period.

What was the name of the band?

45 Houses.

And you played . . . ?

Keyboards, and sang and wrote all the songs.

What kind of band was 45 Houses?

Have you ever heard Young Marble Giants?

No.

Colossal Youth. Great record. You'd love it. Search it out.

Where are they from?

They're from England. They only made this one record sort of at the height of punk rock, and it sounds like it was recorded in someone's basement. The instrumentation was bass, very primitive, artificial percussion, like the sound of a lightbulb bursting over and over again, and a Wurlitzer organ. So it's totally primitive. The songs are kind of bare bones lyrically. They had this dispassionate girl singer, so that was kind of the idea. Songs that were sort of minimal to the point of being almost bereaved sounding.

What was the instrumentation of 45 Houses?

Keyboards, bass, and drums. The drummer was from RISD [Rhode Island School of Design], and she couldn't play at all, not a lick. We had this drum kit that we'd bought at a flea market. It wasn't even a complete kit, and she just kind of hit it on the four.

Did you draw crowds?

Surprisingly, yes. Some people came out. The bar known for bands at that time was the RISD Tap Room, which was the bar on the RISD campus, and we got a fair number of people, a couple hundred.

Did the band interfere with your schooling?

Yeah. Everything interfered with my schooling. I didn't spend that much time studying. I was playing in the band, I was writing fiction, I was acting, I was painting, and when I got around to it, I went to class.

What about the song lyrics? Are you still comfortable with them?

No. They were awful.

Did you write the music first?

Music first and then put the lyrics in. Whatever fit.

And once you had something that fit, you quit?

Yeah, yeah. Absolutely. I didn't bother to revise.

Did you record? Are there 45 Houses tapes laying around your apartment?

I had one but I lost it. The guy that I played with in this other band, The Null Set, is the writer Jim Lewis. He wrote a book called *Sister* that Greywolf published last year. The title is an allusion to an album by Sonic Youth.

See, that would be my favorite Sonic Youth record, but it doesn't seem to be anyone else's choice.

Mine also. *Sister* and *Daydream Nation*.

So we had this tape and I think I loaned it to Jim or something, but it disappeared. So there's no record of 45 Houses.

Of the music, painting, and acting, whether they're hobbies or distractions, which of those do you still . . . ?

Music. I don't do any of the rest of them.

What's your commitment to music now? Playing keyboard in the apartment or more?

Well, I play guitar now so I have an electric guitar, but I write lyrics for a bunch of people. My brother, actually, has a band, so I write lyrics for him and a couple other local Manhattan bands, most notably this band called Fly Ashtray, but that's about it.

Do you take more time with the lyrics now than you did when you were at Brown?

Yeah. My name goes on it.

Have you seen any cash back? Any publishing?

Not yet. It's funny how that works.

Let's back up a bit. You grew up in a fairly affluent community in Connecticut, which is not the setting of Garden State. What gives a writer the conviction to take a set of characters through a whole novel?

I don't know the answer exactly. I would say, from this vantage point, and I don't mean, at all, to be cavalier with respect to the people who love *Garden State*, and there are any number of people who think that it's my best book, but I can't read it. I think that it's an embarrassment frankly.

You know, I started it when I was twenty-six and I finished it when I was twenty-eight, and it took almost two years to sell it, so by the time it came out it was ancient history. It was really about the time in my life that I lived in Hoboken and about a lot of people I knew who were sort of hanging around and not doing terribly much.

It does seem to be a book of characters who don't do terribly much.

Right. So what gave me the conviction was experience at that point. The class dimension of *Garden State* is, to my mind, its most egregious failure. I'm not from the working class, and my attempts to synthesize or imagine that experience don't seem to work terribly well.

That was part of why, when I went to write *The Ice Storm*, I tried to write more emphatically about this social milieu I had grown up in. Once I had accomplished that, the idea was to sort of double-cross again and write about a completely different landscape in the novella and most of the other stories in the collection.

If Garden State *is your least favorite, what's your most successful book?*

I get a sort of feeling of regret about all of them pretty soon after they cool, but I'm pretty proud of the novella "The Ring of Brightest Angels around Heaven." If I had that book to do over again, I would've probably repressed all of the stories and only published the novella. I feel good about it from the point of view of sentence rhythms and compositionally and so forth.

What's the least successful piece in Ring?

The one I like least is "The James Dean Garage Band."

Because?

It just doesn't have aura of conviction about it.

So you were in love with the idea but fell out of love before you finished the story?

I don't even think I was in love with the idea when I started it.

What was the idea? What if James Dean were alive?

Actually, it was more of a challenge. A friend of mine challenged me to write a story about James Dean.

So this wasn't much beyond the wedding cake in the road exercise?

It was a lot like that. There are many people who think that's the best story in the book, and I don't understand why they feel that way but there are those. It's just not my best work.

There are a couple of things in Garden State *I wanted to ask you about. Where does the name Smail come from?*

Well, I just wanted a name with a sort of homely, Northeastern feel to it.

To accentuate the dyed blond hair and the fishnet stockings?

Yeah, yeah.

So the name is chosen more for the daughter than it is for the mom?

Yeah, exactly. One thing I decided long after the fact, when I was thinking about Alice, is that, to one degree or another, all of your characters are reflections of your personality in some way. So I decided that Alice's name is actually a contraction and that actually it means Alice is male. That was my psychoanalytic reading.

Of course, you probably listened to a lot of Alice Cooper growing up.

I did. I would say the best Alice Cooper album is *Billion Dollar Babies*.

How important is Mike Maas to Garden State? *He reminds me of the lady in black that follows the lovers in Chopin's* The Awakening. *He's never far outside the scene because his self-immolation is referred to repeatedly. Is he a warning? A goal? He's obviously idealized by the characters.*

That's a good question.

And a damn long-winded one, too.

I would say just motif, really. I would say that my recollection of that time and the way I was feeling when I wrote it is that it's not surprising that it would seem ambiguous on that point. The name, of course, is borrowed from *The Crying of Lot 49*, the exterminator.

Let's talk about Ice Storm *and the fact that Ang Lee's filming it. Sarah Kerr, who did a piece on Ang Lee for* New York *magazine, writes that because James Schamus's wife knew you from grad school, they "were able to cheaply buy the rights to a book that Hollywood had overlooked." Will you get a raise from "cheaply" if the movie does well? Did it feel cheap to you when they were buying it?*

No, not at all. It did not feel cheap. And I got a raise on the first day of filming, so to me it was a tremendous big deal. As someone else said, the difference between publishing and movies is exponential.

Why do you get a raise on the first day of filming? Because it's actually being filmed?

What they do is they buy an option . . .

So it wasn't really a raise, it was more like a kick in?

Exactly. People's books get optioned every day, and mostly they do it to take the book out of play so someone else won't get it.

Is there another stage when you get another raise or kick in?

The option agreement is that you get X figure upon signing and then you get kind of a large figure if they ever film because the presumption is that ninety-nine out of one hundred cases are never filmed. So I got lucky.

So you're talking double whatever the original figure was?

No, it's more like ten times.

When did filming start?

April 8th.

So you're feeling a little more comfortable now. Of course, you've known they were going to film for a while.

Well, I never believed it was going to happen. I find, with Hollywood, that stuff goes awry so never depend.

If filming started April 8th, when did the check come?

It came. It just happened.

Like the day the filming began, they wrote the check?

But then it has to go through like a zillion agencies before it gets to me.

Is there one more bump if the film does well?

Well, I get net points, but net points are meaningless.

Because of Hollywood accounting?

Supposedly Hollywood accounting practices are a little more lenient than they used to be, but I'm not holding my breath.

What about Ang Lee filming it?

It's great. He's a director I admire a lot. I think *Eat Drink Man Woman* was really a great film and *The Wedding Banquet* also, and *Sense and Sensibility* was pretty darn good. My sense of him personally is that he really has a literary sensibility, and he's not just some movie guy coming in to sort of lay waste to the text. They've spent a lot of time worrying about my opinion of things.

Why is that? Respect for the work? Lip service? They've got their screenplay based on your book, so why invite you around for the filming? What do they have to gain? What are the odds that you'll show up and say, This is exactly how I envisioned it?

None whatsoever. And the script, in some ways, is quite a bit different, and it's difficult to see something you've labored over for such a long time be refracted in that way. I know that they worried I would find the screenplay treatment too liberal somehow, but I think that they wanted to do the book because they were interested in the themes. They preserved the themes, and they feel that those aspects of the story are really important. So they want me, I think, to feel like they're dealing responsibly with what the book was trying to accomplish.

Do they think you may have something to give that wasn't on the page?

Absolutely. They had me talk with the actors and stuff. I went and spent a fair amount of time with the kid who's playing Paul, gave him my yearbook to look at and shit like that.

Whose idea was this? How was this set up?

They said, Come on by. I met with the actors before filming started. I went to the rehearsal studio and I had lunch with them and we sat around for a long time, and Kevin Kline asked me how big my father's lapels were and things like that at some length. I felt, at that time, I was a resource, that I wasn't being trotted out for my own edification.

The set was a different matter. The set is Ang Lee's business, and I'm only there to watch. A movie set, as I've experienced it so far, is of interest to the director and the director of photography and nobody else. There's like two hundred other people wandering around, operating fog machines, production assistants warning passersby away from the scene. Those guys aren't integral to the process as I was not. To that degree, I was unimportant.

Did you meet with the actors individually or as a group?

I met only with the Hoods, actually, as a group.

That's interesting that they would divide it up into the Hoods and the Williams.

That was just how rehearsal went, but it was obvious why I should be with the Hoods.

What's the difference between the book and the screenplay?

Backstory. That's like a Hollywood word, which I must say I find to be a misguided principle, but it's the idea that you have to sort of know everyone's past and ancient history in order for the drama to unfold credibly into the present. It's something I've always fought against in fiction, and I think it's irrelevant really.

But in the screenplay, what James Schamus did was take the implied backstory, what happened in the days before the day on which the novel takes place and some of those other associations, and gear them up into about forty or fifty pages. So the first forty pages of the film take place before the one day on which the novel is set. It's maybe two or three days of narrative time, and it sort of fills in the background in a more dramatic context.

The novel primarily uses a third-person point of a view, but there's a first person. . . . The word intrusion *is coming out of my mouth, and I don't mean it to.*

No, that's fine. That's the right word.

How do they handle, or do they handle, the shift?

They just didn't.

We don't have a Paul Hood narrator at the end saying, This is my family?

No. There's a tiny bit of voice-over for Paul at the outset. They always said to me, We can't do this, we don't want to do this, we're not going to do a voice-over, but I think they found they couldn't live entirely without it. But they haven't dealt with the third- to first-person ambiguity at all.

What about the third- to first-person ambiguity in the novel? What's the necessity for both points of view? Most sections begin with the first person and then shift to an objective, rather than subjective, third person. The voice is much more fair than you would expect Paul to be toward his father.

The first-person narrator, in the sense that there is one, is meant to be writing from a great distance. The last paragraph suggests that he's narrating from a great distance.

A Richard Dreyfuss in Stand by Me?

Exactly. The reason for the ambiguity was, in part, my feelings of allegiance to the experimental fiction of the early seventies. The book is set in 1973. I spent a lot of time thinking in terms of the experimental trade in 1973, so it's meant as a bit of a homage to them.

What can you tell me about Purple America, *the novel you're working on now?*

Well, it involves certain ideas about how to use the novel that I had when I was writing *The Ice Storm*. It observes the unities—takes place in a single setting. The time is even more compressed than *The Ice Storm*. It's less than twenty-four hours. It's fourteen hours.

It's really about two characters, a guy in his late thirties and his mother, who is terminally ill with MS. So it's sort of about euthanasia and sort of about nuclear physics for reasons that I won't get into. And it's highly compressed. It's more realistic than *The Ice Storm*. The idea is to be perfectly realistic and at the same time to try to use language the way I like to use it without formal gimmickry.

How close are you to being finished?

I've got about thirty pages to go, forty pages.

How far in are you?

Three hundred and forty pages. It'll be longer than any of the other books by a little bit.

It's April 29th. You've got thirty pages left. Do you have a pace you can trust?

Sort of. I'll be done in July. It's like a chapter a month.

So two more chapters?

One short and two long chapters.

So it's just a matter of writing it? Did you know the ending when you started?

I always sort of know the beginning and the end and I wrestle with the middle a little bit.

Where does the title Purple America *come from?*

Well, I'll put it this way: There were two sort of impulses to write this book—sort of a sacred and a profane impulse. The sacred impulse was to deal with the physics, with my lay interest in physics and science and what I see as the sort of twentieth-century American interest in empiricism. The profane interest was to write a book that had as much emotion and sentimental feeling as a really drippy Hollywood movie. So *Purple America* has a twofold meaning. On the one hand, purple like *Ghost* starring Demi Moore and, in the other sense, purple as in the cloud over Alamogordo was at one moment purple.

Do you know what you're going to write next?

I'm going to write a nonfiction book actually, sort of a multigenerational saga on the New England ministers in my family. There have been many, many New England ministers.

Did you ever feel that urge?

To minister? No. I have grave problems with the church as an institution.

So you didn't go to church on Easter Sunday?

I went on Palm Sunday and Good Friday. I really love Good Friday.

What's your daily schedule like?

I work in the mornings pretty much. It used to move around depending on the mood, but right now I'm writing in the morning.

Do you set the alarm?

No, I get up naturally. Usually I write till noon and then do business shit in the afternoon.

Do you write every day?

Pretty much. Usually on the weekends I'll take one day off.

What will you do when you finish this novel? Will you take time off?

Usually I take ninety days off. I have to teach in July and August but I'm hoping, in September and October, to go to the Southwest.

How much attention do you pay to criticism and reviews of your work?

I pay attention to criticism a little more than I ought. Reviews get under my skin in a way, so I sort of stopped reading them. I take it back. The responses of my readership are important and are going to help me do my job better, but I hate reading reviews. I'm not trying to cover up the fact that I'm incredibly thin-skinned about reviews.

I've read several reviews of Ring of Brightest Angels, *but I looked for reviews of* Ice Storm *and just couldn't find them.*

The problem was that *The Ice Storm* wasn't really reviewed.

That seems ironic since that's the book in paperback, the one they're making the movie of. Have you sold movie rights to either of the other two books?

Garden State?

I'm just asking.

No.

There are a lot of independent filmmakers out there.

There's certainly a lot of interest in one of the stories in *Ring of Brightest Angels*.

Which story?

"The James Dean Garage Band."

Is that more for the story or the fact they can cast . . . ?

Brad Pitt. The guy who wants to do it is an Indy filmmaker named Michael Almareyda. I think Michael has a certain intriguing vision, so I may yield and let him do what he wants.

Would you work on that screenplay?

I don't know. I can't answer that question yet. He wants me to help. I might help a little bit.

The three reviews of Ring *I wanted to discuss are Amy Bloom in the* Sunday Globe, *Claire Messud in the* Village Voice . . .

I haven't read either of those.

And Madison Smartt Bell in Spin.

I read that one.

Because?

Because it was one of the first ones out and I was unprepared.

Amy Bloom writes, "I wish that Rick Moody's intricate, interesting language wrapped itself around more compelling characters sometimes, and I wish he never used his way with language and structure to conceal his heart, the fine center of his finest work."

Do you think that you might use an inventive style and structure and form to avoid dealing with the emotion of the characters? Or are you dealing with characters who don't have a wide range of emotion? Are you hiding behind what you do best to the neglect of something else?

Yes and no. I think it's a mistake in general to assign this book to a realistic writer. Amy Bloom is the wrong writer to review my book. I think it's like asking Jamie Wyeth to review Mark Rothko. And you know what? I don't like Jamie Wyeth. That's enough on that subject.

To my mind, Madison's review, which opens with a quotation from Brian Eno, uses the quotation exactly backwards. The point of the collection was to demonstrate range. Here's a guy who wrote a novel that got compared relentlessly to John Cheever and John Updike, who wanted to try and move into some different directions and to see what else he can get short fiction to do. I think it's important. In fact, it's like an article of conviction, that fiction can do more than provide feel-good, realistic stories about people's relationships.

To me, if the be all and end all of American fiction is *The Shipping News* and *The Stone Diaries*, that's cool but it's not doing all that it can. I'm much more interested in the *Infinite Jests* and the *White Noises*. I think Nick Baker's *Mezzanine* is one of the finest novels of its period. I think it's an incredibly beautiful book.

You know, I want to see fiction expand and do more. So when Madison says sometimes it's interesting to get the system to do what it's not designed to do, and then says that my systems don't do what they're not designed to do or whatever, I think he's missing the boat.

The idea of the collection was to try and make the short story do what it's not designed to do. That was my intent. If it's true that, to some people, that seems cerebral at the expense of heart—whatever heart means—my response to that is that I don't agree.

In the late stories of John Cheever, ones that are laterally constructed and very odd stories, the emotion comes out through adjacency and stuff. They're very rarely sentimental. They're all about fragmentation and lateralness. To me, those stories are tremendously moving. I thought that I was writing a moving book. I come from an uptight WASP background where emotion is expressed through subtlety and not through *cris de cœur*, so I feel like it's a cultural difference in some ways.

Let me back up to something you said earlier—that Ring *is a natural progression for someone who has been compared to Updike and Cheever and wanted to do something else. But you know you're not Updike or Cheever. As far as I can tell, setting is the entire basis for the comparison.*

Yeah, I agree.

So don't you think it's a little defensive to go off in another direction based on an argument as loosely grounded as one that suggests you write like Updike and Cheever?

I agree with that point. I just don't want to be pigeonholed, and you'll be in the same spot one day.

I was an experimental writer before I ever wrote a book. That was my background, that was my training, and those were my teachers. The most natural thing in the world for me is to want to move in a different direction, so I don't see it as defensive to respond to that level of hype with *The Ice Storm* to want to move in another direction. I will, after *Purple America,* move in another direction still. And I hope that I continue to do that.

In the Village Voice *review, Claire Messud writes, "It would appear that Moody's faith in the short story form is about as healthy as his faith in humanity."*

That's such a horseshit remark that I can't even believe it. I'm glad I never read that. I would say that my faith is evidently abundant.

Because you're trying to expand?

Right. Because I have faith in its capacity.

Back to Bloom for just a second. "His heart, the fine center of his finest work." It's obvious that you and Bloom have a different idea of heart, or your heart at least. What would you consider to be the heart of your work?

I would say language. That's why music is an influence on what I do. Because I spend a lot of time, hopefully successfully, trying to think about how to make language do interesting things. I think when language is used to create music, as I perhaps sometimes exhibit, its connection to human longing and the great humanistic ambitions of literature is self-evident. Language is its own reward. In the same way, those Rothko paintings, with their emphasis on light and color, tell me more about heart than Jamie Wyeth paintings. Language is its own reward.

A Conversation with Steve Erickson

Steve Erickson has chosen a different path. Much of his work has never appeared in hardcover, yet the author has seen more of his words in print than most of his contemporaries. He has written on a variety of topics for periodicals including the *New York Times*, *Esquire*, *L.A. Weekly*, and *Rolling Stone*.

At the time of this interview, Erickson also had managed to publish five novels—*Days between Stations*, *Rubicon Beach*, *Tours of the Black Clock* (which was named one of *Village Voice's* Ten Best of 1986), *Arc d'X*, and *Amnesiascope*—as well as two books of nonfiction, *Leap Year* and *American Nomad*.

Regardless of the assignment, no one writes like Steve Erickson. One particularly apt critic described the work as "science fiction without the science." Time and geography are often subject to alteration, though many readers attempt to recognize the writer's setting as some personal vision of Greater Los Angeles where Erickson resides.

We talked at the Empire Radisson across from Lincoln Center in Manhattan during the summer of 1996.

Your publicist sent me a note that says, "Steve does not read his own reviews" and "does not" was capitalized and underlined, so it seems like a pretty big deal. When did you quit reading your reviews, or when did you decide not to read your reviews?

I decided it with the last book, and I stopped reading them with this book, in part because of the nature of this book. It's a more personal book and I think that, generally speaking, I don't learn that much from the reviews. There are exceptions, but it's a roller coaster. You're getting a great review from *Time* one week and getting it slammed by *Newsweek* the next, and especially when you're out there touring, you don't need it. I've been a lot happier not having read them.

You talk about being better off not having read the reviews, but you obviously have a sense of what they say. Do you have someone else read them for you? Is there a curiosity?

No, I kind of hear about it because I tell people that I don't want to hear about it and they can't resist. They can't resist the allusion or the condolences. I've been more disciplined about it than the people around me, including the publisher.

Including the people who are telling me not to mention reviews?

Including the people who are telling you in big capital letters.

In your Publisher's Weekly *interview for* Arc d'X, *you said that it was your most personal novel, "the one that comes most deeply from my own experience." Can you still make that statement after* Amnesiascope?

No, now that's more true of *Amnesiascope*. Each novel sort of picks up on something that was left unfinished in the last novel, and this novel picked up on something in *Arc d'X* that I felt like I hadn't finished.

I was two-thirds of the way through *Arc d'X* and suddenly a character named Erickson appeared and a few pages later the book killed him off, and both things came as a surprise to me. I hadn't planned on either one and I said, Well, this is kind of interesting, and finishing off *Arc d'X*, as is the case with every novel, I felt completely exhausted, but a year later there's always a nagging whisper of something that you didn't completely address in the last book. *Amnesiascope*, in some ways literally but in more ways figuratively, picks up with that dead Erickson character in *Arc d'X*. The narrator of *Amnesiascope* is at ground zero emotionally and psychologically and creatively and the only thing that's keeping him going is his own sensuality. And as a result, this book wound up the most personal of all.

You mentioned the nagging whisper of something unfinished. I apologize if I'm getting too far into reviews, but one said that if Steve Erickson was a musician, then Amnesiascope *would be a sort of greatest hits compilation.*

In a sense you've brought a lot of your characters back, characters from further back than Arc d'X: *Wade and Mallory, Adolph Sarre, the boat navigated by the man with the white hair, the mathematician who finds the missing number between nine and ten. Is this a trend? The same reviewer suggested that* Amnesiascope *might be a wrapping up and that the next book would be significant if for no other reason than it had to be something different for Steve Erickson.*

That might be true. I won't know until I write the next book. I certainly had a sense of this being a coda of sorts to the books that had preceded it. I mean, I know what the next book is, but it's not a novel. The book that will come out next spring is a book about America in pursuit of its own meaning during the last presidential campaign of the millennium, so it bears some resemblance to *Leap Year* except that it's a different year and a different election and a different country and a different me. But the novel after that—and the book that comes after that one will be a novel—could start at a whole different place or it may not, but I too had that sense of this book either being a coda to something or a prologue to something or a combination of the two.

You mentioned Leap Year. *What's the relationship between your nonfiction and your fiction? What does one give you that the other doesn't?*

What one gives you that the other doesn't is a ready-made story and ready-made characters, but that isn't the attraction. The attraction of it is these are just things that I care about and would like to write about, but as time goes on I realize how all of these books become part of one ongoing book and that even includes, ostensibly, the nonfiction book. I say ostensibly because I find *Leap Year* in the fiction section in a lot of bookstores, and that doesn't bother me at all.

I wouldn't think it would.

It might bother the person who buys it, thinking he or she's going to get a novel, but maybe not. I mean, the new book talks about the presidential campaign and things going on in the country, but it also opens with Viv and the narrator of *Amnesiascope* heading for the canyons outside of Los Angeles, to sort of get away from the approaching apocalypse so it picks up, in a certain way, where *Amnesiascope* leaves off, and then moves into the story of the campaign. I guess my only reluctance in characterizing it that way is that it's going to inevitably sound like a campaign book.

Do you consider Leap Year *a campaign book?*

Avoiding that question, this book will be both more and less a campaign book. There are ways in which it will get more into the nitty gritty of the campaign, partly because I had that experience, with *Rolling Stone,* of covering the campaign. It's also very much a landscape across which the campaign is the main road, but there's always little scenic side roads that the book goes off on, whether it's talking about Frank Sinatra or Oliver Stone or Philip K. Dick, who I think have something to say, in their own way, for good or bad, about the way in America that as we approach the millennium memory becomes disengaged from history.

You said "had" that experience with Rolling Stone.

Yes. *Rolling Stone* and I have parted company now, so I'm going to go back out and cover the campaign on my own beginning with the conventions in August.

What problems do you face doing it on your own? Are finances Okay? Do you have a hard time obtaining credentials?

The second is more of a problem than the first. The advance I got on this book takes into account that it's going to cost me money to do it.

So what do you say, I'm Steve Erickson and I'm doing a book for Henry Holt, rather than I'm Steve Erickson from Rolling Stone?

If I'm really sneaky and weasily, I say that I'm Steve Erickson and I've been covering the campaign for *Rolling Stone* and I'm doing a book for Holt. You wind up leaving yourself all of these legalistic loopholes that Bill and Hillary Clinton would've been proud of.

Obviously, Los Angeles plays a major role in your fiction. What does a reader have to know about Los Angeles to fully appreciate your work?

Sometimes I think it's more a case of what the reader is better off not knowing, so I can create a Los Angeles of my imagination that may come closer to the true spirit of Los Angeles. If you've ever seen movies that are set in Los Angeles, though it's true of anywhere, New York or San Francisco, and you know anything about the setting, you can always tell how the continuity of the movie never adds up. They're driving down one street and then the next second they're driving down another street that you know is on the other side of the city, and it works if you don't know that much about the city.

    The Los Angeles of *Amnesiascope* may make more sense to people who don't know anything about Los Angeles.

In Amnesiascope there's a passage on Shale, the editor, which reads, "In Los Angeles history is one of those things that will obscure your vision more than illuminate it. But at any rate he got to be a fucking expert about Los Angeles in short fucking order and sometimes it gets on everyone's nerves." Do you ever feel like you depend on Los Angeles too much?

My relationship with Los Angeles is touch and go. I didn't set out to write about it so much. It just naturally lent itself to what I was doing.

I got away from it completely for a book or two, *Tours of the Black Clock*. In *Arc d'X*, the city of Aenopolis is identified by a lot of people as futuristic Los Angeles, but that was never in my head. But I was ready to write about L.A. again, in part because, especially in the last five years, the landscape of Los Angeles really came to approximate that ground zero that I was talking about with the main character. It was a good landscape to put that particular character on.

One of the landmarks of your Los Angeles is the Ambassador Hotel. Does Los Angeles feel any guilt or should Los Angeles feel any guilt like Dallas does about the incident in Daley Plaza?

I think the sense of civic identity and the sense of civic responsibility is so nonexistent, and moreover that is so much a part of the attraction of Los Angeles, that there was never that sense about Robert Kennedy's death that Dallas, I assume, has about John Kennedy's.

Didn't the Ambassador take a downhill slide, fall into disrepair, after the Kennedy assassination?

I'm not even sure it's still open. I think it's closed now. It used to be one of the major hotels in Los Angeles. It's sort of a symbol of an L.A. that's past.

Because of location, the time, or because of Bobby Kennedy?

Bobby seemed to be the final blow. I think it was going down before Bobby. Hollywood changed the Ambassador Hotel. It was very much a hotel that was a part of Hollywood like the Coconut Grove used to be. It was where they used to hold the Academy Awards. I think it had already started to go down but probably the location that, on the one hand, came to hurt the Ambassador was a big reason why Bobby was there at all. It was not an uptown Beverly Hills hotel. It was a little toward downtown and a little closer to reality and maybe reality just overtook it.

In Amnesiascope *you write, "There is, after all, no happier occasion for a writer than another writer writing something bad." Do you feel you're in competition with other writers?*

I think writers always feel competition with other writers, and I'm guilty of that, too. That line is obviously a cynical one, but I'm guilty of that. It's one of the things I least like about myself.

Who would you be in competition with? Not to get too much into the area of reviews again, but both positive and negative reviews of your work present Steve Erickson as a writer with a singular vision. Where would the feeling of competition come from? That I'm a better writer than this guy and why is he making more money than I am?

I suppose. That's competition at its pettiest level. Competition is petty by nature, but I just try not to get into that if I can help it. I don't know who my competition would be and whoever he or she is, there's got to be room for both of us.

I'm assuming there's a touch of cynicism in this line, as well. In Leap Year *you write, "The great novels of the past thirty-five years have had titles like Chuck Berry's* Great Twenty-Eight *and* Blonde on Blonde *by Bob Dylan,* Where Are You *by Frank Sinatra and* What's Going On *by Marvin Gaye, Bruce Springsteen's* The River *and Little Richard's* Grooviest 17 Original Hits!*" You're definitely making a point about where contemporary art comes from, but the fact that you used the word* novel *but only included albums seems to take a rather negative view toward contemporary fiction.*

It does, and I've said in interviews that there has not been an American novelist in the past thirty or forty years more important than Chuck Berry, and that makes people angry. My agent gets angry calls from other authors who assume I'm specifically talking about them.

That seems a bit egotistical.

I think so. It's kind of assuming that this particular shoe fits their particular foot. But I came of age at a time when Bob Dylan meant more

to me than John Updike. I think that for the most part, since World
World II, most of the interesting fiction has come out of Latin America
or Europe, certainly not North America. That's not to say there haven't
been important North American writers, but there have been very few,
in my view, on the level of Milan Kundera or Garcia Marquez. It's just
that Bob Dylan and Lou Reed and Otis Redding and people like that
meant more to me than a lot of contemporary novelists. They meant
more to me in terms of firing my imagination or telling me what's going
on in the world.

What's the last contemporary North American novel you've read?

Right now I'm reading a man by the name of Charles Willeford. Have
you read Charles Willeford?

No.

He's dead.

How contemporary is that?

Well, he's recently dead and was, in fact, writing right up until the time
he died. He's a crime writer. He writes very eccentric crime novels. The
camera's not really focused on the middle of the scene. It's a little bit
off. They're not plot driven or language driven, which makes them really different from most major crime novels. They're character driven
and cunning in a very eccentric way. I find myself, more and more, reading around the margins. Willeford writes crime novels that are that
genre's equivalent of Philip K. Dick's best science fiction novels. They
don't really fit into the genre.

*Since we're discussing genre, what type of fiction do you write? One reviewer
called it "science fiction without the science."*

In terms of my reaching an audience, I think the problem with my writing is it's not fish or fowl. It's not fantasy, it's not surrealism, it's not magical realism, it's not mainstream, it's not avant-garde, it's not

conventional and, God knows, it's not hip. It just doesn't lend itself to a niche. I would like to think, in the long run, that will be for the good, but I think for the short run it makes it harder to find an audience.

You said that Amnesiascope *is your most personal book. What do you share with the novel's protagonist?*

I think that probably whenever there's a character in one of my novels that I personally relate to in the sense that that character is sort of the stand-in for me, the surrogate for me, it's always some aspect of me pushed to an extreme. It might be some aspect of me that is pushed as far as I wish I had the courage to go, or it might be some aspect of me pushed someplace where I have the conscience not to go.

Could it be the same aspect?

It might be. It might be. That probably accounts for why people who know me a little bit are sometimes startled by my books, because my books are more aggressive than I am, and the surrogate is going to be more aggressive than I am. He may be more aggressive about his sexuality as opposed to sensuality, he might be more aggressive about his despair, he might be more aggressive about his dreams, but he's some aspect of me pushed further than I'm actually going to go, so therefore I don't always want to be held accountable for what I write or for how the book reflects upon me. The book is always going to reflect upon me, but it's going to reflect upon some part of my life that, for whatever reason, I may not actually live if that makes any sense.

When you talk about not wanting to be held accountable for what you write, are you more at risk personally with your nonfiction than your fiction? Does the word fiction *grant you a release in any way?*

Theoretically it does, but certainly in the case of *Arc d'X* and *Amnesiascope,* which were transparently more personal books, those two little words on the title page, *a novel,* don't really provide a lot of cover to hide behind. I think that's why these books become more difficult for me in personal terms, because I realize that I am revealing, usually, the darkest side of myself, and it often has ramifications around me. Particularly in the last two books, I've certainly pushed myself a little further in terms of personal revelation.

Does it take a few published books, being accepted as a writer, to be able to allow yourself to take those chances?

I think that from a tactical standpoint, if *Amnesiascope* had been my first novel, I never would've gotten it published, because the realities of the publishing world right now are that if you are not female, or a writer of color or gay, a baldly personal story is not as viable both in the commercial sense and the critical sense.

Is the lack of viability for a first novel? That you have to deserve that leeway?

You know, I wrote a number of novels before *Days between Stations*, which was my first published novel, and several of them, I think most of them, were in the first person, and I can remember being strongly advised, at the time, by agents and editors, that it was almost impossible to get a first novel published in the first person. Now I think in the twelve or thirteen years since, that has changed a little bit, and it has especially changed for kinds of voices that used to have a much more difficult time getting published.

But I think I had to get to a certain point in what I am always reluctant to call my career before I could kind of get away with *Amnesiascope*. And the irony was that in getting to that point, writing a book like *Amnesiascope* entailed a whole different array of risks. For starters, it was considered by people who had followed all of my other books to be a radical departure, and it was clearly a work that was tilted more toward the experiential than the imaginative. I know that that really flummoxed some of the readers I've had since *Days between Stations*.

You mentioned, briefly, the worry that people who barely know you might be concerned about the aggressiveness of your characters. Which of your major characters would you feel uncomfortable with? Have you created characters that scare even you?

I think the protagonist of my third novel, *Tours of the Black Clock*, a character named Banning Jainlight, is the darkest character I've created, and he would probably be the character I would feel the least comfortable with. But he was also, at least until this last book, the favorite character of mine that I'd created. And the paradox, though I imagine at some subconscious level it's not all that paradoxical, is that the same things that made me uncomfortable are also the same things that attracted me to him.

Both Banning and Wade come to mind as being capable of physical violence, but neither seems close to you in an autobiographical sense. I think I wanted to know whether you would be more uncomfortable with a character's physical aggressiveness or whether a character pushed to the edge of your own character would cause you greater discomfort.

Well, I think both of those characters do both. They're violent characters and they go to an edge, violently and sexually and in a lot of other ways. I think that Banning is the more fully developed of the two in that regard. The physical violence is the part of that character that is the furthest away from me because I'm not a violent person, and so the way in which that physical violence becomes wedded to a certain psychic violence is intriguing to me and probably provides the components that both attract and repel me.

Let's talk about the women in your fiction. In Arc d'X, you write, "Sally was already the most beautiful woman in Virginia. As is true with any such beauty, it was lit from within by her obliviousness of it. It stopped men where they stood and pushed to the edge of violence the friction between husbands and wives." There seems to be a similarity between Sally and Catherine from Rubicon Beach in this regard. Are these women examples of Steve Erickson's idealized woman?

I don't know about idealized.

They're not as close in some ways as, say, Viv is. They don't share the life. They seem to be approached from a distance, so I'm using idealized in that sense.

I think that both of them verge on the abstract and dreamlike. They are women who have stepped out of sort of a collective male dream, or what I perceive to be the collective male dream, as opposed to Lauren in *Days between Stations*, who is a little more of this earth, and Banning's wife in *Tours* and Viv in *Amnesiascope*. I personally think that Viv is certainly the best female character that I've created.

Define best for me. Is Viv the most realistic? Is she closer to the Steve Erickson fantasy than the collective male fantasy? Best in what sense?

She's the most vivid in terms of her impact upon the reader. That would be my guess. That seems to be reinforced by responses I've gotten to the book. A lot of people who've read the book miss Viv as soon as she vanishes. She holds her own as a character. She has not stepped out of somebody's dream. The only dream she has stepped out of, if she has at all, is her own.

When you use the term collective male dream, is that like calling a personal book fiction? Is that a disavowal of the Steve Erickson dream, or is Steve Erickson part of the collective male who dreams about a Catherine or a Sally?

Oh, I think I'm part of it. I think if it's the collective male dream as I imagine it to be, then I'm definitely in there. Again I think that Sally and Catherine are one kind of character, whereas Viv or Dania from *Tours*, who may actually be my second-favorite female character, are different. Maybe that means that I feel closer to and more affection for the women who are more real as opposed to the ones who are more dreamlike.

What about the "spiritual strip joints" mentioned in Leap Year, Arc d'X, *and* Amnesiascope? *What's the fascination there?*

I don't know that I really want to analyze that too much. I know that I'm done with it. I know that's a motif that I felt was fully exhausted with this last book.

The stripper, Sahara, from Amnesiascope, *is described as "perfect and remote," which seems to fit the Catherine/Sally mold.*

Yeah, but of course once we get a little closer to her, as opposed to Sally or Catherine, she becomes a little less remote. She's not a particularly interesting person.

Like Cricket in Leap Year? *That's nonfiction and, I believe, the first reference to strippers in your writing. Is this a continuation of the collective male dream? Do you enter the strip joint looking for the well-educated stripper who's able to carry on a conversation while being gorgeous and naked and in control of her own sexuality?*

I don't know. I do know that part of my fascination with the phenomenon of the strip joint is that, while on a superifical level the stripper is being objectified by the men who watch her, the thing that struck me in these places is that the women are in complete control and invariably they realize that. The stripper realizes that and the men don't.

You sound like a man who's visited a lot of strip joints and has just about had his fill of them.

I was assigned to do a story on strip joints for an alternative newspaper about ten years ago or so, and I became fascinated with the ritual of it. I became fascinated by the way, on an immediate conscious level, it was an experience almost completely without eroticism, that whatever eroticism the experience had sort of invaded the subconscious like a virus, and I was fascinated by the role of the man in the experience, which I found to be at once absurd and pathetic, and the role of the woman who was completely in control of her own sexuality, to get back to the question two or three questions ago, and at some point that phenomenon stopped becoming fascinating.

How long has it been since you've been to a strip joint?

It's certainly been years. It's been enough years that I have to stop and think about it.

If you knew there was no chance that you would end up writing about the experience, could you go into a club now without being either depressed or embarassed? Are you saturated to that point?

I could certainly go in without being embarassed or depressed. I think my response was usually more depression than embarassment, but the last two or three times I went into a strip joint I ended up leaving after about twenty minutes because I got bored with it. I think listlessness would be more the response now rather than embarassment or depression.

But just like putting the words a novel *on a book, entering the club with the idea that you are a writer who has come to write about the experience rather than being just another male patron did grant you a certain amount of distance, didn't it?*

Yeah, but I didn't ever pretend to myself that I was just investigating something for a novel. It was a more personal interest than that. Even though the experience winds up being as de-eroticizing as anything else, it was certainly an erotic interest that drove me to go there, along with the intellectual fascination with the experience, so it would be complete horseshit for me to tell you that I was going there because I was investigating a novel. But I guess my point was that my interest and fascination existed on a lot of different levels, and now I doubt that that would be true.

In Amnesiascope, you write, "When we're this confused about women, we turn to the only option left us: we write." Is frustration a motivation for creation?

Yeah, sure. Absolutely. It's certainly not the only motive, but I think that repressed sexuality is definitely there in the mix.

What does give a writer the conviction to write a novel? Is it something different for you each time?

It's different in the sense that each novel is different. It's both more difficult and less difficult each time in that, especially as I get older, I have less energy for doing it. On the other hand, I now know that I can do it.

And theoretically, there's a payoff at the end?

I don't begin a novel until I've thought about it a long time and until I've worked up a head of steam for it. When I now begin a novel I know that, barring something creatively or physically unforseen, the novel is going to get written and it's going to get finished. It may or may not be good. It almost surely won't be what I'm conceiving of it as but it's going to get written, and knowing that has removed one of the great psychic roadblocks to doing it. But I've got to say, in all arrogance, that I never thought I couldn't do it. Going back years and years and years I just knew that, for better or worse, whether I'd do it well or not, this is what I was supposed to do, so it was never a matter of having the guts to do it. I just knew that this was what I was supposed to do.

So there wasn't the fear that once you completed a novel it wouldn't have been worth the investment of time, of yourself?

Oh sure. There's constantly that fear, but there has never been the fear that I couldn't do it, that I couldn't begin and follow through and finish.

When you say there was never a fear that you couldn't do it, is "do it" write a novel or write a good novel?

Well, it's certainly the first. The second is just more complicated because I'm always going to agonize about it being a good novel. I have not agonized about any novel as much as this last novel, which was a much bigger novel, for starters, in my head, than I wound up with.

Bigger in the sense of longer?

Longer and more expansive. I was sure this was going to be my longest novel because I thought that I had all of these things to talk about, and I did have all of the things to talk about but because the novel was so personal and because it therefore was always going to risk solipsism, self-indulgence, self-involvement, self-loathing, self-promotion, self-aggrandizement, because it was always going to risk those things I knew that the balance between the various components had to be exactly right, and I knew that I couldn't afford to make mistakes that I might have been able to afford with the earlier books. I finally started calling it the Incredible Shrinking Novel because the more I wrote, the shorter the book got because I kept going back and cutting and cutting and cutting and making it tighter and tighter and tighter and at the end of it, and this is still the case, I wondered what I had left out, and I wondered about how I had fallen short with it. Even this very afternoon I was thinking about something that maybe I should've followed up on in the novel, and I suppose at some point I'll finally let go of it but it's a harder book to let go of than all of my previous novels.

To get back to the original point, that self-doubt about whether the novel lives up to what you want it to never goes away and probably, if anything, I had more self-confidence, misplaced as it may have been, when I was younger than I do now. I'd like to think it's because, as I get older and as I do it more, I've come to know enough about writing to know all my flaws and all the ways in which I fail.

What's your greatest flaw as a novelist?

My greatest flaw is I'm really not as careful an observer as I should be, and my books wind up being a little too imagined when they ought to be better observed. I expect that's because I've spent a whole lifetime living inside my own head, and I'm more comfortable there. I'm more fascinated with my own head than I am with the world around me. There are a lot of bad things that journalism does to one's writing, but one of the good things is it does force you out of your own head and forces you to record the world around you in ways that I wish I was better at than I am.

You destroyed the first five novels you wrote, didn't you?

There's not really a lot to say about that. I'd gotten *Days between Stations* published and I was at a point where I was either going to go forward or go backward, and I decided I should go forward and that meant burning the bridges behind me. There are occasionally little scenes from way back when, imbedded in my subconsciousness, that kind of pop loose and float to the surface of something I've written, but there's really not much more to say about it. I certainly don't want to sound self-mythologizing.

No, not at all. I don't know that I consider audience all that often but I believe that most people who read literary interviews have an interest in the process and possibly a moment of shared experience. And if aspiring writers read that you're someone who wrote six novels before getting one published, then they might feel they're not in such bad shape.

You have stated exactly the reason that I tell the story. I know there are struggling writers out there, and it just seems important that they know that I wrote six novels before one was published. I'm probably, if anything, a somewhat extreme example. I'm sure there are writers out there who have written seven or eight novels before getting one published, but I don't happen to know of them.

Here's a hypothetical question: If Days between Stations *hadn't been published, would you have set the fire?*

I have asked myself that many times and I don't know. When I wrote *Days between Stations* I was aware, while writing it, that I was breaking through something, that I had taken my work to another level, and when I finished I said, and everybody who read it said, Man, if they don't publish this. . . . But the fact of the matter is, it took two years to sell that book. It was rejected by five agents and twelve publishing houses, including the one that eventually bought it.

You spoke earlier about building up a head of steam in order to start a novel. Do you ever make yourself not write, resist the temptation because you feel like it's too soon?

Yes, I do that with virtually every single novel. I hold back until I'm really sure that it's time, and I wind up resisting a lot of feelings of wanting to get on with it. I think that has become part of my particular process actually.

You mentioned that you believe your novels are more imagined than observed. In Amnesiascope, *you write, "I love having nothing left to hope for but the cremation of my dreams." Are any of the dreams of your characters actually your dreams?*

Yeah. I'd have to go back and look at them all, but I think virtually all of the dreams in Amnesiascope are dreams that I really had, including the dream where I almost threw myself out a hotel window. I actually think reading about other people's dreams is really boring and it was just one more thing that tormented me about *Amnesiascope,* and I cut out a couple of dreams and I distilled and abridged some of the dreams that I did write about and basically retained what I felt was absolutely essential to the book.

Dreams in this book were really mine. I'd have to go back and look at the dreams in the other books, but I'd imagine most of those were really mine, too.

Did you agonize more over having a character named S., similar to yourself, appropriating your dreams than, say, a more disparate character?

No, I think what I agonized about was just using more dreams, and fearing that the reader would find it as boring as I often find other people's dreams. Dreams are just so subjective that I think the symbolism always holds a certain importance for the dreamer that doesn't always translate to someone hearing about them.

Do you dream in black and white or color?

I don't know. People have asked me that and I can't remember. I don't know. I think they must be in color because in an odd way I think I would be more likely to remember if they were in black and white than I am to remember them in color.

I want to get back to your Great Novels quote in Leap Year. *We talked about that statement as an indictment of contemporary fiction, but isn't it also an indictment of contemporary music? I know* Leap Year *was published several years ago, but the most recent entry on your list is Springsteen's* The River, *which is now fifteen years old. So is the statement also an indictment of contemporary music, or have there been more "great novels" since* Leap Year's *publication?*

That's a good question and the answer is yes, but I'm not sure that they're in the league of those records that I mentioned. I wrote that in 1988 and just in the time that's gone by since I wrote that I might even revise the list that I included, but I don't know how much I would update it. I suppose *Nevermind* is probably a Great American Novel. That's the only one that springs to mind.

Have you heard Liz Phair's Exile in Guyville?

Okay, that might be a possibility, too. I love that novel, that record, actually.

Especially when we've been talking about the empowerment of women, that album is singular, I think. Of course, it's awfully early, but that record's been quite influential already, and if it doesn't have a long-term influence it would be a damn shame.

That's a good candidate, and I like that album a lot. That was my favorite album that year, actually.

I know you've mentioned Faulkner as an influence. How have you been influenced by his work?

I remember how the chronology of Faulkner's work would tick more to the clock of people's memories and dreams than to the clock of literal time. Works like *Go Down Moses* and *The Sound and the Fury* were doing things with memory and consciousness that made a big impact on me when I was eighteen years old. A book like *Light in August*, where the central plot is really framed by the subplot rather than vice versa, which is the way you would usually structure it, and thereby gave the book a whole different kind of resonance, that made a big impression on me. I was also impressed by the fact that my English teachers in college would say that Faulkner's a great novelist but he doesn't know how to structure his books, and especially as an arrogant eighteen-year-old I just knew that was horseshit. It was obvious to me Faulkner knew exactly what he was doing.

While we're on the subject of structure, in Tours of the Black Clock, *when Dania is dancing, you write, "By intuition she didn't strive to control her body but to risk losing control every place she took that body, every place in her own psyche that thundered with gleaming buffalo. 'But there's not structure to her form,' one of them argued, or perhaps he said there was no form to her structure. Young laughed, 'She's inventing her own structures, can't you see?' He detested the way they supposed that the structures they didn't recognize weren't structures at all." Is this passage a defense of your own writing?*

No, it's a defense of Faulkner's writing. That's exactly what I'm talking about. That's what impressed me about Faulkner. The same thing that impressed me about Faulkner was the same thing that drove critics of his time and English teachers of my time crazy, and I was really impressed by it. I was impressed by the liberty he took and the way he co-opted anarchy and made it work for him and was completely in control of it while always sort of dancing on the edge of loss of control.

Faulkner's been dead about thirty-five years. Has anyone since Faulkner served as an influence on your work?

The most obvious answer to that is *One Hundred Years of Solitude*, which I read when I was around twenty-five or six, and it is clearly influenced by Faulkner, which Marquez is very upfront about. What struck me was the way Marquez had taken Faulkner's lessons and incorporated them into his own fictional universe and made all those things work in a way that was true to him. It never seemed derivative in the way other books did, and that made a big impression upon me. You didn't, in other words, have to be writing about the American South to get something from Faulkner and for the things that Faulkner was doing to be true to your own experience and the way you saw things. Faulkner impressed me not on some rarified cerebral level but just because there was something about the way he wrote that just made sense to me. I grew up in the San Fernando Valley, as far from Yoknapawtapha as you can get except for maybe the jungles of Colombia where Marquez was, so that made a big impression upon me.

Similarly, Philip K. Dick's best six or seven novels, taken as a whole, made an impression on me. He certainly wrote a lot of bad novels, but there was just something about the way Dick looked into the clockwork of reality and humanity and memory and history that just clicked with me, that made a certain sense to me, and I think that's probably the truest definition of an influence—where you read somebody and they make an impression on you because they're ringing a bell that's already there.

Pynchon was a very strange influence on me because I had always found Pynchon very intimidating, and so I kind of avoided reading him for a while. And I was intimidated, not just by the largeness of his vision, but by something that, almost by osmosis, I knew was there but couldn't put my finger on. I just kind of avoided him. Finally, after my second novel and people kept making the Pynchon comparisons I said, Well, I guess I better read this guy, so I read V. My original reaction to the Pynchon comparisons had been very defensive because I thought, I can't be influenced by Pynchon because I've never read him, but I finally read V. somewhere between writing *Rubicon Beach* and *Tours of the Black Clock* and I saw that people were absolutely right, that I had somehow been influenced by Pynchon, kind of like Joyce. His influence was so pervasive, it was so much in the literary air, that I had breathed it without knowing it.

Were you as intimidated by meeting Pynchon as you were in picking up that first novel?

Well, first of all I should say that I've only met him once, and it was relatively recently. I think there may be an impression out there, which I've unwittingly contributed to, that I have more of a relationship with the man than I do. He certainly doesn't set out to be an intimidating figure, and one of the appealing things about him is that he really seems to have no sense of his own mystique, and doesn't place any value in it as far as I can tell. He's just a private guy. And he was very nice. He was a very sweet guy and a very kind, gentle soul, so meeting him was less intimidating for that reason but, you know, he's still Pynchon.

The last direction I want to take you in is the separation between writers and young writers. In Arc d'X, *you write, "Now at the age of forty, his father and his youth and love all passing at the same moment . . ." Is forty a significant age in a writer's career?*

I think it was significant in my life simply because it happened to coincide with a lot of personal stuff. If a writer stops being young, it's probably more around the time of his fifth or sixth book than around the time of his fortieth birthday. I think I am actually commonly perceived as being younger than I am.

Why do you think that is?

I think it's because I got published late and yet I got published with a book that was sort of seen as a new thing and so the newness made me be seen as young. While thirty-five is not old, it's not twenty-five. It's not what people usually think of as a really young writer.

Are there different expectations toward you as a writer now as opposed to when you were called a young writer?

I don't know. I think you would have to ask the people who have those expectations. I'm certainly aware that you can't be a promising writer forever, that after six books you've certainly stop being a "promising" writer and at that point something is going to happen or not happen, and I don't know if it's going to happen to me. Down in the darkest corner of my soul I suspect that it's not, and that's what a lot of *Amnesiascope* was about.

I don't know what people expect and, as I'm sure you know, or can imagine, getting caught up in people's expectations is really deadly. The people who have been reading my novels all along expect a certain kind of novel. The people who found my earlier books difficult expect a certain kind of novel. The critics expect a certain kind of novel. The publisher expects a certain kind of novel and, especially when you're a novelist and your readership is as hard won as mine was, which is to say that millions of people are not buying my books and therefore I really value the ones who do, to defy their expectations is hard.

Did Amnesiascope *defy their expectations?*

I'm guessing it did, but that's really hard for me to know and it's probably just as well that I don't speculate about it.

A Conversation with Robert Olen Butler

Robert Olen Butler was born in 1945 in Stone City, Illinois. From 1981 to 1996, he published seven novels (*The Alleys of Eden*, *Sun Dogs*, *Countrymen of Bones*, *On Distant Ground*, *Wabash*, *The Deuce*, and *They Whisper*) and two story collections, the 1993 Pulitzer Prize-winning *A Good Scent from a Strange Mountain* and *Tabloid Dreams*. Butler was on his last stop of a month-long book tour in support of *Tabloid Dreams* when I met him in New York in late November of 1996.

The author studied theater at Northwestern University and obtained a graduate degree in playwriting from the University of Iowa before serving in Vietnam as a translator. For some years he lived in Lake Charles, Louisiana, where he taught at McNeese State University.

Butler is a personable, gracious man who is more than giving with his time. The day before his reading at the 92nd Street Y, he conducted a seminar for literary aspirants entitled "Fundamentals of the Creative Process for Fiction Writers." Years of teaching and countless literary discussions, reinforced by a straight month of public appearances, combine to yield a sense of preparedness, not unlike an actor who is intimate with his own lines. Almost every question, both in his seminar and in this interview, receives a ready, studied response.

We talked in an alcove off the main lobby of the Hotel Intercontinental in Manhattan while Butler's wife, the novelist Elizabeth Dewberry, wrote in their room upstairs.

When you won the Pulitzer Prize in 1993, you were a relative unknown, and many articles focused on the question Who is Robert Olen Butler? Who was Robert Olen Butler when A Good Scent from a Strange Mountain *won the Pulitzer?*

Well, I was, at that time, the same writer I am today, and that's really kind of the point. I published six novels in the 1980s, which received wonderful critical acclaim in certain limited circles, but they were not widely reviewed and not selling much of anything. Indeed, the novel just before the Pulitzer, *The Deuce*, which was published with Simon & Schuster, received a better than half-page rave review in the Sunday *New York Times Book Review* from Scott Spencer.

Was that the first time you'd been reviewed in the Sunday Times?

No, no. The *Times* had always been very good to me. But that Scott Spencer review appeared very near publication day, and was a rave, and the book went on to receive seven more reviews total. And the book sold 1,086 copies. But that was no new phenomenon. That was pretty much typical.

So long before I won the Pulitzer I had reached a point, and I had been published by Knopf, and in the early days Horizon Press, so I had good, name publishers, but I had reached a point where I had thought, Well, this seems to be my lot. And so I realized that I would go mad if I were to worry about the critics and worry about the sales and worry about the book prizes, so long before the Pulitzer I had just decided, To hell with it. I'm just going to write the books I'm given to write and whatever happens happens. That I would be as daring and as personal as I wished to be. I'll write what I see about the world.

And then the Pulitzer happened and all of a sudden I had the same attitude but for a different reason, you know? Hell, I won the Pulitzer Prize. I don't need to worry about anything else. The fourth through the seventh words of my obituary are already written so to hell with it. I'm just going to write the books I'm given to write and I'll be as daring and as personal as I wish to be.

Interestingly enough, in terms of the work, in terms of the aesthetic, in terms of my attitude toward all of that, I feel very much the same. Robert Olen Butler is the same now as he was then. I think you can see a trajectory in the work, but moving through, always, the same concerns, moving through the atmosphere of certain fanatic preoccupations, which continue to drive me.

What, if anything, has changed since winning the Pulitzer?

What's changed is now, instead of a thousand copies of a novel, I sell thirty-eight thousand in hardback and readers who all along, I'm certain, would've been responding to my work have now had their attention drawn to it and are actually finding the work.

It pleases me. I'm just coming off a very long book tour for *Tabloid Dreams* and it pleases me now. I feel that *Tabloid Dreams* is my best work. I feel like with every book I've stretched myself more and accomplished a more complex vision of the world, though I reread all of my six pre-Pulitzer novels a year or two ago when they came back out in paperback and I wouldn't change a word in any of them. Each of them represents, for me, a full and complete, organic expression of what I saw at that moment.

But it pleases me that I have had fans come up, frequently, at stops on my book tour, with stacks of my books, and they have collected and read all of my work, and many of them feel like my later work's my best, but not infrequently people will say, Oh man, this one's the best, or This one's still my favorite, and they put *Sun Dogs* in front of me, or This one's still my favorite, and they put *Alleys of Eden* in front of me and so forth. The difference is the people who I feel would've responded to me all along are now doing it. They have a chance to. Their attention has been drawn to me.

It's interesting that you went back to your first six novels. I don't know that I've run across too many writers who go back and reread their early work. Was it difficult at all?

No, it wasn't because the stuff that would've been difficult to read is still in drawers. Before I began publishing, I wrote five dreadful novels and about four dozen ghastly short stories and a dozen truly awful full-length plays, and thank goodness I made my serious mistakes in private. By the time I began publishing, I had done a lot of writing and I finally found my way through to an understanding of where I had to go in myself to write well.

Is the Pulitzer the best thing that could've happened to your career? Is there anything better that could've happened, not to your writing but to your career?

No, I think not. On the morning after I won the Pulitzer, at six in the morning I was in my hometown of Lake Charles, Louisiana, sitting in my car in front of the local liquor store, which is the one place where they have all of the magazines and newspapers, and a guy in a seed cap stepped out of his pickup truck, with the gun rack in the back, looked at me, came over, and knocked on my window. I rolled it down, and he stuck his hand in the car to congratulate me on the Pulitzer Prize, which, at that point, was a banner headline in the paper.

The Pulitzer has a recognition value on the street that I think no other book prize does short of the Nobel Prize, which is another world entirely of international politics, but the Pulitzer is certainly the best thing that could've happened to my career.

There seems to be a definitive line between the five early novels and Alleys of Eden. What was the turning point between those five novels and your published work? Did a light go on in your head?

Well, I think, in fact, if I can pick up your metaphor, the light went off in my head. That was the critical thing. And I find this to be the problem with almost every manuscript I've ever read from any nascent, aspiring writer. That is that the impulse is indeed to write from your head, that is, from your intellect, from your own abstracted set of beliefs, philosophies, ideas. And to construct objects, these books, that are driven and inspired by that rational faculty, is entirely the wrong thing to do, and that's what was wrong with all the bad writing that I did.

Are the five early novels thematically similar to your published work? Is it just the process that's different?

Somewhat. That's an interesting question. To show you the destructiveness of the mind as a source of inspiration, some of those books did indeed draw on what could be seen as the same thematic material as the good books, so it's not a matter of I had a certain set of ideas in my head and then in another place. That's the key. I stopped writing from my head and I went to my dreamspace, my unconscious. That's where art is created. Not from the head but from the dreamspace. And even though some of those books written from my head did deal with the same stuff that clearly was roiling in my dreamspace, because it went through the willful, analytical faculties, the work came out badly. It was only when I was able to let go of the thinking mind that I was able to write well.

It's interesting. I have a friend who's an assistant athletic director at LSU. His name is Greg LaFleur, and he's a former tight end for the then-St. Louis Cardinals NFL football team, and he and I have discussed the similarity in process for his work and mine. For him to race down a football field with three linebackers or safeties converging on you, to crush the life out of your body, and in his case, Jim Ray Hart thirty yards upfield launching this bizarrely shaped projectile into the air and Greg throwing his body out and extending his hands and that projectile falling onto his fingertips and him pulling it in—for him to be able to do that he had to be, as the athletes call it, in the zone. And what in the zone means is, for them, is not to think. The moment you become self-aware or self-conscious and reflective and thoughtful in the process, you are unable to do it. And for the artist, it's the same thing.

I think psychologists call it the flow state, that state of trance that you get into that puts you in connection with your unconscious. It's from that white-hot, unconscious place that art is created.

What makes fiction art?

Well, the artist, it seems to me, is someone who encounters the chaos that is life on planet Earth with considerable intensity and, like a lot of other people, feels somehow that there is order behind that chaos. In this respect the artist is like a philosopher or theologian or scientist or a pyschotherapist or whatever, but all those other folks are very comfortable in understanding and expressing their vision of order through the mind, through abstractions, philosophical principles and theological dogma and scientific law and psychoanalytic insight or whatever, but the artist is deeply uncomfortable with any expression of that vision or order that is abstract or ideational. The artist is comfortable only with going back to the way in which the chaos is experienced, the way in which life is experienced on planet Earth, which is moment to moment through the senses and pulling out bits and pieces of that sensual flow of experience and reshaping it, recombining it, and giving it back to the world as if it were bits of experience, as if it were experience itself.

As a result, the way in which the artist communicates is by setting up a kind of harmonic in the reader, a resonance. You do not understand a work of art rationally and analytically, you thrum to it. That's the artistic impulse. The important thing here is the artist does not understand herself what her vision of the world is until she creates the art object. That's the way in which she comes to understand what it is she knows about the human condition. The act of creation is as much an act of exploration as it is of expression.

So you reached that flow state while writing Alleys of Eden *that you hadn't reached before, and when you arrive there you know that it's right?*

Yes.

Can you point to a time or a moment that caused you to make the transition? Was it a conscious decision not to write consciously?

It happened from the beginning of that novel. I don't know what it had to do with, to be honest with you.

Subject matter?

Subject matter certainly had something to do with it. The character and the relationship of that deserter and the Vietnamese woman that he loved and the ambience of that back alley room in Saigon, which provided the kind of cultural vacuum in which this love could grow, some of that.

It seems that what Cliff has to learn from Lanh, especially while they're still in Vietnam, could, in a sense, contribute to the zone or the flow state.

Cliff is deeply engaged with Saigon, with the sensual world, and he was particularly suited for me to get inside of and then look around the world through his sensibilities because he is deeply sensual and engaged with that world. It is the thing that allows him to desert in this place that most Americans would shun. And so, I think in that sense, Cliff led me to abandon the thoughtful processes and get into the sense memories, which is really the essential content of that unconscious.

If we were to select from your work the character most amenable to this flow state theory, the character most likely to write and write from a flow state, then Cliff would have to be pretty near the top of the list.

I think you're right. I think you're right. I hadn't thought about it until you asked the question and we talked this out, but I think that's probably one thing that allowed the breakthrough to happen. I think there were probably other forces, too, in my personal life. I was ready to enter that unconscious. It takes a while for your courage to reach a point where you can do it.

The great Japanese film director Akira Kurosawa once said that to be an artist means never to avert your eyes. Aspiring artists, nascent artists have spent most of their lives protecting themselves, defending themselves against the chaos that they sense around them and inside them by resorting to their intellect, their reason, and it takes a while, even if you wish to do it, even if some part of you knows instinctively—and some part of you must know instinctively—that you have to go to that place and not flinch, not avert your eyes. You have to face down all those demons.

Even if you know that, even if you wish to do it on some level, there are so many layers of resistance and defense that you've built up all your life that will try to stop you and will succeed, will trick you into thinking that you're doing it and you're not, so I think there's just a certain amount of writing that you have to do, trying to get there, and it will be inevitably flawed writing or bad writing. I think there's just a certain amount of that I had to go through as well.

Is it easier to achieve this state now? Did you ever falter in later books?

No. Once I was there I stayed there. I now know instantly. Of course, every day there are forces that want to drag you back out of there. The challenge of that, the difficulty of it, the scariness of it never goes away, but what you finally have is a sensor in you that will alert you whenever you've slipped out of it.

Did you have concerns, early in your career, of being labeled a Vietnam writer?

Oh yeah, I certainly did. With *Sun Dogs*, I slid out of Vietnam for the venue though I used a character, Wilson Hand, who was a secondary character in the *Alleys of Eden*, but I set it in Alaska. Then my third book, of course, was set in Alamogordo Desert and I began this fictional city, Wabash, in that novel, so it wasn't until the fourth novel that I got back to Vietnam. Nevertheless, I was often called a Vietnam novelist.

My feeling about that has always been that I am a Vietnam novelist the way that Monet is a lily pad painter. Vietnam, for me, and for any artist who's written there, it's the same for Southern novelists, which I'm now being called, it's a metaphor, a locale, it's a source of characters and situations, but my focus is not on Vietnam in any political or sociological or anthropological way. It's on the deeper truths of the human heart.

Is there one book that captures the Vietnam experience?

I don't think so. The Vietnam experience for me was quite different from the Vietnam experience for virtually all of the others who have written about it. The nonfiction is always focused on the political complexities of that whole event and rightly so, but virtually all the novels have been written from the combat point of view. That's understandable because combat soldiers were there with the intensity of experience sufficient to motivate them to be writers, but in reality fewer than 20 percent of all the men who went to Vietnam ever saw any combat. For that 82 percent or so who did not see combat, I think the Vietnam experience was something quite different from the issues that are at the heart of the combat novels.

It's that experience that I'm interested in. And I'm able to see from both sides being both an American but an American who spoke fluent Vietnamese when I was in Vietnam. That issue is the collision of cultures, the ongoing intense, enforced definition or redefinition of who is your own and who is the other, who is the friend and who is the foe. That was the issue that most Americans truly encountered in Vietnam. And it's the issue the Americans sitting back in their living rooms and watching the war and watching their children or their brothers and sisters out there in the streets, that's the issue that they encountered. It was a drastic reevaluation of self and other, and that's the Vietnam experience as I see it. And there's not much on that subject.

That reevaluation of self and others had repercussions throughout all of our society: in race relations, in gender relations, in foreign relations, in spousal relations. That is a prime central human issue, and for Americans it got drastically roiled up and complicated in that era.

You tell your students they should write every day. I assume that you take your own advice.

Yes. Absolutely.

You're finishing up a month-long book tour. How difficult is it to not only get into your zone but to simply write every day?

The woman I'm married to is a remarkable literary artist herself, and so it's helpful in that we both reinforce each other. We both understand the necessity for writing every day and we do that. It's kind of a shared thing for us, and we can sit in a hotel room at opposite sides of one of those round tables and write for two hours in each other's presence which, I guess, is rather rare, so that helps a lot.

It also helps that my early years of writing were spent coping with very difficult situations. I was trapped in a very bad marriage, kept there for the sake of my son who I paid complete attention to when I was home, and I was living in Sea Cliff, Long Island, and working in Manhattan and so to be the artist that I was driven to be, and this was before laptop computers, I had to write all of my books on legal pads, by hand, on my lap on the Long Island Railroad. And once I learned how to do that, by necessity, once I was disciplined enough to do that, I could do anything. I write on airplane tray tables, in hotel rooms, airports, so that toughened me and it's made it possible for me to continue to be productive, even accepting the burdens of celebrity that the Pulitzer has brought.

Have you ever felt any guilt over the insistence of that time, two hours every day?

I'd say two hours is about minimum and about maximum, too. That's just about the right amount of time. Guilt in terms of family, friends? No, there's no guilt. You learn to pay yourself first, your art first, and two hours is not a tremendous chunk of the day. The amount of concentration that it takes to be in your dreamspace for two hours a day is tremendous. I mean, that's enormously hard work but it's intensely concentrated too so, as far as the rest of the day is concerned, you can give to whoever you need to give to with those other hours.

Do you ever use background music when you write?

I almost always do. I carefully select music for every work that I'm doing.

The music depends on the piece?

With *The Deuce*, for instance, there was a dance club single called "New York, New York" by the Microchip League. Fabulous, driving dance music, post-disco dance music.

For *They Whisper* I used Mark Isham's score of *The Moderns* and some Ravel like "Le Tombeau de Couperin." It varies pretty drastically.

For Good Scent, *would you have a different piece of music for each story? There's a sense of place that carries throughout that book, and I don't mean place strictly in terms of setting. I can imagine two or three pieces of music could carry you through that entire collection.*

That's exactly what happened. There were slight variations of mood. I used the soundtrack of *Mishima* and I used some New Age stuff, a woman composer, Lucia Hwong, I think. I used some music that had strong associations with Vietnam, Jacques Ibert's *Escales* and Ravel's "Alborada del Gracioso," which is more focused on Spain but I associate it with Vietnam because it felt exotic and I listened to it on the balcony of the Metropole Hotel over and over at night, watching the sun go down over there out in the distance with Saigon roaring past my window. Those were pieces of music that had strong personal associations with Vietnam.

I would think Tabloid Dreams *would be more scattered, a different piece of music for each story.*

It was. It was.

Tabloid Dreams *comes across as more modern than* Good Scent. *Was the music more contemporary, as well?*

That's true, though I used some Satie in there, which is kind of art deco, twenties music. Some of those French composers of the twenties had a hook into the popular culture of that time and that worked for me, but there was more pop music although I tend to prefer nonvocal music for obvious reasons.

Let's talk about point of view. You've used the first-person point of view in your last three books: Good Scent, They Whisper, *and* Tabloid Dreams.

Actually four. *The Deuce* was just before *Good Scent.* The first five novels were all third person. *The Deuce* was the first book written in the first person.

Point of view is as intimate and organic a decision in the specific work as anything else so you cannot really generalize about point of view. However, I'm about to. It's hard for me to think of myself going back to third-person point of view in a work. Just knowing the nature of how I see the world and how I'm accessing it, first person feels like the point of view I still wish to continue to explore.

Does your theater background help you with the first-person voice?

Oh, absolutely. Absolutely. The first-person voice was the breakthrough for me to give me access to parts of my vision that are appropriate to short stories. The key was that I was able to take the short stories as little dramatic monologues or soliloquies. And I am able to submerge myself very much as I did as an actor in a role, submerge myself into the role of this character who is speaking into my computer, so I certainly feel that strong connection between the first-person voice and the theater training that I've had.

Is it dangerous for beginning writers to work in the first person? I've heard several teachers warn students away from the first person, but I don't think I've ever heard a writing teacher warn someone away from the third person.

Oh, I would. If I were to warn somebody away from one point of view or the other, and I don't, because, as I say, for the artist, any preconceived effects, any rationally arrived upon attitudes, effects, ideas, whatever, in the work, are going to begin to destroy the work of art, and to make a decision about point of view rationally, intellectually, separate from an intimate consideration of all the other organic elements that are roiling around in you that want to be this work of art, is the antithesis of the artistic process. So to warn someone away from a particular point of view a priori is bad teaching it seems to me.

But if I were to warn anyone about anything, I'm always warning them about not distancing themselves, about not going back into their heads, into their minds, into their rational faculties. And the danger of the third person is that's where you place yourself. Pull back. Keep the intensities of the story at arm's length because of the distancing effect for yourself of the third person. And so I think there's a serious danger with the third person as well, a danger that I think is more dangerous ultimately.

You've said that you have five or six more books in your head that you're ready to write. Will all of those books be written in the first person?

Yes. They're first person because that is the voice that needs to be used to get at the vision that's there in each of them.

Tell me about the balance of male and female voices in both Good Scent *and* Tabloid Dreams. Tabloid Dreams *literally goes male-female-male-female in terms of sequencing.*

Good Scent *does, too.*

Good Scent, *I think, has a small break in the pattern. There's a male-male there with "In the Clearing" and "Ghost Story."*

Oh, you're right. You're absolutely right.

What's the underlying reason behind this order? You obviously feel a need for balance.

Yes. And the reason we slipped out of that alternation is that there were deeper connections here from one to the other. It's the governing aesthetic principle for making the decisions you make. Neither of these books is a short story collection in the traditional sense, where you've written a lot of totally freestanding, independent stories and now, as a kind of a matter of convenience, you pull a bunch of them together and put them in a book. Every story in these two books was conceived within a few days of the beginning of the book, and so they really do function. There's a gestalt to them. I carefully worked and reworked the order of the stories. I'd forgotten that they were not strictly male-female though that was the kind of dialectic of male-female sensibilities, part of the aesthetic of the ordering of the stories, but there's much more than that as well.

To move from, for instance, "In the Clearing" with the father telling this fanciful creation myth to his putative son, and for that fairy tale, that fantasy tale to end with his desire for his son to think of it as true, to put that in montage, you know I use the montage effect here of movies, juxtaposition of things. Next to that, "A Ghost Story" with a man much more bitter. The man in "In the Clearing" is deeply sad that he has been exiled from his own family, from his own son, and the man in "Ghost Story" seems further down the road of that kind of exiled bitterness and again, telling another fanciful tale, but now instead of a beautiful creation myth of Vietnam it's the horrifying urban belief tale of this ghost story, so there was that much deeper kind of connection between those two stories. I think one can examine all the stories in both collections in terms of their sequencing in that way. But a strong consideration in that was the dialectic of male and female sensibilities.

I think the conception of Good Scent *and* Tabloid Dreams *needs to be talked about. The* New York Times *called* Tabloid Dreams *a "new collection of high-concept stories" and* Time Out NY *said that "the idea may be a little gimmicky but its implementation is nearly perfect."*

The *New York Times* also used the word "genius."

What about the assertion that the concept is gimmicky?

Of course it's a gimmick in the sense that these manifestations of our pop culture are sitting there in front of us every day, and to take them and turn them into something quite different could be called a gimmick, but for Sophocles to take the existing mythology of Greece and create a drama out of it is just as much a gimmick. And there's a reason for me saying that because I think that tabloid headlines, not only the bottom rack at the grocery store, the fantasy apocalypse rack, but even the rack up from that, the scandal and sexual peccadillo rack, and the correlary media, *Hard Copy* and *First Edition* and the extremes of *Court TV* and *Jenny Jones* and all that stuff, that cultural expression of our country at the end of the century, I think, is deeply connected to mythology and folklore, which are cultural manifestations that nobody takes seriously in that all of those impulses in human beings go back to the desire to project the intensities of our daily lives into a much larger, dramatic situation, or into personages bigger than life, or into extreme circumstances so that we can be reassured that the feelings that we have in the quotidian are not insignificant but are a part of some larger universal human reality. Indeed, artists must come to terms with the popular culture. These so-called postmodernists have approached the popular culture as well with their own kinds of gimmicks, but it's almost always from a position of irony or sarcasm or scorn, and I think that you have to use the popular culture as a way into those enduring themes of art.

To go back to Sophocles, if you think about *Oedipus Rex*, it's really "King Inadvertently Marries Own Mother, Plucks Out Eyes." *Hamlet* is "Prince Sees Ghost of Dead Father Who Fingers Own Murderer." I think all the enduring works of literature can probably be expressed as really good tabloid headlines, but what I've done is simply reversed the process.

It's all in the execution. It's not a gimmick to take *Ulysses* or *The Odyssey* and take an Irishman on a twenty-four-hour trip in the quotidian around Dublin and to follow his days if it were that kind of epic. The execution is everything, and it's what you do with those things that are in front of you culturally, the things that are natural expressions of the nonartistic culture, the natural expressions of the popular culture or just the flow of normal and daily life. You take those things and you transform them. You allow the deep and universal impulses and truths behind that to show through so, in that sense, all powerful and deeply connected art can be seen as having a gimmick of some sort.

I realize that "gimmick" is an easy term, especially in reference to Tabloid Dreams, *but is the concept idea itself a gimmick? You said the artist must encounter the world and perceive the chaos but not know beforehand how the world is to be ordered, that the artist must explore.*

Let's use Good Scent *as an example since it gets us out of the realm of tabloids. Is the preconceived concept of the book itself a gimmick? How does it work that an artist cannot possess previous knowledge of how the world is ordered, yet all fifteen stories were conceived in a matter of days?*

You begin with something and what you begin with is character, and what you begin with is characters about whom you know one thing, and this one thing is at the center of fiction as an art form. Fiction is a temporal art form. It exists in time. And it's about human emotion. Now, you ask any Buddhist how difficult it is to exist for even thirty seconds of time as an emotional human being on the planet Earth without desiring something—my favorite word is *yearning*—without yearning for something. I think inevitably, just because it is a temporal, narrative art form about human feeling, fiction is inevitably and inescapably about human yearning and so, for me, every work of art begins with the presence that I sense in my dreamspace, in my unconscious, of a character who embodies that paradox of art which that character, I know, is coming from, is born from, that deepest white-hot place in me, in my unconscious. And yet the character is the other. It is me and it is not me. It is of the deepest part of me, and yet that character has a separateness or otherness to him or her. And the one thing I know about that character before I can begin to write, the one thing I must know, and I know it as a kind of intuition, but a strong one, is that I know I intuit what the yearning is of that character, and so I made a list of seventy or eighty tabloid headlines.

So these are real headlines?

Some are. Eventually, when I began to write, I changed some of the headlines and some are actual scoops. You will read "JFK Secretly Attends Jackie Auction" nowhere but in *Tabloid Dreams.*

In *Good Scent from a Strange Mountain,* this place Versailles and Southern Louisiana, and this circumstance, exiled from this culture, from a life and land that is deeply embedded in these people, in both cases those sets of circumstances, these headlines and this situation, suddenly resonated into the voices and lives of a number of those characters kicking around in my unconscious.

But still, that's not a whole collection; that's a number of characters. It's not like saying, here are fifteen story ideas and now all you have to do is write them.

No, no. It did not occur like that. I had eighty headlines and I worked through them and worked through them, and some of them I thought would happen but didn't. When I went to the unconscious, it was not ready. Maybe they will be, but these are the twelve that emerged from that much larger list.

Are there leftover stories?

Oh yeah. Oh yeah.

From each of the books?

Yes, there are.

What happens to those?

Well, there are leftover stories from *Tabloid Dreams*, certainly, that I expect, eventually, to write.

Let me back up. I know there are leftover ideas. Are there leftover written stories?

Oh, written stories. No.

From neither one?

From neither one. The ones that were not connecting dynamically to preexisting characters in my unconscious I did not will into being. That was the sense I was talking about earlier. I started to write, I started to think about writing "I'm in Love with Pig, Says Smitten Farmer" and "Baby Born with Angel Wings" and "Cleaning Woman Sent into Outer Space by Mistake." Those are three that I thought were ready to be written, and I was dreaming into them ready to write and I realized they were not there yet.

But that doesn't mean they're gone.

That doesn't mean they're gone, they're just not ready to write. They may never be ready to write. There may well be a character in my unconscious with whom they are connected but they are not yet. The connection's not complete enough for me to write. I never did write a story that didn't make the cut.

The Washington Post *review said that* Tabloid Dreams *is "an unrepeatable feat."*

Well, I can repeat it. I'll certainly repeat it sometime.

Is that what you're working on now, or is that one of the five down the line?

No, that's one of the next three. I have a novel that I'm almost finished with, which is going back to Vietnam as a metaphor. It's a tense, present-day love story with a deeply mythic metaphor at its center. Then I will be doing a major novel for a publication on the eve of the turn of the millennium, a major novel further exploring, further wedding the high and low culture, the comic and the sad or dark, a novel that will try to deal with an expanse of time backwards, at least through the century if not the millennium. And then the third book, which will be called *More Tabloid Dreams Found on Mars.* The first novel is almost done and even as I'm writing this other major novel I will also be turning out, at times, stories. There are headlines that I'm still collecting, like "Tribe of Al Jolson Lookalikes Found in Amazon Jungle," for instance. I hear the voice of a middle-aged white guy from the Midwest in black face in the Amazon Jungle seeking authenticity at the end of the century and not succeeding very well, but seeking his Mammy.

Tell me about the conception of Tabloid Dreams.

I had not long before finished *A Good Scent from a Strange Mountain,* and the deepest issues in that book were still kicking around in me, and indeed they're the deep issues in most of what I write—matters of cultural exile and loss and aspiration, the search for self and identity, the yearning to connect. And one late night I was standing in line at the twenty-four hour Kroger grocery store in Lake Charles and there were actually, at that hour, past midnight, two people ahead of me in the one open checkout lane, and I was stalled there at the tabloid racks, and my eyes fell on that bottom rack and those themes leaped out and attached themselves to a headline down there, and I think that night it was "Boy Born with Tattoo of Elvis." I might be wrong but I think it was that one. And I suddenly understood that those papers were typically getting the headlines right and the stories all wrong. This book sets the record straight. Twelve issues of burning importance in human life. Not quite so facetiously, I heard the voice of that boy and it was a voice that was already there in my unconscious, but this was the circumstance which allowed it to speak. I did not know that he had a tattoo of Elvis on him until that headline showed me that.

Was that the first story written for Tabloid?

Yes, it was.

What was the last story written for Tabloid?

The last story written was "Titanic Survivors Found in Bermuda Triangle."

Is that telling at all? Can a reader learn anything from which was first and which was last?

Not quite. The first one, "Tattoo," really was the one that started it, but it's not a pivotal story in that sense. The fact that "Titanic Survivors Found in Bermuda Triangle" was the last one, I think, is appropriate. I knew that it would be the last story in the book. As soon as I wrote "Titanic Victim Speaks through Waterbed," I knew that there would be another story and it would be in her voice and that she would be taken up out of the Bermuda Triangle whole. That's another one of the scoops in the book, by the way.

Was there a similar moment that allowed you to begin Good Scent?

Yes. I was just finishing *The Deuce* and that was, as I mentioned, the first book I'd written in the first person, and I got a phone call from National

Public Radio asking me if I wanted to contribute a short story to *The Sound of Writing*, which was a series they were putting together and I said, Sure, of course, and I hung up the phone and as soon as I did I went, Holy shit, what have I done? When I finally had the breakthrough with *Alleys of Eden*, I was very strongly convinced that the breakthrough was for novels only, that I still really couldn't write short stories and, you know, it is rare that a writer is equally adept at short stories and novels. It's a quite different form.

Do you think you're better at one than the other?

I personally don't think so. I would put *They Whisper* up against any novels, and I would put these stories up against any stories. I think both forms are equally interesting to me because my vision of the world has enough complexity to it that there are certain things that I see that can be told only in novels, and there are certain things that I see that can be told only in stories.

But after I hung up the phone and thought I was in big trouble, I went back to those four dozen terrible short stories. I was a little panicky at that point, and they were even worse than I remembered.

What happened then was there was a little bit of Vietnamese folkway that I had thought might get into *The Deuce* but at that point I realized was not going to. It had to do with the propensity of Vietnamese boys to catch, collect, and train crickets. And so I took that little bit of Vietnamese folkway, and I thought about it, and then I heard the voice of a Vietnamese father trying to come to terms with his thoroughly Americanized son on a boring Sunday afternoon by trying to get him interested in cricket fighting. So I sat down and took the first-person voice again and that was the key. As I said earlier, the first-person voice was the thing that gave me a handle on the short story form. I sat down, went into this character as I would've as an actor twenty years earlier, and I wrote the story, and six and a half hours later I got up from my computer and there it was and it was really good. And then twenty-four hours later, I had ideas for every story that was in the book and some more that didn't work out. I had two dozen ideas.

What was the last story written for Good Scent?

Again, the last story in the book, the title story. In both cases there was kind of closing a loop. And so then I called my editor, Allen Peacock, who's the best editor in the world and to whom *Tabloid Dreams* is dedicated, and he said a remarkable thing. I said, I've got this little story. I read it to him on the phone. He loved it. And I said, Well, I have a bunch of these other ideas, and he said, Great, do a book. And so I did.

You mentioned earlier that in the writing process you needed to write about the you that is you but is not you. Is there any particular character in your work that is particularly autobiographical?

I don't think so in the sense that they've all been transformed, but I think that perhaps Ira Holloway represented the kind of dead end that I'd run into. Ira comes to recognize that he is not whole, and in a kind of lost way, because his Holy Grail, Karen Granger, that little girl whose feet he convinced to stick into the machine in the shoe store when they were both eleven years old, she's long gone and impossible to find and yet that image of innocence and intimacy still drives him on though it will, perhaps, probably forever, elude him. And I had reached a kind of dead end artistically and personally in my life at the completion of that book and so in that sense, perhaps.

Which is not to say that any of the characters in *They Whisper* are autobiographical because art comes only from the things you have forgotten. Graham Greene once said, in effect, paraphrasing, All good novelists have bad memories. What you remember comes out as journalism, what you forget goes into the compost of the imagination. And you must forget. The unconscious is full of all the things you have forgotten that have broken themselves down into their basic sensual components to be reshaped by the imagination.

But when you talk about things like a ghastly marriage, living on Long Island, and taking care of your son, Ira begins to form an image not too dissimilar from Robert Olen Butler.

Right. It's just that the characters have been so transformed in detail that there's no resemblance to what the reality was, or very little to what the real autobiography was. But in terms of the state of soul, he was pretty close to where I was at that point.

So in They Whisper, *Ira yearns for intimacy, or wholeness?*

Wholeness ultimately. I mean, he comes to understand that that's the issue. He thinks it's intimacy. He thinks it's a matter of understanding, sorting out the deep drive, the deep appreciation of almost any woman he sees he finds beautiful, the pursuit of that secular sacrament of sex. And that sorting out, that articulating of the voices of the women he's loved through his own voice. But the thing he finally comes to understand is that as close and as intimate as he feels toward so many women who continue to live in this internal landscape of his, that was not enough. There was something that eluded him, and part of what drives him on is the absence of that thing.

The Washington Post *review of* Tabloid Dreams *says, "The overarching theme of the book, a theme echoed in many of the stories, is that of passion's failure." Do you agree with that?*

Oh, man. As an artist I am deeply uncomfortable with abstractions and generalizations. You know, for me, which is not to invalidate what's being said there, but it's for others who think like that and who speak like that to come up with as complex an abstraction as they can to try to talk about the book in what I see as an ultimately artificial way. Necessarily artificial, but still artificial.

The only meaning, the only true answer to What is *Tabloid Dreams* about as a book? or What does it say? or What is its theme? or What does it mean?—the only true answer to that is to open the book and read you those fifty-four thousand words again. For me, a work of art is irreducible.

Now to try to describe in other terms the ways in which you thrum when you read it, that's part of it certainly, but I don't even think about the book in those terms.

You teach a class in Contemporary Fiction. Do you not utter the word "theme" in that class?

Oh sure. When I teach literature, what I do at the beginning of the class—and I think these two things should happen in every legitimate literature course taught in this country—the first thing you have to say is, What we are about to do is a totally artificial and completely secondary activity. In other words, the analytical approach to this work of art, to describe it in abstract, generalized, summarized, analytical, interpretive terms, whatever those terms may be, but we're going to do this not because the artist is an idiot savant who really meant these abstract, philosophical things but wasn't able quite to say it directly and so we've taken this object he's created and we're translating it into the real terms. That's not the process. We're doing this artificial, secondary thing simply in order to tune up the instrument inside the reader that thrums. You add some strings to the upper and lower register, tune up the strings.

And then the last assignment in the class should be, and is always when I teach and should always be, I think, at the end of the class— your last assignment as you walk out the door is to forget everything we've said, because if you do this when you read, I will have taught you how not to read, how not to respond aesthetically to a work of art.

In as far as *Tabloid Dreams* is concerned, I may have to eventually talk in those terms, but I don't know what those terms are.

If you walked into someone else's Contemporary Fiction class, a class operating with those guidelines, and Tabloid Dreams *was being taught, you wouldn't be uncomfortable to hear the theme of passion's failure?*

I think that's part of it, certainly. The failure of passion is part of it, but it doesn't get all of it. We yearn for self and to define ourselves, and then we yearn also to connect to the other.

If passion's failure is the thematic concern of Tabloid Dreams, *is it not also the thematic concern of* They Whisper?

Yes, it is. Absolutely. There's no one more passionate than Ira. He is the antithesis of the typical cocksman because, for him, women are not objects. They are profoundly and beautifully their own individual selves, and the bodies of these women are simply metaphors for the deeper, inner self, the inner voice, which is what he truly wishes to connect to. And he does so with great passion and delicate responsiveness, and it's not enough. It's not enough.

    Yeah, passion's failure is certainly an important issue in *Tabloid Dreams* as well. My hesitation beyond the kind of philosophical reaction to abstraction is that I think that the focus is as much on the striving as on the failure. The striving for self and the striving for intimacy is a redemptive thing in itself in some ways. And when passion fails, even in the striving, there is an expansion of the human spirit that is very much a part of what the books are about.

A Conversation with Gordon Lish

"I believe that we all want to stick out in the world," Gordon Lish once said, "that the least of us has a profound impulse to distinguish himself from everyone else." "Sticking out" is the least of Gordon Lish's accomplishments. He is a near-mythic figure within New York literary circles as the most visible teacher and editor of American writing in the past thirty years.

Lish worked as an editor at *Esquire* and Knopf and was founding editor of *The Quarterly*. He taught at Yale and Columbia before taking his fiction workshops private, and several articles have referred to him as "the most sought after, most expensive" writing teacher in the nation.

As a fiction writer, Lish has published several books, most notably, *Dear Mr. Capote* and *Peru* as well as *Epigraph*, released just prior to this discussion. In the previous year Lish had signed an agreement with New York publishing house Four Walls Eight Windows to publish his new fiction, as well as revised editions of his earlier books.

This interview attempts to focus attention on Gordon Lish's writing rather than his other exploits. We met at the offices of *The Quarterly* on Manhattan's East Side in December of 1996 and, not surprisingly,

talked for some time of writers and writing before the tape recorder was
turned on.

----

*You've done many interviews that have focused on your role as an editor and
a teacher, and those roles can't be ignored in this conversation, but I would
like to, as much as possible, focus this discussion on your writing.*

Rob, I'm delighted that's the case. I'm all too often, I think, made to
make responses in respect of my having edited and taught. In both of
which instances I'm probably as despised as I am as a writer. I mean, it
doesn't really matter. I'm not going to do any better in this category, but
it's refreshing anyway. It's new.

*Your influence as an editor and a teacher has been well documented, but what
writers have had an influence on your own work?*

I think if I were to speak to the question of writers that have influenced
me, it would be convenient to deflect the force of the question by cit-
ing philosophers I read who have, in fact, influenced me enormously,
and I cite one of them, in fact, in the novel that brought you to my
doorstep, *Epigraph*, which is to say Julia Kristeva with specific respect to
her book *Powers of Horror*. But it's fiction writers that you're looking for.

*Not necessarily. Kristeva's obviously important and I'm certainly curious as
to her influence. You mention her as far back as* Zimzum, *and she has the epigraph to* Epigraph.

I want to make it very clear that her fiction certainly has not amused
me in any kind of way, but I'm able to read it. But, of course, I wouldn't
even attempt to read it given that I would have to then be reading into
English and I'm willing to take the view that any writing of any
prospect of making its way with me would have to have been done in
English. The kinds of things I'm looking for in a piece of writing can
only have been put there by somebody writing in English, or writing in
American English.

I read and reread Gilles Deleuze's *Thousand Plateaus*. I read everything I can read by Deleuze and Guattari. Giorgio Agamven I've read all of and reread and am rereading now. That would be true of at least two Kristeva titles, *Powers of Horror* and *Strangers to Ourselves*. I think I've read that one three times. I've read all of Bloom several times. That is to say, I'm not interested in Bloom, the critic, but Bloom, the theoretician, yes. I've read all of Donoghue. I don't think there's anybody writing English sentences that produces better ones that Donoghue.

The authors that you mentioned, except for Bloom and Donoghue, all write in other languages, yet you said that you were only interested in American fiction writers. That rule obviously doesn't apply to philosophy.

Yes, all are in translation with the sole exception of Bloom and Donoghue.

Among fiction writers, living fiction writers, none would be more immediately retrieved by me across that paddle of responses that would count more than DeLillo, surely. And then secondarily, Ozick. I would be a liar if I were to fail to remark the affection that I have had for certain of Harold Brodkey's short pieces, so called. As he himself was given defensively to observe, not all that short. I rather imagine that certain of Brodkey's short pieces probably surpass, in magnitude, my own novels, thinking of "Largely an Oral History of My Mother," of the story "S.L."

These pieces, incidentally, appeared, and one wants to underscore this observation, for malicious reasons, in *The New Yorker*, under the editorship of Bill Shawn. One wonders if *The New Yorker*, by implication I suppose my observations suggest, would publish such work now. I know they were happy and delighted to publish Brodkey's pieces on his dying of AIDS, which I didn't think quite filled the bill for me.

But in any case, I read Brodkey's novel, *A Party of Animals*, in manuscript, over the course of one night, starting as soon as I got home from my office, having been given the manuscript by Bob Gottlieb, not by Brodkey, whose editor I was officially at the time, and the gist of that is that Brodkey's delivering his manuscript to Gottlieb was his way of severing relations with me, although later on he elected to repair that severance. Not all that effectively certainly, and not in a way that would interest us here. But the point is that I took the manuscript home that night, started reading it about seven and, despite the distractions of family life, stayed with it, I suppose, pretty incessantly until ten that morning, having completed the reading of well over a thousand pages and coming to the view that this was the surpassing novel by an American of the century.

I would now amend that view, holding Cormac McCarthy's *Blood Meridian* for that post, for that distinction, if my reading of these things has any value at all.

You're speaking to me on a day when I feel myself rather more vacant from myself than I have ordinarily felt, but each day I'm getting the sense of my losing my purchase on that personality that I had sought so hard to disguise myself within and to present myself under the auspices of, and I don't do that anymore, or I'm losing my grasp on that presentation of myself, and I'm willing to therefore offer, with my comments, the ironic interpretation that they may be completely without value. I mean, everybody else may come to that view, but I know I have come more and more, certainly, to that view.

But anyhow, "influence" is a considerable word and requires every kind of examination, and one does not want to give it, but in an "in my face" or "in your face" kind of way, Brodkey's fictions and DeLillo's fictions and Ozick's fictions and McCarthy, with particular respect to that book *Blood Meridian* and alternatively *Outer Dark*, I find them unbudgeable acmes of expression in the language and cannot claim that, as distant as my work may seem from any of the aforementioned, that they are not, to a greater extent than anything else I might posit, on my mind as I write. Is this work, in its appetite, rather to say its absence of appetite, does it make a legitimate claim to a place in the national literature alongside a *Blood Meridian*? That's a most disturbing question.

What I'm trying to get at is that what I want from my own activities as a writer is, to put it plainest, everything. What I want is some kind of sufficiency in reply to the incommensurable insult of death. I want everything from the page and reckon that, even though my everything may be an entirely different coloration than McCarthy's every-thing, there is an absolutism, or an ultimacy, in which these artifacts can be measured, one to the other. To find oneself insufficient in the face of that, insufficient in the face of DeLillo's 1,414-page manuscript for the novel *Underworld* or DeLillo's *Mao II*, which I've just read for the fourth time, is distracting at the very least.

Is it disabling? Not quite disabling. So it appears because I con-tinue to scribble away, and not without, I beg you to believe, the in-tention that the mark made by these works will be competitive. I don't wish to make the claim that my aims exist apart from what is also in that category. I'm not willing to say that I write for myself. I'm not willing to say I write for God. I'm not willing to say I write without a great con-cern to see the work translated into time and space and therefore oc-cupying, maybe not making, a place for itself with other works that have made themselves.

I don't think I will ever, given on the one hand the terms of my ambitions and on the other hand the terms of my limitations, however much I may believe absolutely in the Swinburnian notion that one stands on his limitation, one stands on his limitude, and in standing on his limitude one shall be as lavish as one requires. It's only from stand-ing on one's limitude that one can achieve that absolute lavishness. Despite all that, I'm not disabled but am much dismayed to reckon with my failing limitations, my failing powers to face my limitations, as measured against these acmes that I've remarked: DeLillo, Brodkey, McCarthy, and Ozick.

What is your greatest limitation as a writer?

I'm a small man. I believe that the body is continuous with the sentence at its best. I don't have the stamina, the physical strength to produce the kind of text that persons in better position of their bodies would have.

You know, my friend DeLillo can get out and run six miles. He's not as big a man as Brodkey is or as Cormac McCarthy is. I've seen McCarthy and he's a fairly sizable fellow. There's something to it, in my judgment. How does this speak to the matter of gender I immediately am made to wonder, but we're not going to engage that topic, I do hope. But I can make the claim for myself that my body precedes me out of the page, and with all of the vicissitudes that have always interfered with its translation into what's exterior, my having had disfiguring skin disease all my life, my having been a little guy, and therefore extremely, extremely dexterous in beating big guys in games until I got to a certain age when bigness mattered more than skill mattered, more than adroitness mattered, or deftness mattered.

What I think is my defect now, as I'm able to examine my experience as a writer now, is that I've passed that point where mere adroitness, mere deftness will do, and massiveness, size, bulk, and all of the vulgarity of that notion is certainly the ground on which I hold myself to failure. And the work will always fail on account of that.

Then wouldn't logic argue that your earlier writings, when you were likely in better physical shape, not come closer to the vibrancy, the absolute you're trying to achieve?

It doesn't. I've looked at it. I've had the luck, under the agreement made with Four Walls, to look at the early work and revise the hell out of it, and I know I'm infinitely more able now than I was then, but that ability is all craft. It's not desire.

The ability is deftness?

That's what it is. It's just adroitness. I know the moves now. I know how to make it down the court and elude those who would interfere with me, but whether I can make the kind of score that I wanted to make, that I set out to make, producing on the page the vision that brought about the impulse, that's another question entirely.

My physical response to *Blood Meridian* is, Gee, that's my kind of stuff. That's wall to wall my kind of stuff, and I would be competent of being driven by a notion like that but absolutely incompetent of bringing it to bear, bringing it into any kind of compositional reality. I couldn't do it. And if I produced five hundred pages of that, I'd probably end up reducing it to fifty pages.

But the fact is that Blood Meridian *is beyond the capabilities of 99* 44/100 *percent of us. Is it a sin that neither you nor I will produce a* Blood Meridian?

It is, Rob. It is. For me, it is. If we take the view that the only reason to do this is to somehow make a reply, make a reasonable reply to the unreasonable character of existence, to time, because that's what animates me, then we're in the realm of ultimate matters. We're in the realm of absolute matters, and it's precisely that McCarthy does what 99 44/100 percent cannot do that makes it the only thing to be done. It's necessity itself to somehow seek to surpass McCarthy.

Doesn't that take us too far into the realm of competition?

I'm all about competition. I'm all about competition. The horror of that is, since I invoke that, it's precisely that view that undoes me. If I could take a more libertarian view about myself, if I could be more forgiving, if I could say, Well, there's a kind of thing that I do and it's forgivable if I do that kind of thing as well as I am able, I'm left entirely dissatisfied with the experience. It isn't enough for me. I'm the kind of person who if I come to the shopping mall, when the sign says, Something for Everybody, I immediately want to rewrite that, to revise the statement to read, Everything for Gordon. And that's the only kind of shopping mall I want to be in.

But aren't we doomed to failure if we realize at the outset that we cannot achieve Blood Meridian?

But somebody did. But somebody did, you see. Somebody did. A man did it. Somebody wrote *Moby Dick*, one has to remind oneself.

But isn't there pleasure in achieving as absolute a work of fiction as you yourself are capable of?

Only defeat. Only defeat because it is, again, the affirmation of nature, of time that you are not enough. You are not sufficient. You are defective through and through. You die. No, it is not acceptable to me that I be served up my portion since the receipts that I will eventually be given by time exceed my portion. All shall be taken from me, and I need all right now.

I want all the women. I can recall when I was twelve, thirteen years old having the view that the only prospect that was reasonable would be that I would bed all the women. I don't know what this meant to me at age twelve and thirteen. I know that there was a joke that was commonly about in those days about a guy that was whacked out who had precisely the same vision. But I've been locked up twice and probably not for trying to bed all the women but for having notions that it was a doable thing.

I continue at age almost sixty-three to feel that it's a kind of no-option situation since my construction of life is a sort of no-option situation. Nevertheless, given the alibi of psychopathology, I'm not daunted by this. I mean, I'm not daunted by the absolute numbers, by your making the claim that, Well, Gordon, *Blood Meridian* was done by the rarest fellow under the rarest circumstances in the rarest moment. He may not be competent of that accomplishment now. He probably could not do it again. But I have yet to exceed myself, to cross a line as uncrossable as that.

I think that's the only thing. I'm not satisfied with anything less. If I were a larger man, then maybe. This is where we return to the weird politics of body. I've made the claim that the accomplishment of the unaccomplishable act may be a function of body, a sufficient body, and I feel I have an insufficient body. If I were a larger man, I might be willing to forego that absolutism in respect of accomplishment. I might be willing to be satisfied with less than myself on the page, feeling I had more of myself in reality. But I feel myself actually excavated. I feel myself, placed by reason of circumstance, on the margins in both realms, and I have in me all the frustration, all the rage, all the anger, all the viciousness of temperament that is the result of that sense of myself having been thrust to the margins, by reason, not of ability, but of the given.

You mentioned your presentation of yourself. In your fiction you consistently mix the obviously autobiographical with the not-so-obviously autobiographical. Is this an attempt to re-create or remake yourself?

Everything I do is an effort to remake myself. I'm not interested in re-making anybody else, and I'm not interested in re-creating anything outside of myself. I'm interested in finding, in the page, a replacement for what I feel I've been deprived of in actuality. But I beg you to believe that when you say "obvious autobiographical elements," I would refuse that observation and say "apparent autobiographical elements."

Well, I'm referring to more than using your own name as the name of your protagonist. I'm talking about things such as using your own neighborhood as the setting or the names of your own father and mother as the names of the protagonist's father and mother.

I have two ways of answering this, or three ways. Let me give you three notions that I think probably apply to what I'm up to. One is, if I can set forth certain facticities that are somewhat known of me, then I can buttress the force of authority in those absolute inventions that I'm going to set forth. So that's one trick. In the case of *Peru*, for example, I dedicate the book to my mother and father, gave their actual names so I could use the actual names in the book to give some sense of authority to the claim that I had, at the age of six, or the speaker had, at the age of six, done away with another boy. I gave the name of the person who was presumably assassinated in the course of the book, Stephen Michael Adinoff, and his dates, trying to lend a certain verifiable force to the fictions that have been assembled around those facticities.

I do it, too, because I think it's pointless to invent certain points. The energy that is consumed in the invention, I think, is quite uselessly consumed. Why bother to invent? The whole thing is a fiction by my lights. Everybody knows it's made up. Why play that game? If it's a novel, if it's being promoted as a novel, it's being put out there or sponsored as a novel, then presumably it's all made up, is it not, so why bother?

While you're at this point, "being promoted as a novel," in what way is My Romance *a novel?*

In what way is it a novel? Only because I said it's a novel. I think the book says it's a novel. It may not be a novel. I don't know how I would define what a novel is. I know people spend a lot of time with that activity. I don't know if it's interesting anymore.

I read recently a book I'm rather fond of, Seamus Deane's *Reading in the Dark*. I'm told that it was originally published as a memoir in England or in Ireland and is being published as a novel here. Does it interfere with my savor of the text any to know that in one instance it's to be viewed in this category? I must say, Yes. Yes, it does. Had I known it was viewed as a memoir and then later published as a novel for reasons that may or may not have to do with literary gamesmanship, I might not have been so disturbed by the discovery.

These books that I put out are only novels by declaration. Are they novels by definition? Are they novels by construction? Heavens, I would be the last one to be competent to say. Certainly any of the critics that I've named that take their chicken and peas in the United States would say no. I mean, I imagine that Harold Bloom and Denis Donoghue would say that's just Gordon doing what Gordon does, but it's scarcely to be viewed as a novelistic enterprise. But I think I might persuade Julia Kristeva of a different view, or I might be able to persuade Giorgio Agamven, certainly, of a different view.

I don't think anything on that score, this is just to remark by the by, is particularly new, by the way. I mean, this has been done for a long, long, long, long time. I'm not a scholar with sufficient information to give you names and addresses, but what I'm up to, or what I appear to be up to, the seeming actuality of so much that I put on the page, as in *My Romance*, has been done for a longish, longish, longish time while under the rubric of novel or imaginative writing.

My Romance turns on my turning my father upside down while he was perceived to be coughing, undergoing a coughing fit, and dropping him while doing that, and having had the inspiration to turn him upside down by reason of his having told the story over and over again of having done so to a brother who was choking on a peanut or a sourball or a piece of jelly apple or something in the park. The observation I might make about that, and this is interesting to me, is that it represents that particular mechanism, that device, precisely the mechanism that I apply in *Epigraph*, and I see it everywhere in me, the inability to escape my own devices.

Clearly, clearly, what study of any of these works sufficiently would discover, as I am now discovering since I'm revising them all, is that I'm quite unequipped to escape certain rather well-worked grooves in my personality when I perceive myself as the one speaking. These are the things I say, and I say them again and again and again and again, hoping each time to say them somewhat more ably than I have said them. But the fact that I am saying them over and over again certainly speaks to an authenticity in them. It certainly must speak to some kind of deeply positioned autobiographical stance. So I can't deny it, can I? I can't deny it. So there they are. Even in the effort to reinvent and write another autobiographical novel, as *Epigraph* might be construed to be, I'm back in the same place again.

I've only got two or three, not even themes. I've only got two or three, not even tales to tell. There are two or three bits that I can't let go of because they won't let go of me. But let me put this to you. The force of their fascination for me is certainly vouchsafed by my inability to escape them. I do try. I do try to elude the purchase taken on me by that which has developed in me, the jeopardy of the gaze. I do try to do that, but I don't succeed. Does anyone succeed at this? I'm not a close enough student of anyone's writing, or I'm too polite, despite what's claimed of me, to offer an observation yea or nay. I'm not willing to believe I'm unique in this respect.

I might have been able to get away with it better had I been a poet. I read Wallace Stevens a lot, since you asked about influence. I read Stevens's letters a lot. I'm eager to find all sorts of connections between Stevens's life and my own, right down to, and I'll put this to you, my extraordinary discovery not long ago that the face on the coin, on the half dollar coin, and on the dime that I gazed at so often as a child in honor of my idea of an American woman, since I come from an immigrant family, what a great American woman looked like, the one that you would have to bed in lieu of all the other women you could not bed, turns out to have been modeled for a sculptor who was a landlord in Chelsea. He was, actually in fact, Stevens's landlord when he and Elsie Kachel, his wife, were living in Chelsea, and the design on the coin was modeled by Stevens's wife, so that it's fair to make the claim that I was infatuated with Stevens's wife, or at least her profile, from the time I was five or six or seven years old. You looked at the dime, you looked at the half dollar, and you saw Stevens's wife, amazingly.

When I say influence in this respect, what got me on this stream of discourse was what I would take to be repetitive fascinations, or fascinations surfacing again and again and again and again, in Stevens. I think we're rather more willing to forgive the poet than we are to forgive the novelist. But I'm probably not a novelist, and I'm probably not a poet either. I'm on the page.

Talking to you now, the responses I make to you, as much as they seem to rush out of me without very careful consideration, are very practiced. I'm not surprising myself. I'm not saying anything that I haven't really probably said, one way or another, before. What I produce for the page probably comes a little closer, a little closer, to getting rid of, or squandering, something actual in myself and the pleasure I take from this, the way in which it answers the aggressivity in me, to use Kristeva's term from the first epigraph, is as close as I'm going to get to the sublime. I feel good with it. I've come to the view, with the work that I do, that it has finally become absolutely necessary for me to do it and that if I am made to see, five years after the work has achieved print, that I've simply iterated, yet again, an earlier reiteration, I'm not dismayed by it.

It seems to me that if the task is to write my name onto the surface of the earth, which I take to be as hard a surface as we will find, then the effort of scribing the same mark over and over and over again might leave some kind of trace. And I think that's what I'm doing, writing the same mark over and over and over again.

When you say writing the same mark over and over again, are you making the same effort, are you using the same muscles when you begin a novel that you use when you're rewriting, for example, Dear Mr. Capote, *which you've recently done?*

Best question I was asked, Rob. Best question anybody ever asked me. I use my dick, mainly, to write the first time, and I'm using my brains to do the revisions. I mean, not my brain. I'm using rather practiced sequences of motions that have to do chiefly with mind or chiefly with know-how. I'm trying to stick it into the page the first time out. The twenty-eight versions of *Epigraph*, each of which was disposed of and each of which, I would argue, is a distance from its predecessor. I disposed of them entirely because I'm trying to create a blank, but I couldn't create that blank, quite plainly. Never could create that blank. They were done with an effort to jam it in as deeply as I could.

There in fact is, it occurs to me now, quite felicitously, a little moment in the book when the speaker, which I find to be the delicate way to mark the narrator, is discussing the pressure that is produced between the unmentionables, I think is his word, his own unmentionable and his sex partner's unmentionable, by reason of her gesture with her heels. She's able to enact some kind of gesture with her heels and his ankles such that the contact between them is tighter. I'm always looking for that tighter and tighter and tighter contact. I find that in actual sex, it's never quite considerable enough. And I'm not talking about a psychic or a spiritual or an emotional experience. I'm talking about simply the body being in contact with its other never being quite sufficient to satisfy me. I never feel like I'm in enough, man. I'm always afraid that's she's going to say, Are you in yet?

Does the analogy hold true with the work? Are you ever afraid that the book is going to voice back, Are you in yet?

Oh, man. Do you know what? This is it. Given the terms that I've invoked by reason of everything I've said, I think you've offered the supreme reply to my work.

I would like to not only put the steak and potatoes out there but to gobble them all up, gobble up everything on the table, and everybody else's food, too, put my hands on their plate and eat their food, as well. So yes, the book's saying, Yes Gordon, tell me when you're in. That's probably it. I'm just going to have to deal with that. I don't know what else to do.

But you know who's in? Certainly McCarthy. Certainly in *Blood Meridian*. I would say he's really in in *Blood Meridian*, and DeLillo's really in in *Underworld*.

I want to talk about the revision process and editing your own work but, while we're talking about Epigraph *specifically, you said that there are twenty-eight. Would we call them drafts or versions?*

I wouldn't call them drafts. I never sit down with ambition to produce something that I'll then rid myself of or keep some semblance of and work through and improve. No, I write it as ably as I can, as truly as I can, as carefully, as closely machining a sentence with ferocity of attention that I would hold to be as good as you're going to get, as good as I'm going to get, ever.

So there were twenty-eight previous versions of Epigraph *before the one that was published?*

What you're holding in your hand is twenty-nine. It's a completely different undertaking. From start to finish a different rendering. This is the only one that turned out to be epistolary.

Really?

It never was epistolary until I did the last one and then that I revised and revised. The process I undergo usually is when I get it back in type the first time round, I do about 80 percent of it all over again.

Is Epigraph *your greatest accomplishment as a writer? Is it the closest you've come to that absolute as a writer?*

Oh God, I hope not, man.

If you had to hand over one of your books as an example of your finest effort toward the absolute, which one would you choose?

I won't dodge the question because I'm always of the view that I'm about to crap out and whatever I've gotten on the record is it. It would be improper to point to something yet unwritten, and the work presently underway, *Arcade*, even though I'm up to rather a lot of pages is, God knows, not for the record yet. But there's a book called *Self-Imitation of Myself*.

I can't recite the title without offering the observation that DeLillo abominates that title, and maybe that's the reason why I insist upon it now, so as to avoid any taint of being influenced by DeLillo although he's influenced me a lot in respect to very specific matters. I asked him recently about an epigraph for the novel *Arcade*. It's a completely contrived epigraph, by the way, but assigned to somebody. I do that from time to time. I'm a bad guy, Rob. But that's all right. I mean, it's a novel, right?

It's a book that, in fact, Four Walls has their hands on. I finished it about a year ago, I think it is. I finished a novel called *Chinese* and a novel called *Self-Imitation of Myself*, and I haven't read either one of them. I don't really want to read *Chinese* at all. I imagine I'll be much displeased when I do read it, but I have a sense that *Self-Imitation of Myself* would probably be that book that I would put before you as that object, making the claim that it not so much expresses my best token in the game, but it probably encompasses the heart of me better than anything I've ever done.

Will the words "a novel" be printed beneath the title?

Yes, otherwise I'd probably be put away in jail forever. Now I haven't looked at it, mind you, in that occasion of desire when I believed I was in as far as I could've got in and she was screaming with completion and perfection of all of her wants. When we have a look at the matter, she may make the claim Were you there? Did anything happen? Tell me when it's over.

So Self-Imitation is still a dick book?

It's a dick book. All my books are dick books.

But much time has passed since the original appearance of Dear Mr. Capote *and you've gone back and revised it. Doesn't that make the reprint a brain book?*

It sure does and they all will become, but you know they're infinitely better reflections of my concerns for cadence, my concerns for the syntactical relations that might be achieved. They've been spot cleaned of their errors to the extent I'm able, but the initial error, the original error, where I wanted to put my dick in the first place, there's the thing. Where do you want to put your pencil in the first place occurs to me as critical, and it's probably there that I'm never going to escape.

Here, I'll tell you something I haven't told anyone. My original fascination, the thing that set me in motion, the thing I wanted to write about with this book, *Epigraph*, was produced in a glance. I think it's referred to in the most passing way in the novel that now obtains, or the work that now obtains if you'll grant me that, but at a certain point, at the initial point, when the originary moment was upon me, this was it. My wife was being held aloft by two nurses and a third person. It may have been a mother. I don't know who the third person was in the room with her, but there were two nurses and a third person. She was strangling on her saliva. All the material in her bowels was running out of her anus. She was urinating. Everything was coming out of everywhere. Suction tubes were in her everywhere. She had tubes in her chest, two tubes in her chest, and because she could no longer flex her feet, given the nature of the disease which had made her muscles in her feet useless, they had fixed in a certain position. She was positioned on her toes. The most excruciating pain one would imagine. She could no longer speak, of course. She could not even scream her agony. And I was rushing back and forth from the closet in the kitchen to the bathroom adjoining our bedroom, where my wife was, with towels. We always had stacks to clean up and clean up and clean up. And she must have, at the time, weighed forty, forty-five, fifty pounds.

I've never seen anything like it, never imagined, and I've been in two bughouses, been in jail. I'm willing to look at anything. I've looked at hard things in my life, but I never imagined I would see anything quite so close to a transfiguring moment as this. This was as close as I would ever come to seeing the unseeable. I looked at this thing and felt such shame in looking at it. I had the sense of such deep-seated shame in looking upon her nakedness in this way. This was a nakedness of the spirit. I don't even have that termed. I would have to try to write it out and write it out and write it out.

But that's what animated me in the moment. I thought, That's the thing. That was the aspect. Not my wife, not the three people, but just what I was able to sense, the "on the toesness." Her "on the toesness." "On the toesness" is the only way to say it. It was her "on the toesness." It was the bones. It was the deathhead, the mouth open and everything rushing out all over the body. I wanted to make a book out of that. I wanted to make a book out of that and my looking at it. I wanted to make a book out of my sense of being unable to achieve contact between my unmentionable and that unmentionable. I wanted to make a book about my being kept out of it, at a distance from it, and because of being kept out of it, at a distance from it, everlastingly ashamed, everlastingly damned in my judgment. Damned.

I couldn't do that. I tried. I don't know how many of those twenty-eight books we've been talking about were efforts to do that, but I certainly couldn't get anywhere close to it. I beg you to believe all of them were efforts to reduce the whole of the event to a wispiness of it that I'm not even competent to describe to you. All of it achieved in the glance, and certainly vividly. I mean, I'm still able to look exactly at the thing I was looking at then, and able to revisit the same feelings I had then. It's not as if I've lost it, but what has occurred is a failure before it, an insufficiency before the force of the object, and it's important that I make the point, the object is not something which would be describable by anybody else but myself, and only to be seen in capturing that fraction of a second when that certain composition of elements was as it were and as I was in relation to them. That's what I mean by the object.

Is the incapability of rendering that moment, that vision, that feeling of shame—is that a temporary incapability? Is that something that you couldn't achieve with this book? Is that something you will ever be able to capture?

Rob, I don't know. I will try. I will try. I'll never have another one like that and I can't do that one again. I failed that one. I contaminated it. I can speak to it as I'm doing with you now. I may find myself speaking to it, but I'll never render it.

Now, I beg you to believe that part of that sense of failure certainly derives out of my knowing, absolutely knowing, that DeLillo, that Brodkey, that McCarthy would not fail in the face of those objects. They could do it. I certainly would include Ozick in that, but I'm not prepared to go beyond that and say that Denis Johnson, for example, who we both admire very greatly, could do it or any other persons we've been naming could do it.

I think maybe Barry Hannah could do it because Barry Hannah has an enormous heart and he's afraid of nothing. I recall Donoghue once saying about Barry Hannah, when I think I was publishing Hannah's *Airships*, Barry Hannah is afraid of nothing in experience. I try to be afraid of nothing in experience, but I'm really afraid of everything. I try to adopt this disguise I'm afraid of nothing. I like to say I've been in the bughouse twice. I've been in jail. I've done some heavy stuff. I've driven across country a number of times with Cassady, that kind of shit, but the fact of the matter is I'm afraid of everything. Everything. Principally, I'm afraid of her saying, Tell me when you're in, you know. That kind of thing.

I'm terribly afraid of anything exterior of myself and have always been. I've never not been afraid. I've always been uncomfortable. I've never not been uncomfortable. I've always been uncomfortable with my body. I've always been uncomfortable with the earth, and I can't seem to ever find my way on the page outside of the pressure of those repressed powers, of those repressed forces in me. That's what I'm all about. I'm all about my fear. I would like to make the claim that the desire in me is adequate to displace the fear in order to produce a text but always, at the end of the text, when I come back to it, and I'm coming back to *Capote* now, I see that fear really won out.

Fear affects your writing, but does or did fear ever affect you when you acted as editor?

No. I'm tyrannical. I'm certainly reported to be tyrannical and everybody can't be wrong.

I'm assuming that no one else edits your work.

You know, I was edited once. No one edits my work in the sense that I have edited others, line-by-line editing, no. But I'll tell you one time I was edited and I knuckled under, and it kills me that I did it and it's lost now forever. I can recall being told by somebody when I told the story that I should answer now with revision, but I couldn't do it when I got *Capote*. But it had to do with *Capote* and it had to do with the editor then, Billy Abrams, calling me at the last minute because I had gone through many, many revisions, and then saying, You know, I don't want this last one. I want the one before the last one.

I said, No, no. The last one is the one that's the way I want it, and I just can't have it any other way, and what the last one was was a kind of frame over the frame over the frame, the unfolding of the guy who was claiming to be killing people. He suddenly shuts up in mid-sentence, and a letter to Mailer occurs and it's myself writing to Mailer about a bet we had about memory, trying to recall some responses to some trivia questions about soap operas and the claim being made to see if the narrative structure will produce recollections of a kind. It had to do maybe with what Ben Bernie would say or what Ben Bernie's sign-off was, I can't recall, but you get a letter to Mailer, a quite civilized letter to Mailer, about that discussion we had, and we had the bet, and I win the bet because here, in fact, is the proper answer to the question. And then it comes back to the novel as the novel is going forward again, and then it comes back to Mailer again and it was very, very carefully worked out. Minor, minor citations in a novel that was going along become major citations in the letter and vice versa, so that what was foregrounded was backgrounded, what was backgrounded was foregrounded. It was kind of a playful thing like that.

But Abrams said, No, no. Nobody can read that. Nobody will ever get that and I don't know why you want to do that, and I don't want that, and it can't be that way. And I said, I'm sorry, it can't be any other way but that way. And Lynn Nesbitt, who was my agent at the time, in essence she and her colleague suggested to me that I was being a fool, but I think I was a fool for allowing them to suggest that to me and for taking their counsel but did as told and Abrams had his way with it, and I always have been displeased.

When I've told the story, I think I've told it once or twice, I told it to one of my children once, and that child said, Gee Dad, now that you've got a chance to do it your own way, do it your own way, and I couldn't. I couldn't. I thought about doing it when I redid *Capote* and I couldn't. My heart wasn't in it anymore. I just couldn't. No, that's an unsatisfactory way of making the statement. The fact of the matter is I couldn't do it. Mechanically I couldn't do it. Whatever intricacy then obtained in the making of that device required of me a kind of faith I no longer had.

I want to talk about the dualities you mentioned in relation to fear restricting you as a writer. Can you not get Gordon Lish the writer out of the room and leave the manuscript with Gordon Lish the editor? Is it impossible for you to achieve that objectivity?

I can't do for myself what I have done for others. And I say with some satisfaction I've done some remarkable things for others.

And you don't trust anyone else to do it for you?

I would be willing, perhaps, to do so if someone would volunteer, but nobody really ever has.

Have you asked or are you expecting a knock on the door?

Well, I always knocked on doors. I knocked the house down. I was unwilling to get out of the picture. I had to have it right, my idea of right. Otherwise I couldn't put my name on that contract as it were. And I no longer have that kind of ferocity.

In your short story "How to Write a Novel" from What I Know So Far, *you say to buy the first one of whatever it is because the maker of it is never going to knock himself out like that again. And yet you're rewriting your previously published books. So, should I believe you now, or should I believe you then?*

Don't believe me anytime, Rob. Don't believe me anytime. Don't believe me anytime. I don't think I'm worth believing. There's no profit in believing me. The only thing you can get from it or not get from it is the pleasure of the time, the savor of the time. Because I'm a frightened man, because I'm essentially a weasel, because I'm essentially a swindler, because I'm a wheedler, because I'm always looking for a way to escape, I'm not reliable. I'm not trustworthy. I would make that claim of myself with anything I say, but in my life, in my relations, I've proved remarkably reliable. A good old loyal dog. I would never leave a wife. I've been left by wives. I would never leave a friend. I've been left by friends. So, reliable in human relations curiously but not reliable in what I say.

Language, for me, is something that belongs to other people. In the same way I feel that my body represents a bad judgment made on me. I should've looked like Alan Ladd. That was the notion I had as a kid. I should've looked like Alan Ladd. That would've been fair, that would've been just it seems to me. I should've been able to hit a baseball, I should've been able to knock them down the way Joe Louis could knock them down, that's the sense of sufficiency I have. I'm an American boy like that, and I think we're all American boys like that. My complaint is, that when it comes to language, because of the kind of circumstances I came from, where English was not really the language that was exquisitely managed in the household, everything in me, always, everything in me is an effort to grab onto what I feel I was deprived of.

I can reduce it to the personification of Miss McEvoy, who is really Miss Donnelly in *Peru*. There really was a teacher I had named Miss McEvoy who was everything I understood Americans to be. She looked like Wallace Stevens's wife on the fifty-cent piece, and she sounded like Miss McEvoy, and she had the elocution of Miss McEvoy, and she had the enunciation of Miss McEvoy, and she had the syntax of Miss McEvoy and all of that. And because I feel myself, when I'm with the language, concerned only with how the language manifests itself through the conduit of Gordon Lish, I'm indifferent entirely to what's said. I don't even know what I'm saying half the time. I'm only saying it for the sake of saying it, for the sake of saying something, hoping that

I can keep talking until I can get out of there safely, without somebody capturing me, without somebody seizing me by the throat.

You know, there's a story by Philip Roth that deserves reading. It's called "On the Air." He never quite finished it, I don't believe. And that tale concerns the terror of the Jew who's captured by the non-Jew, and all of whose Jewishness is really the consideration at hand. We got you now. You can't escape. We're going to measure your balls now.

At a certain point he crosses the George Washington Bridge. He thinks he has an engagement with Einstein at Princeton. Einstein's become the Jewish answer man. He feels there's an insufficiency of Jews on radio. Einstein's the smartest guy in the world. The Jews will have an answer man. So he's on his way to meet with Einstein to produce this program and never makes it. On the way, he's captured and dragged into a back room somewhere, and he's made to have his testicles weighed to see if they measure up.

Now I'm telling you, this is choice. It must be, in every Jew's terror, that this will be his destiny, that this will be fate. Somehow the most intimate part of himself will be measured against other men and found wanting. See? That's the thing. And whether it has any kind of reality to it, whether it has anything other than just simply phantasm to it, is not the point. The phantasm is good enough for me. I've been that way all my life. All my life. And language would be the domain in which I would fear myself most likely to be exposed.

I have seen myself on television and I'll make some error. I'll say something either factually wrong or rhetorically wrong or grammatically wrong and even be corrected, or I'll stop myself and make the correction or the interviewer corrects me. I'm always at the precipice of being convicted.

How do you rationalize the difference between your feelings of responsibility for the spoken word and the written word? What's the difference between your feeling for the spoken word and your feeling for the written word?

Well, I'm better defended in the latter case. I'm much better defended and therefore the aggression in me, because, really, my fear must be, certainly, a version of my aggression. I'll answer your question in a moment. There's an observation I have that interests me a lot, and I've only made it recently about myself.

I walk along the sidewalk always, certainly in New York where the sidewalks are canted so that the rain runs off into the street. I try always to hold to the higher ground so I will, as I pass people, appear to myself to be taller than I am, so I will always seek to walk inside toward the storefronts. When I was in San Francisco recently, I felt how awful it was to be deprived of that advantage because the sidewalks weren't canted in the same way, so that you were often, likely, on the same footing as everybody else and I didn't like that. I wanted a little advantage to what I felt was my insufficiency.

And while I was thinking about that, as I was making my way, I was uncertain about where I was going. I would stop and ask people and, the most curious thing, I'm invariably smaller than the persons I'm asking, irrespective of gender, and I imagine myself as a mild and gentle and pacific man but invariably, and this has been true all of my life, I felt on the occasion of coming up to somebody to ask the question, that I'm somehow dangerous. That they perceive me as dangerous and that I have to, in the asking of the question, somehow give them to understand they are not to interpret my behavior as dangerous. And when I had this notion of myself, when I suddenly realized something about myself, because I'm not, despite evidence to the contrary, evidence you may take to the contrary, I'm not an introspective person at all. I don't sit around thinking about myself. I'm not competent. I would rather hide from myself than think about myself, so this came to me as really news. Wow! Why do I always think I'm dangerous when I'm a little guy? And I do think of myself as somehow dangerous to others. I don't doubt that it's because of the enormous aggression within me or aggressivity within me.

But you're not bothered by that perception at all. Aren't you in a sense flattered that others would see you as dangerous?

Yes. I'm not so sure other people see me as dangerous. I see myself as being dangerous and trying to, in the moment of contact, disabuse them of the notion that I'm dangerous but really, probably, as you quite rightly surmised, relishing that this is an issue, relishing the prospect of this being an issue. And I probably have presented myself that way all whole life long. It's probably what got me into the jams I've gotten into in my life, gotten me the reputation I've got. Probably certainly what's gotten me able to be pals with certain persons you wouldn't think a New York Jewboy would end up being pals with. Probably because I've projected an air of a certain danger or recklessness or willingness to cross certain lines.

Now, I must beg you to believe, nothing in others is more terrifying to me. But I used to ride with guys like this. I was a wrangler in Tucson. I used to ride with whacked guys who didn't use saddles and didn't use regular tack and hit the horses with sticks and didn't come from Wyoming. They came from Long Island and couldn't wait to hurt somebody. I seem to have, in me, by reason of my sense of being tiny, of being small, of being insufficiently large for the case, an awful lot of violence and hence my absolute devotion to *Blood Meridian* as the supreme American text.

Let's go back. You seem to be able to let the spoken word fall where it may yet you're extremely careful with the printed word.

I'm careful with the spoken word, too. I'm just very good at this. You've got to understand, man, you're talking to somebody who gets up once a week and talks for eight hours nonstop and sometimes does it three or four days in a row, so either I'm very good at it or I think I'm very good at it.

You don't ever find out what you think when you've heard yourself say it?

I would like to. I would like to. I'd like to say I'm going instead of I'm coming. I'd like to call out the wrong woman's name.

I tell you this. I didn't even surprise myself when I was captured the first time and put in a nuthouse. I must've been about sixteen, seventeen. I was as gone as I think I'm going to get, but nothing I did really surprised me, and I ended up thinking it was just more theater. I ended up thinking even the craziness was feigned and what got me locked up in manacles and chains in Florida and kept on bread and water for two weeks and that kind of thing, in serious lockup, I think it was all an act. I don't think I surprised myself with anything. I think I was pretending. I think I've been pretending for as long as I can remember.

Nothing I say to you, as much as I would like to give it the appearance of vehemence and immediacy, has surprised me. I may be completely transparent to others, and you may be sitting and surmising what I'm up to, maybe saying, I can read this guy through and through, and how come he can't read these conclusions that I come to, but I don't know that I'm escaping. I don't know that I'm ever going to elude the surmise or elude capture as it were. I can't speak to that. It's not within my power to know, but I get the sense, that's all I require, that, Gee, I got through with that. I got through with that without making a shambles of things, without delivering myself up to some kind of deep, deep, deep shame, or I preempted the shame. I preempted the moment. I delivered myself to shame before that person could deliver me to shame, before that person could say, Hey, you don't make it. You're not in yet. Before that person could say, Are you there? I said, I'm probably not there. So that suffices for me.

I suppose, with how I'm read, both on the page and how I'm read as an editor, and how I'm read as a publisher, and how I'm read as a teacher, it's that the surmise that I think that I've, in an approximate kind of way, produced for you today, isn't the surmise that's mainly made about me. I'm willing to take the rap for what I think my crimes have been, and I think I certainly have committed crimes, but I'm not infrequently, I think rather more to the point, as paranoiacally as I can, the view of me that's posited as the authoritative view, the thing just doesn't square with reality at all. And I don't think it's got by people that have ever had any kind of touch with me at all.

But you like your reputation.

I've got to like it. It's what I'm stuck with.

You don't have to like it.

I've come to like it. I've come to like it, I suppose. I've even come to like the price I've paid for it.

Let me see if I can steer you back by using a different course. You would never hand over Chinese *and allow me to edit it.*

No, I wouldn't. You got me, man.

But these words now are your words and, in a sense, I will be editing you. What's the difference?

What's the difference? What is the difference? First-rate question, first-rate question because I wouldn't cede to you, or anyone else, the authority to revise *Chinese* or any of my work. I won't even let you look at it. I don't even want you to fucking look at the goddamn thing until I fix it. I write all kinds of insane letters trying to govern the ungovernable. My God, man, please, please, I'm only giving this to you now in case the plane goes down. I don't even want that record in place because I have my pride, my pride and my vanity.

Well, gee Rob, I don't know that it's going to be possible for me to answer it with any adroitness. You've got me captured.

Probably because my valorizing of this episode in speech is very different from my valorizing of the other. That's plain to see. I don't know what you're going to make of this, this exchange between us, but whatever you make out of it, the very best you can make out of it, it will have been a collaborative effort.

Does the fact that this is a collaboration absolve you of a certain responsibility?

That's it. That's the word. That's the word. That's the word, man. That's the word. See, I wrote about twenty books before *Capote*, under other names, and as long as it was under another name, I didn't give a shit what I'd done, what kinds of errors might be in place. I never have looked back. And I did a lot of work under other people's names, too, when they got fame for it, a lot of fame for it, and I, even in those instances, and there's one instance in which I don't think I could've conceivably have labored with a more finely grained tooth comb, that's the expression, with more fine-grained attention than I did. We were revising and revising and revising it over and over again for each edition, taking such pains with every utterance that came out of my mouth in that writer's name. I, nevertheless, am willing to say, although I have acknowledged that I could not edit myself as successfully as I could edit somebody else, or revise myself as successfully as I could revise somebody else, that unless my marriage to the inviolate center of myself as it comes into play by reason of my written utterance, that's to be in touch with the only God I'm ever in touch with. It's the only thing, in all of my experience, that's even perspectively sacred.

But there's a sanctity that you bestow on the printed word, and in the case of at least two of your works, soon to be all of your works, the printed word changes. I guess what I'm asking for is ungivable, even if you have the desire.

You've published dick books and brain books, but the separation seems to be caused only by time. Why is Epigraph, *after twenty-nine tries, still a dick book? When does it become a brain book? When did* Capote *become a brain book?*

Time's the big fucker, man, and these designations we're offering as if they are polarities, dick and brain, really aren't, as both of us know.

Is time the only thing that can provide the distance?

No, no. I don't think so. I think intellect has got a lot to do with it. There are some people who are smart. If I were to speak of my friends, DeLillo and Ozick, they're both really fucking smart, really smart, you know. I would never make this claim. I'm always prepared to argue with my students that smarts has nothing to do with it. That the mind can, in fact, be in your way, but as I measure, after the fact, my life, because I see my life after the fact now, those persons that have done nobly and really work with respect to the page, given that polarity that has been invoked, dick books and mind books, they're all smart. The ones I have named are really fucking smart. They're sure as hell smarter than I am. I don't like having to concede that. I would rather think that cleverness, I would rather that think devotion would do, stamina would do, that desire would do. I don't want to be seen as good and smart. I'd rather be seen as the supreme swindler. I'd rather be seen as the grand artificer.

Then you've pretty much got what you want, haven't you?

Well, you're very genial to offer that observation. From your mouth to God's ears, even though God doesn't exist for me, Rob. You make me grin. But I don't, really. You see, the people I named, they could get that thing down that I told you I couldn't get down. They could get anything down. As I read through DeLillo's *Underworld*, I came again and again to the altogether unpleasant recognition that this guy can do things I can't even imagine getting words around.

There's a moment in his book when he's writing about the major dump out on Staten Island, and it's just a bit. I remember it exactly in the manuscript because I was reading the thing and I said, I'm not going to call. I'm not going to call him until I finish the whole damn thing, you know. It was deep in where he's offering you up the behavior of some seagulls over the dump as they are suddenly fastened in the air and he follows the word, "regardful, ready to fly."

Now, I couldn't do that. First of all, I couldn't look at seagulls moving anywhere, in any circumstance, even imagined seagulls, and render them. I couldn't give you the sense of a seagull, and I couldn't give you that sense of a seagull as it comes to its pause and then begins to fly again with the word "regardful." That kind of looking about that one sees in the seagull's behavior. That word "regardful" would never ever be rendered to me. I could seek its deliverance the rest of my days and would never get it because I could never study the object with the form of attention required to produce the word "regardful" from it. I could never get it.

That's not a matter of character because I've got character in spades. I think I do. I'm not chicken shit. I've never walked away from a fight. I'm willing to stand up to any fucking thing, really man, I am, to be killed on it. I believe in the writing of a book and signing your own death warrant. That's how it should be if it's to be a proper book. But DeLillo can get that "regardful" because I think he's got an intellectual power. He's got mind in amplitude I'm never going to have. I can say the same about certain other parties including McCarthy. And I feel so damned deprived on account of it.

I used to pal around with James D. Watson, the double helix guy, and I've known one or two really pretty smart cookies in my life, and it's okay to be around Watson, or people like Bloom. There are people like Bloom who can start reciting all of Murphy to you, backwards. Bloom can recite all of Murphy to you. I mean, you want Beckett? Bloom can give it to you out of his head. I've never seen a mind work faster than James D. Watson's mind. Or Neal Cassady. Cassady could talk around seven different things at the same time and give each one its due. One's a scientist, one's a critic, and one's just a guy on the street, you know, but DeLillo and Ozick and Brodkey. These are unforgivable. They're writers and they bring to the task of writing an amplitude of intellect.

Don't you have an appreciation for them, as writers, if for no other reason than that they can do things that you can't as a writer?

They should be there as my models, as what I posit as the heroic, because I'm of the same category. Is that what you're saying?

No, only if you need to render a seagull should you hold them up as models.

But I don't need to render a seagull. Who needs a seagull? I want to write about what's in my heart and what's inside me. I don't want a seagull. Seagulls are in the world. Anybody can look at it. Anybody could look at it, but you see, he could've looked at my shit, any of those persons named could've looked at my shit, whatever my interior shit is, and rendered it. You see, that's the thing. They could do a better job. They could deliver that moment, that glance that I took, that peek I had, when I looked on the unpeekable, the unlookable, when I looked at Barbara Lish when she was in that condition, in that circumstance I described to you, and they would get it out. They would get all of it.

No. They can't be more Gordon Lish than Gordon Lish.

I would like to think they wouldn't have seen it in the first place. I would like to think they would've seen something an instant later, an instant before, and not seen the very thing that I saw.

Because you want that moment for yourself.

That's right. That's right.

Didn't you remark that Epigraph *was a book of a man driven insane by grief? Or am I misquoting?*

I don't have a problem with that. Is he driven insane by grief? He's ultimately a swindler. I'll stay with that.

He's a swindler early on.

He ends a swindler. He seems to become more and more revealed as he speaks. He seems to have removed a certain number of veils, but I think he remains quite wonderfully clothed. He's shrewd to the end. But I don't think I can even read it now. The only true thing in that book, the only true thing in that book, honest to Pete, Rob, I didn't even say, and that's Nietzsche at the very end of it. That's the only true damn thing in there, and that's the last page in the book.

There seems to be a falling off though, and calling him ultimately a swindler suggests that the man is in control. Don't you have to be in control to be a swindler? The narrator of Epigraph *comes apart in the same way as the narrator of* Dear Mr. Capote *comes apart, but in* Epigraph *it's a contrivance?*

Yes. Don't you think that control is false? That the equivalency between control and fraudulence is apt? What you want, we're talking now about the others, saying, not with a withering measure, Are you in yet? We want the other, driven quite beside herself in fulfillment of what it is that's being offered, so that one wants the reader somehow beside himself in response to one's manipulations but one is forever manipulating.

One's probably never going to be in enough, probably isn't even in to begin with, is always trying to develop the apparition of being in, the appearance of being in, putting something in the place of what, if you put it in, you may never be able to bring back out again.

I'm a guy who could get in a car with Cassady and drive like a lunatic, but get to the destination. Some people get in the car and they don't ever get out. You know what I'm saying? I want to get where I'm going. I don't want to lose myself along the way. I haven't gotten lost yet and I'm almost sixty-three. I understand the authority of that exultation—let's get lost. I understand the beauty of that, the exorbitance of that. I would posit this as the sublime for all of my students, but would I ever take myself there into it? No, no. I want to get there.

So the narrator of Epigraph *doesn't lose his way? The narrator of* Epigraph *is as much in control at the end of the novel as he is at the beginning?*

Yes, absolutely.

What about the narrator of Dear Mr. Capote?

Ditto, ditto. You know, the narrator being myself. I mean, after all, I'm Davie.

But don't you need a separation between narrator and author?

If I offer the separation then yes, he lost himself more, he loses himself more. You know, *Peru* ends with that kind of moment, that moment when he's seeking escape from all of this and calls out about the cab driver and all of that. Though you may have seen a very bad version of that thing. It pains me. That novel, it seems to me, as I read it now, seems to be a very homosexual novel. That seems to me to be really altogether about that, about the speaker's falling into the colored man, falling into the taxi driver. I think it's all really about that. As I read the book now it seems to be quite absolutely about these matters, but he nevertheless remembers, you know, his father's telephone number. He's able to produce his father's telephone number. He hasn't forgotten.

See? This would be very like the revision I want to insist upon. I'm going to get it back for another run through because I see now that the number comes up twice. I must've inserted that when I did the paperback version of it because the number wasn't there at all in the original version, I do believe. It only comes up in the very end, so now the right number comes up twice before: Lackawanna 4-1810. The last time the number appears, it ought to be wrong and I can still catch that. It ought to be wrong.

So Peru's not rewritten yet?

Not yet. I just got it from the exchange we had right now. I have revised it, but I'm waiting for the third pass to come back to me, and by Christ, the last time that number is uttered it ought to be wrong. It ought to be wrong. Shit, I got to make two changes in that thing because I also want to add a name to the dedication. I've fallen in love, you see.

But now you've proven yourself wrong because you said you never surprise yourself.

Yes, I just did now. But you furnished the occasion for it. I never would've thought of it had we not been talking. You're my editor. I never would've had the idea.

I don't want to try to equate Peru, *and* Epigraph, *and* Dear Mr. Capote *with Faulkner's* As I Lay Dying, *but in that novel Darl loses control, and he is, in effect, the narrator of that book.*

I tried to read that book recently, about a summer ago.

The circumstances are not dissimilar. Granted, there are more voices, but the progression is similar and Darl does lose his sanity by the end. He loses control. He's no longer being manipulative. In my mind, he loses control of his rational being when his family turns on him at the graveyard and sends him off to the asylum. They get rid of him to save the money for the burned barn, and it's that betrayal that causes him to lose control, but you're telling me that the narrator of Peru *and the narrator of* Epigraph *and the narrator of* Dear Mr. Capote *are still as in control at the end of those novels as they are at the beginning, and so therefore they do not have that moment of loss that Darl experiences.*

They are because I am. They are because I am. And I've tried to get rid of my mind.

I'm really surprised that you don't insist on more separation between author and character.

I'd be a fraud.

How is that different from putting the words "a novel" on the title page?

None of this, really, is reportable fact. My God, none of this is reportable fact. Certainly I'm making no effort at all in the reading of these things, after the point of composition, in the reading of them, to find some kind of moral plane different for myself than I would find for the narrator. I mean, I'm prepared to answer for the narrator as if I were.

I recall a time when Bellow was asked about Augie March in relation to Reaganomics. He was asked the question in some interview, How would Augie March behave during the Reagan period in relation to Reaganomics? And he made a reply as if what was ink on paper somehow existed as an authentic being that would have an authentically stable response to conditions. I thought nothing could be more preposterous, nothing could be more ridiculous, but I didn't invent Augie March. I only invented a version of Gordon Lish, and I can tell you exactly how Gordon Lish would feel in any circumstance, and I don't want to make the claim that there's any kind of distance, any real distance, any statable distance, between myself and the name I'm using for myself in my books.

But you see the problem I have. I don't see how claiming a separation between author and narrator is any more fraudulent than putting the words a novel *on the title page in order to present it as a work of fiction.*

There are certain frauds one is more comfortable with than others. I think it was becoming sort of modish not to make a designation of any kind when I started to put out these books. Is it still in the mode? I don't know. I know in 1984 with *Capote* I had the sense that it was getting to be modish to leave off a designation, and I always work against the mode, whatever the mode was.

Were all previous twenty-eight versions of Epigraph—*even though no others were epistolary—what could be described as a type of monologue?*

Yes. Oh, absolutely. That would be true. That would be true.

Is the monologue a congenial form?

You're discovering my only form, I think. It better be congenial.

Are you capable of writing another type of novel?

Oh, I have, under other names. A standard kind of novel? Third person and all that?

Yes, in another point of view. At this moment.

Oh, now? Under my own name? I wouldn't in a million years. Wouldn't in a million years. The only novel I've got under my own name that presumably doesn't have me as a fixture in it is the novel *Extravaganza*, which I will presently revise, I suppose. But that novel's just a stunt. It's a bunch of jokes.

But I don't think I could, Rob. I've started several just as Cynthia Ozick has lately started a book in the first person and has some misgivings about a book in the first person. I would start a book in some other point of view. There are many, many points of view aside from the ones routinely cited. There are all kinds of ways of producing once removed and once removed. There are all kinds of tricks, but the only point I want to make is that I rather imagine that, in due course, I would think better of it, having made my way into the text feeling that somehow I was hobbling myself and that it's not worth the hobbling. Just to be able to point to a book that was rendered by reason of another kind of device wouldn't be worth the price in not getting far enough in.

So it's a moot question. It doesn't matter whether the monologue is a congenial form. It's your form.

I'm my object. I'm my character. I've got no other. I don't believe in any other.

A Conversation with Stephen Dixon

Stephen Dixon was born in 1936, and since 1963 he has published nearly 500 stories in such magazines as *Paris Review, Harper's, Atlantic Monthly,* and *Playboy.* This extraordinary feat works out to roughly one published story a month. He has published, on average, one book each year since his first collection, *No Relief,* appeared in 1976. Dixon has been recognized with a grant from the National Endowment for the Arts, a Guggenheim Fellowship, the Pushcart Prize, an O. Henry Award, and by the American Academy and Institute for Arts and Letters. Two novels, *Frog* and *Interstate,* have been nominated for the National Book Award. Stephen Dixon may well be the most decorated unknown writer in America.

Generally, critics recognize Dixon as an urban stylist whose narratives are propelled by protagonists not too far removed from his own biography. Before joining the writing faculty at Johns Hopkins University, Dixon worked as a junior high school teacher, bartender, salesclerk, waiter, artist's model, and reporter, among other jobs, and many of his earlier characters share similar employment histories. The writer is married with two daughters, as are the protagonists, most notably, of *Frog* and *Interstate.*

I spoke with Stephen Dixon in his New York apartment, around the corner from Columbia University, the morning after his reading at the National Arts Club in support of his novel *Gould*.

You're quoted, in the preface to a Glimmer Train *interview, as saying, "'Frog's Interview' says most of it for me." To me, Howard Tetch is more cross, ornery, and cantankerous in that chapter than in any other part of the book. Is that a fair assessment?*

Yes, it is. But since I was writing it as a short story, I wanted to make it dramatic and funny and interesting, and if he was just benign and uninteresting it wouldn't have been a good story. It doesn't serve truth as well as it serves fiction.

So what is your opinion of the interview process?

Oh, I don't like the interview process at all. I would rather not be interviewed and, if anything, that sort of reflected my sort of interior cantankerousness, my covert rather than my overt cantankerousness. I would prefer not to be interviewed but I interview, selectively, because people ask me to and it's probably good for the work.

What's the current count of published books?

A very small press is publishing my twentieth book later this year. It's my first completed novel, the one that I first wanted to get published and never could. It's called *Tisch*. I worked on that between 1961 and 1969, so this book is thirty years old, and a small company in Palmdale, California called Red Hen Press is coming out with it. It's a very small contract. They wanted a book of mine, and I always wanted to publish this book.

Did you rewrite it?

No. I'm not going to rewrite it, and it's a book that I only would pub-lish with a very, very small house so people would know that it's an old book rather than a book that follows the newest book.

What's the story count?

The story count is probably about 425 now. I lost count. I've had about fifteen stories published this year and fifteen last year. The last time I counted I was at about 350, and that was three or four years ago.

If you've published 425 stories, how many finished stories do you have?

Well, I have, lying around, about another fifty stories. I threw out a whole bunch of material, but they weren't really finished. Those were really sort of first or second drafts that didn't work. I would say, alto-gether, about 500. I'm still writing them left and right.

In any article or review of your work, the number of published stories is al-most always mentioned. What does publishing a story give you that writing alone doesn't provide? Is there a different satisfaction in the publication?

No, once I finish writing the story, the satisfaction is over. I don't worry about getting it published. I just send it out. I don't get any satisfaction in seeing it published. I just like to write it. I don't waste any time think-ing about a story once it's over with.

You mentioned that Tisch will be published thirty years after you wrote it. Are there any other unpublished, longer works?

Yeah, there's one that I love. It's called *The Story of a Story and Other Stories*. It's a short one, 160 pages. I wrote that in 1974 through 1976, but nobody's ever wanted to publish it. Asylum Arts was interested, but then they took something else. It's a very sort of experimental work, you could say. Maybe too many tricks for one publisher.

Your face lit up just mentioning the title, but your contention two minutes ago was that you didn't care about publishing, that there was no extra satisfaction.

Well, the stories, no, but the novels, yes, because so much time is consumed. That's almost the difference between the short story and the novel. The novel, if you put in one, two, or three years and it's wasted, at the end of it you feel that it's a piece of junk. You really feel that three years of your creative life were for nothing except maybe learning what you shouldn't do. But a short story, you can write it and spend two weeks or thirty days on it, or for a very long one, two months, and if nothing comes of it, well, it's a short amount of time.

But *Story of a Story* I love because it's a one-of-a-kind book. I would love to see it published someday because I still think it's fresh, while *Tisch*, although I take some chances in it, I'm doing more for historical purposes than anything else. I still feel that it's a valid, funny novel.

Your first published story, "The Chess House," appeared in Paris Review *in 1963. When did you first start writing?*

I started writing a little when I was in City College in 1957. I wrote about two or three stories and submitted one to a college magazine contest in which the winner would get fifty bucks. Of course, I didn't get the prize. Not only did I not get the prize, but the teacher scribbled all over my story saying what a piece of crap it was, even changing the title from "Miss Turvy" to "Topsy Turvy," indicating my prose was like that, and then I stopped writing for two years.

I really started writing when I was a newsman in Washington, covering the Capitol and other places. I wasn't making much money and I had nothing to do at night except drink and read, and so I just sat down and wrote a story about a guy in a similar situation. That was the first time that I really enjoyed writing.

When was that?

That was in 1959. That's when I decided to just give up everything as soon as I possibly could and become a fiction writer. From then on I would just work until I had enough money saved, unless I was canned first for some reason or another, and give myself periodic sabbaticals to write.

Do you think you have an obsessive personality?

Well, obsessive mainly for writing. I am still obsessed with finding the time to write, and if I'm away from my typewriter for more than a day or so I feel uncomfortable, although what it does do, this obsession and this discomfort, is make me write harder when I do get to that typewriter. Again, there are lots of things that keep me away from the typewriter: work, my family. But I'm compulsive about writing, finishing the thing that I'm doing and getting on to the next thing.

I think my question came not so much from the number of stories you've published but from your phrase, "I decided to give up everything."

It's not that I'm prolific, not really prolific. It's not that I've written a lot in a short time. I mean, I've been writing constantly since 1960, so that's a good thirty-seven years of writing, and if one does that one's going to build up quite a lot of work.

Since you used the word "prolific," let me read some other words critics have used to describe your writing or you as a writer: quirky, experimental, uneconomical, self-indulgent, versatile, cynical, funny, rapid-fire, unstoppable, cunning, emotional, manic. Do any of these hit a resonant chord?

I think they all do.

You'll admit to all of them?

Sure. And more.

Are any of those words particularly apt?

Well, unstoppable I like. Unstoppable, to me, sort of describes my compulsiveness to write. I've never had a writing block in my life. Nothing has ever stopped me from writing. Only illness and hangovers have stopped me but not for very long.

Tell me about your method of composition.

Well, with a short story, which is an easier example, I sit down 95 per-cent of the time with nothing in my mind as to what I'm going to write and I start typing. Sometimes I sit down with a line that appears to me the day before or an hour before. Just a single line can send me off writ-ing. And then I usually write, without getting up, the entire first draft for a period of a half an hour to an hour and a half, and then I set it aside and I think about it. I mean, I don't even have to think about it. It's just there and I think about whether I want to continue it, whether I want to spend the next fifteen to thirty days rewriting it, putting the story into final draft, and I'll know that by the following day. If I think that I don't want to, then I just sit down and write another first draft, or some-times two or three first drafts.

If each first draft is something that I feel that particular day is not something that I want to continue, or something that I've already done in style or story, then I throw it away and start something else. Usually I'll do three or four first drafts of different stories in one day if the first one or the second one doesn't work. By three or four I tell myself, Well, you've put in a good writing day and today's just not the day. Do it to-morrow. And usually the next day the first draft will be the one that I'll start writing to its completion.

I start on page one of the first draft and I rewrite and rewrite and rewrite that page thirty or forty times until it's finished, and then I'll go to page two. Page one of the first draft could turn into ten pages of the final draft, and I've had stories that were fifteen pages in first draft and I've written entire novels from them, two or three hundred pages, and never even got to page ten of the first draft of the story. Most of my nov-els have started as short stories.

And that's how I do it. I just rewrite and rewrite and rewrite that single page until it's perfect in my mind, and that's the signal for me to say okay, now you have to type a clean page of that. Even though I'll type a clean page, I'll have to retype it five or ten more times. I'm a fast typist with just four fingers, and I usually get a page a day done, three hundred a year.

Do you listen to music when you write?

Never.

You want absolute quiet?

Absolute. I had a friend who used to play jazz—said it was the only way he could write—but the ideal for me would be no sounds whatsoever except the sounds of my typewriter. But definitely no music, no intrusions.

    I do drink a lot of coffee when I'm writing, or tea. There's something about having a hot cup. I just can't think without picking up something and sipping it.

One of the adjectives used to describe your writing was "rapid-fire." Does your method of composition, typing an entire draft at one sitting, affect or cause your style?

Yeah. I like stories that are fast, or the language is fast, and I try to make a very spontaneous sounding story. Rhythm is very important to me, among other things, the way a story reads, and when I rewrite the story I try to maintain that spontaneity of the first draft, although refining that spontaneity, maybe even making it more spontaneous. But rapid-fire? I have stories that aren't rapid-fire.

Does the style, the spontaneity cost you anything? Is there anything you would like to do with your writing that this style, this method might sacrifice?

No. I feel I've done many, many different styles. What other way could I write? By taking notes for a story?

The burst, for lack of a better term, is something that you don't find with every writer. I've read interviews you've given where you talked about the ten pages in a half hour, twenty pages in an hour, and I think what might have been missing is your statement that when you go back and redo that page, that one page might grow to ten. You might have assumed it would be common sense on the reader's part that one page might grow, but I think earlier interviews suggest that you write a first draft and that the draft pretty much defines the length and structure of the story, that the rewrites are more particular because you refer to word-by-word edits. I don't know that your point that the first page could turn into ten pages ever came across.

I might miss something by not trying to contain the work, but I let the work sort of move in its own way.

There does seem to be, in reading both the interviews and the fiction, the impression that you give the work a wide rein. One example might be that the chapters of Frog *appear sequentially as they were written. Was there any thought of reorganization, or do you just trust the organic quality of it?*

Well, a lot of the stuff in there is style changes, too, so I'm not only telling the story, but it's sort of giving the example of the style following a certain chronology. I mean, if I'm going to move stylistically in the book, then I'm not going to rearrange the style to make a more refined work, or even a more cohesive one. It's more important to me to just sort of follow the style chronologically and put the stories in the way I wrote them.

That's not too clear, but it just seemed a better idea than to make a kind of a perfect novel. I'd rather have a perfect page than a perfect novel. Besides, the way I write novels is not the way other people write novels. You know, the story follows a certain pattern or formula or regimentation in most novels. I mean, something happens and then something evolves and you follow it through, and every now and then somebody's doing alternate chapters. You see that a lot. Or going back into the past, whatever the term is for that.

But I've devised a way of sort of including the sort of odd way that I write, which is *Frog* or *Interstate* or *Gould*. Whatever I'm writing is fine because it's going to make one cohesive work at the end by the two main characters, really, being principals in just about every single scene. If something happens four years before or two years before, I'll make sure the reader knows when this is happening.

Frog is all over the place, it's true, but I feel that thematically it's sort of harmonized by the principal character and his imagination. I mean, my early novels, *Work* and *Too Late*, proceed chronologically to the end. I've never much cared for flashbacks. I use a little dream life, but I don't want to just tell the chronologically tight story. I want to be all over the place.

You mentioned that you use a little dream life, but in some of your later work, especially, you present the reader with alternate realities. Interstate would be the main example, but there are many others. You also say that you'll let the reader know what's happening. In a few of your short stories, I've read variations of the line, No, that didn't happen, but we don't get that line with Interstate. We don't get that line with Frog.

Yes, that was "Goodbye to Goodbye," but how many times can you use that? I like alternate realities, in other words telling the same story two or three different ways. After all, a novel is a work of the imagination. It's letting the imagination tell the story differently. In my new work, the mother dies three or four different ways. Same thing with Frog dying and the child dying, two children dying in *Interstate*. I mean, one dies five times and the other dies once or something like that.

But is it the same story?

It's sort of the same story. In *Interstate*, you never know whether he's imagining the whole thing during a car trip. That's my safety valve— whether it's a story imagined by a man driving a car with two children, a man who's somewhat paranoid and very protective paternally so he's thinking of the worst things possible, perhaps to be able to face the worst things possible if they ever happened. The same thing with the deaths of the mother in the new work, imagining that it's going to happen sometime, and so it's a man sort of using his imagination to imagine it happening, to possibly alleviate the pain when it finally does happen.

It's like *Frog* in that it's like a challenge to the reader. How could the wife die and be alive in the next chapter? How could he die? I mean, the guy's just imagining his own death and the death of his wife and sort of projecting them to see what he thinks his reaction will be.

In "Goodbye to Goodbye," the story that you referred to, no, this didn't happen; the key is that what happens at the end is what really happens, which is a very benign good-bye compared to the very volatile good-byes that precede it. You know, pushing the guy down the stairs or punching him in the face or his wife saying, What a man you are. I mean, all this is just his imagination. What he really does to stop his wife from going is nothing, but that story holds a key to my writing.

In what way?

Of all the different projections a man can make about the same situation and the reality of the act itself, which is quite bland in comparison to the imagination.

But in that story the reader knows the reality.

Well, if the reader knows that the last one is what really happens.

You threw an "if" in there.

Well, people have asked me what really happens in that story and I say, Generally trust that the last thing to happen is the thing that happened, that all the other things are the things that he wishes could've happened.

In which case Interstate *would be a happy story.*

Yes. Right. Well, *Interstate* is either something that did happen and so the ending is imagined by the man or else, and I know I'm contradicting myself with the "Goodbye to Goodbye" example, or else it's a story imagined by a man and the ending is what actually happened, that they did get there safely. So either the girl did die and he just reimagines the thing over and over again, which is what somebody would do, no doubt, if someone's daughter died the way she did, or else he imagines all these different versions of her death during a car ride, and the ending is simply what really did happen. They got home safely.

In his Times *review, Alan Friedman wrote, "One doesn't exactly read a Stephen Dixon story, one submits to it." Is this a fair assessment? Is it a flattering statement?*

Yeah. Oh, I think it's flattering because I would hate to just write a story that was this or that. I don't mind sort of writing a story that most people will resist, that they have to sort of fight to accept. What am I trying to say? It's a different kind of story. It's not even something that I'm doing. I'm just writing the way I'm writing. I just sit down at the typewriter and I write, and if it satisfies me that's all I'm worried about.

I know that the stuff is different than other people are writing, although not difficult to understand. The language is different, the rhythm, the long paragraphs now, and it would generally set a lot of people off from the work but once, it seems, they begin reading it, a lot of people like it, I guess, for its difference.

So is Stephen Dixon the ideal reader for Stephen Dixon's fiction?

Maybe the only reader. I'm certainly the only ideal reader. I know I have nobody in mind when I write. I just have myself in mind. I'm just having a lot of fun at the typewriter putting together words and sentences the way I want to and that appeal to me and that would be the kind of stuff that I would like to read.

Anthony Quinn wrote that Gould *"may not have an altogether reader-friendly style." Is that a concern for you?*

Oh, no. I like quotes like that because, first of all, it's accurate. A reader-friendly style is something that people are used to. My work is something that people, even good readers, are not used to. I'm not saying it's anything far out or anything like that, it's just that it's not a typical way of writing. I never wanted to be typical. I never wanted a single cliché or a single sentence that sounded like anything anybody ever wrote. I make a point, when I write, of not writing like anybody.

Certain authors are noted for a particular type of protagonist. There's an accepted Hemingway hero, for example. Is there a prototype Stephen Dixon hero?

No, there's a Dixon antihero. The only thing heroic about my characters, except for Gould, and that was more of a novel about the sexual life of a man for about forty years rather than anything else, is that they sort of do the right thing. They try to do the right thing, and what I like to do in my fiction is to show the problems or the difficulties in doing that. I try to show the consequences of doing good. You try to do good and then you get sued for it or something like that.

I actually was, once, given a certificate, an award from New York City, for being a Good Samaritan, the Good Samaritan Award. They even paid my broken head bills with the doctor because I stopped a robbery. I mean, I've stopped lots of robberies. A lot of these characters are following sort of my own urban heroism, you might say, or just deep feelings that man's on this planet not to just benefit himself but to step in when the situation calls for it and the consequences that he's confronted with by doing this. In other words, I haven't, in the past, done any of these things to get a story, but I have gotten stories from things that I've done.

Do you call this figure an antihero because the character is so close to yourself?

That and also the standard hero is kind of a dull, self-righteous, pious, predictable character, and I like my characters to stammer, have difficulties finding the right word.

You've got a line in Frog where Howard is dead and his daughters are remembering him. They say, "He didn't trust anyone who didn't hem and haw."

That's not a bad line. See? My characters get the good lines. I get the bad ones.

You know, in "Frog's Interview," you know the thing he says about this guy Stein, "If you want a good interview, go to Stein." To me, Stein is just a representative of all the fellows who are interviewed for the *Paris Review* who come out sounding so perfect and polished.

Have you published in the Paris Review *since "The Chess House"?*

Oh yeah, four times probably. The last one was "Goodbye to Goodbye." It won the John Train Humor Award, but they haven't taken anything since. I have a love-hate relationship with the *Paris Review*, but let's say it's love-hate on their part. With me it's just submitting. They say terrible things sometimes. Somebody once did an article on me and called up George Plimpton, and he said, You know Dixon sends us so many stories he thinks we should change the name to *Dixon Review*. Things like that. I don't send them so many stories. I send them a story and they don't respond in about six months, and I send them a letter asking yes or no.

But "Frog's Interview" kind of takes a shot at the Paris Review *and publishers as a whole, the idea of literary life. I know part of the discomfort with being interviewed comes from interviewers trying to establish fiction as fact, but the episode of Howard having a story accepted, being asked to rewrite and rewrite and rewrite, visiting the magazine's office near the East River. That incident would be pretty hard to deny.*

It happened though.

So does that make it fair game?

I would say so. I thought it was appropriate for the particular story that I was writing, so I guess they've been fair game for me and I become fair game for them when they're questioned about me.

In your interview with Yemassee *you mention quite a few writers and Barth is really the only one who escapes unscathed.*

Well, he is my colleague and gave me a job.

What writer can you speak positively about?

Thomas Bernhard. I'm reading him now. He's an Austrian writer, 1931 to 1989, who I got interested in only about three months ago. I tried to read him before, but I didn't think he did the long paragraph very well. His books are usually in single paragraphs, but then this book had Glenn Gould as a character so how could I not read it?

What's the name of it?

The book is called *The Loser*, and I like it very much. Bernhard's very interesting and unconventional in the way he structures the book in that single paragraph, but he's both funny and, at times, touching and intelligent. I don't know what it is that sometimes a writer just hits you, so now I'm reading a book of his called *The Woodcutters*, which I also like very much. I'll probably read three or four or five more of his before I'm done with him.

There's a writer by the name of Leonid Tsypkin who has just one book that was published in English. It's called *Summer in Baden-Baden*. He's an unconventional writer, but the conventions that he breaks are not tripping me up or setting me off against the work. They're working. His unusual style and the way he tells the story is making it a more interesting read to me because I like more unconventional works if you're talking about the late twentieth century. I mean I'll accept the conventions of another time easily, Dostoevsky and Tolstoy or Chekhov.

Well, Bernhard died seven or eight years ago. Can you give me an example of someone living whose works you admire?

Nobody. Bellow's work I did admire and respect. I thought he was the best American writer in that last thirty years, but I haven't really enjoyed much recently, except *Him with His Foot in His Mouth* had two very good novellas in it. He's a really intelligent guy, but the last works are terrible.

What's Bellow's best book?

Seize the Day, and then I would say *Herzog*. No, *Augie March*. *The Adventures of Augie March*; that's his best book.

The problem with Bellow and Barth is that they are too philosophical, too indulgent, and they try to impose their ideas in their books. I think books of philosophy and essays are the place for that. Novels should have real live people, and too often with Bellow and Barth it stops and just becomes a catechism sometimes. It's not interesting. *Seize the Day* is part that but it's really lively and *Augie March* is quite funny, but today I can't think of anybody that I like. I really can't.

How much do you read?

I'm reading all the time. I like newspapers, too. I like to read newspapers in the morning, and in the evening I read my books, but they do take me much longer than when I was a single person. I would read perhaps a book a day.

I also like Solzhenitsyn. Not the historical novels, but I thought *Gulag Archipelago*, which is not a novel but it's like a novel, was a great book. Some of Isaac Bashevis Singer I really like. He became a little schmaltzy, but one long novel that I forget the name of was a great novel.

But if I ask you what was the last good novel you read your answer would be Bernhard's The Loser?

Yes, definitely, and before that, which would be two years before, it would be Leonid Tsypkin's *Summer in Baden-Baden*. Those are the two best books I've read in the last four or five years. They're the only books that have excited me in the last four or five years, and I've read a lot of books. I'm sent a lot of books by publishers and colleagues but nothing sort of interesting.

If you only come across two good books in five years, why do you read as much as you do?

I've got to read. I'm always looking for a writer who I'll really like, and if I do, as with Bernhard, that means I've got a lot of books of his that I might like. I mean, I'm excited. The thing that I want to do is to continue to read his books, and I don't have that feeling with most writers, nor with most stories that I read.

I pick up *Best American Short Stories*. People say, Boy, that's the best *Best American Stories* that they've read in years, but they all sound alike. I pick up *O. Henry* and I think, How did those stories ever get in there? Of course, once Stephen King is the best *O. Henry* and Joyce Carol Oates is the second and Cynthia Ozick is the third—I think that was the last issue—that sort of says everything, doesn't it?

But I read poetry. I read the Bible and novels and newspapers, and that's what I read.

What's your best short story collection?

The best one is *Love and Will*. Of course, the big collection you can't consider a short story collection, it's an omnibus, but the best of mine is *Love and Will*. With *Love and Will* I went through, oh, a hundred unpublished stories to put those together, and then it was rejected by about thirty publishers, or forty. I'm sure thirty of them rejected it because it was a story collection, and ten rejected it because they didn't like it until British American bought it.

What's your best novel?

I really can't tell. I like them all. Truth is, I like all my collections, but I would say *All Gone* is not as good as *Love and Will*. Certainly *Long Made Short* is a different collection than anything I've ever published. It's a totally different piece of work. And *No Relief*, the first one, I loved. There's some really spunky, lively, funny stories, and tragic stories, too.

Best novel? If one would consider *Frog* a novel, maybe *Frog*. That seems to be the opinion, maybe because of its size. It was written over a period of time where you get a good spectrum of my writing style because it took five and a half years to write, but I like *Interstate* a great deal. Each of them has something that I wouldn't try to duplicate in another. One reason is I'd be repeating myself. I only work on one thing at a time. One story at a time. One novel at a time. Whatever I'm working at, it's one at a time, and I try to do everything I possibly can at the time that I'm doing it, while I'm working on that thing.

Fall & Rise? I love *Fall & Rise*. I thought it was wild. I loved it. I was in love with the book. It took me three and a half years to write it and it got dumped. Two little reviews and it disappeared off the map. Nobody ever talks about the book, but I loved it because the stories go from man to woman. It really captures the urban life, and also because stylistically what it does, but I like them all. I really don't have a favorite book.

While we're on the subject of Fall & Rise, *that was the first novel that you sat down to write with the idea that it would be a novel. What's the difference in sitting down to write a novel?*

It's a concept, and with *Fall & Rise* it was a very, very simple, one-line concept, and that is it's going to be a novel about a man who meets a woman on the first page and then she disappears on about the second or third page, and he doesn't see her again until the end of the novel. So it's what happens in between. That's all I had in mind.

With *Interstate*, I knew in my mind that I wanted to write a book about an event that happened and that was told in different ways and where the man would gradually get closer and closer to his objective, which was his home in Baltimore.

When you sat down to write the first day of Interstate, *did you know that there were going to be different outcomes?*

Yeah, I did.

Tell me about that. When you sit down to write a short story, you write a complete first draft and then go back and rewrite those pages until the story is where you want it. With Interstate, *did you follow that process and treat each chapter as a story?*

Yeah. I wanted to start off, first of all, with the novella, and then everything else after that would not be self-contained. The first part is a book in itself, "Interstate 1." It's the life of a man from a certain point until his death and then a little after that. And then everything else would evolve from that first chapter, although he would be a different person with the same name in subsequent chapters. It just seemed right, at the time, to start off with a self-contained work and then everything after that is not self-contained, but the entire work would be contained. I also had the idea, at that time, of writing a book not only in third person but in first person and in second person, to sort of do all the persons and perhaps all the tenses.

So even though you have the concept for the entire novel, the first chapter is written and finished before you move on to chapter 2?

Yes, but the truth is, I didn't know how many I would do. I knew there would be several. The truth is, I only thought I would write it in first and third person and then after I did first and third I thought, How could you not do second? Well, I don't like second person. It stinks. It's the worst person in the world, but that was a challenge to me. I had set up my own challenge to face and overcome, but I thought with *Interstate* that if it didn't work, because I was trying something different, that if the subsequent chapters didn't work I would still have my novella to publish.

I'm assuming that Interstate *was written like* Frog, *that you wrote "Interstate 5" before "Interstate 6" and so on.*

Yes, because with each one they get closer and closer to the city.

At what point did you know that "Interstate 8" would be the last one?

Well, I'd written "6" where the youngest daughter dies, and so I decided to have the oldest daughter die to sort of change it around and see what his feelings would be there, to not only die but not to die accidentally, and perhaps even to die because of his mistake. See, I was covering another facet of projection and after she dies, well, what was I supposed to do? Have him die? No, it seemed logical for them to come home safely.

Also, I wrote that last chapter because I knew that the reader needed relief. This was unrelentingly depressing, this book. This is a book that I would never recommend anybody to read. If anybody had gone through all seven chapters, they needed almost a sentimental, soft release at the end, that everything came out okay. Maybe they could justify in their own minds that this was just an act of imagination on the narrator's part.

When did you realize that the reader would need that relief? And how did you know that was the end?

It just seemed logical that one chapter would cover the good part. All you needed was one chapter where they get home safely. I felt that it had ended on such a sweet note, saying good night, telling them a little story, acting very fatherly, so sweetly, that it was just a wonderful spot to end.

So did you know when you sat down to write "8" what the outcome was going to be, that you're going to get them home this time?

Oh yeah. Usually when I'm halfway through or two-thirds of the way through a novel, except in *Too Late*, I sort of have an idea in my head of how it's going to end. For instance, in *Frog* I wrote the notes for the title chapter, which is number 21, two years before I wrote it. I was in a car, my wife and two kids, going to Maine, when the idea came to me. I told my wife, Listen, I can't write this down, so my daughter wrote the notes that I dictated. The last line even. The same last line.

I'd been writing the book for three years. I was three years into the book, and maybe two-thirds of the way into it I had the idea for how it would end, so I took those notes. Really it was about sixty words of notes, and I put them underneath my manuscript, and those notes were underneath the last page of the manuscript of the first draft.

How far along were you after three years? Do you remember what you were working on at the time?

It was probably during "Frog's Mom."

Did you know the title of the novel before you had the idea for the last chapter?

Yes. The title was always *Frog*, but I knew that I would have to explain. I knew I would have to write a story that would explain why it's called *Frog*.

Explain to the reader or explain to yourself? When you sat down to write "Frog in Prague," did you know what Frog meant?

No. The words "Frog in Prague" came from my daughter Sophia. We were in Prague. It started in Prague. I wrote the first draft of "Frog in Prague" in Prague and I called it "Frog in Prague" because she would say "Frog in Prague." She was two and a half years old. You know how kids get fascinated by the sound of things. Frog rhymes with Prague, so I decided to write a story called "Frog in Prague" about my experiences trying to find Kafka's grave, and the minute I finished that first draft I felt I was onto something.

Of course, I always have to be through with something to start something. I don't work on two things at one time, and so I had gone to Europe having finished *Fall & Rise*; well, *Fall & Rise* was coming out at the time in America, but I had finished some other stuff so I was free to start something new. But I didn't bring a typewriter with me to Prague. We were just there a few days and then we were going on to other places, but after that experience of looking for Kafka's grave, when my wife was sleeping, my child was sleeping in the hotel room, I wrote the first draft, in pen, of "Frog in Prague." And then I rewrote it, subsequently, over and over again to make it clear. It didn't really build up because I wasn't working on a typewriter, but over and over again during our month-long trip I was rewriting it and rewriting it, and when I got back to America I wrote the story in a day. I just retyped it. And then I knew, with that first story, that I was onto something, that I had a good character, you know, with a wife and a child, and that I would try number two.

When we came back to America, we went immediately to Maine and so I wrote the second story, "Frog Remembers," in Maine. I wrote that because my wife, who was pregnant with our second child, had gone to a movie and was late coming back, so I began projecting the possibilities of what could happen to her.

There's a line in "Frog Fears" that seems to foreshadow Interstate. *Howard imagines his wife on the road, wonders where she is, and remembers telling her of the trick where someone points at the wheel of her car as if there's something wrong with the tire.*

Oh yeah, in fact, if you look at the last line of *Frog*, that was intentional. They head back in the car in the first line of *Interstate* so they're back on the road.

While we're talking about Frog, *let me cross a line. In what ways are you different than Howard Tetch?*

Well, I don't die. Of course, neither does he. Nor am I reborn. I'm not as nervous or clumsy, nor, at times, as articulate. For instance, in "Frog's Interview" he says all the things that I would not have the ability at that particular moment to say. I'm probably not as sexy or as good as he is often in the book. He's just a character in my head who lives out many of the things that I have, but he's not me at all, although occasionally his children sound like my children.

Tell me about the leap from "Frog Walks Out" to "Frog Made Free." "Frog Made Free," in a lot of ways, seems to come out of nowhere.

That's a tip-off. That story's a tip-off that this novel is composed with a great deal of projections from a man's mind of the worst things that can possibly happen to him. What he does is project himself into another decade. Since he's Jewish, this is what would've happened to him if he was living in Poland, let's say, as his ancestors did, certainly my wife's family who lost just about all of their family, my wife's mother and father. So I was writing a story about that. That's a tip-off that, Well, this is impossible. This happens forty years or so before.

Then another tip-off, to use your term, occurs with the very next chapter, "Frog Takes a Swim."

Oh yeah. Exactly. I took a lot of flak for that because a lot of people felt that, What happened to the girl?

Do interviews make you uncomfortable because there's an opportunity for the interviewer to try to match what is true in your life with what's in your fiction?

Because there are similar incidents and facts: dentists, odd jobs, breaking up robberies.

Two daughters.

Characters who seem to be the same character resurfacing with a different name, as in the case of Evangeline in Gould. We've seen this character before.

Sure.

Does it matter how much is based in real life? Whether they are based in literal experience or an imagined one?

I don't think so, but I would think that these books, rather than being about my life, are about the projections of my life. Sure, some of the things are things that have happened to me, but they've been rearranged, or changed, to make them not so much fictional, but to make them sound like fiction. I'm not changing them to hide.

The story is that Hemingway created Jake Barnes by projecting what his life would be like if the shrapnel had hit him an inch from where it did.

That's true. What is fiction very often but What if? What if this happened to me? What if this piece of shrapnel had gone further? What if then I was a paraplegic rather than ambulatory as I am now? What if my daughter had been hit by a car rather than my warning her at the last moment to stop?

There's a story, for instance, in "Frog Fragments," which is just sort of filler. It's like the mortar for everything that precedes it, and that was the intention, to sort of fill in the gaps with these fragments. My daughter did disappear from the house, and to me that's like the quintessential piece in the whole book, that little story of about four pages. I know it's four pages because when I read for the National Book Award they wanted something under five minutes and I read that. But there she was, heading right for the road after she had left the house. It's a fairly accurate portrayal of how I felt, but it doesn't relate the story in the actual way that it happened.

Without boxing you too far into the autobiographical, there's a lot of fear in your fiction, possibly due to the urban setting, but it seems to increase almost exponentially once the protagonist becomes a father. Do you see yourself as a fearful person?

Yeah. Yeah I do. Certainly for my children. Not for myself. I'm fairly fearless for myself, but I'm definitely fearful for my children. I'm writing something now, a collection called *Thirty*, and the last one, unfortunately, is sixty pages. They were meant to be short shorts. But one is called "The Plane," and for that one I got the idea when we went to France in November. In this story the plane disintegrates and he's the only one saved, so it's just, again, a projection of the worst thing that could possibly happen. And I thought that the worst thing would be that the man would survive and have to live with it, the loss of his two children and wife, more than having died. So in the story he tries to kill himself, and maybe does kill himself, but in the end he's on a raft.

You say that you're relatively fearless but yet you experience fear for your children. What kind of transformation has occurred now that you can't be fearless because you have children?

Well, I'm more cautious for myself, meaning I have to drink less so my liver doesn't fall apart before they're grown up and on their own.

Do you stop less robberies?

Well, it's a very interesting story. On West 72nd Street I was with my father-in-law and my mother-in-law and my two children, and we had just come out of a restaurant and I actually saw two holdup men go into a Korean grocery, and they had their guns out and they were going in, and then the Korean grocerymen put up their arms so I immediately jumped. I started to go into the situation to stop it. I remember my father-in-law putting his hand on my shoulder and saying, You're a father now. You can't do that. So we just stayed on the sidewalk and they robbed them and jumped into a car and drove away. This is true. It happened at the Korean grocery on 72nd Street between Columbus Avenue and Broadway.

Is that frustrating for you?

No, I realized it was ridiculous, senseless what I was going to do. You see, *Work*, for instance, that actually did happen, where I did chase robbers down the street and the police came and caught them, having seen me chase them, but then I wasn't married or anything like that.

What's the greatest honor paid to you as a writer?

You got me. Probably the National Book Award nomination. I haven't gotten that many compared to a lot of writers. A lot of writers work for it, you know. I've got a Guggenheim, but I applied five, six times for a Guggenheim.

After 425 stories, do you still get any kind of thrill when you go to the mail-box and find out a story's been accepted?

The biggest thrill I ever got was not with the first story that was accepted by *Paris Review* but the first story that was accepted by *Atlantic Monthly*. That was the biggest thrill because I was twenty-eight years old and I didn't think I had a chance in the world of getting a story published, and I was broke and suddenly I have a check for six hundred bucks and an acceptance from a highly esteemed magazine. Up to then I'd only had one story published in my life.

    The second-biggest thrill was not the *Playboy* story because even though *Playboy* was pretty good and they paid well for the story, I knew I'd be sharing the magazine with a lot of naked ladies, or half-naked at the time. The second-biggest thrill was with *Harper's*, the first story with *Harper's*, because then again I was broke. I couldn't afford anything. I was walking upstairs with my girlfriend with this envelope. It was also the way it came. It was an envelope, a 9 by 12, which is the envelope that I sent the story in, you know, the self-addressed. And I said to her, late in the evening, Ah, another rejection from *Harper's*, and I opened it and it's the galleys to the story. I don't understand. It's like it's sort of the dream experience. And a check. A check. And the galleys. And nothing else. And I said, Well, they had to have accepted the story. Why else would they put my story in galleys and give me money? So I called them and a mistake had been made since there was no letter with it.

The third-biggest thrill was when I, again, had no phone. I was living in the same building and the mailman rings me from downstairs. We had no intercom. And I come downstairs and he says there's a letter from N.E.A. and this was 1974 and it said five hundred dollars which later turned out to be five thousand dollars and I was so excited because all three came at a time when I sort of needed to be validated by someone else, which a writer shouldn't have, but listen, you write long enough and you get many, many rejections and then suddenly some very validating organization validates you. It was very exciting.

I haven't become jaded to acceptances. I mean, the other day *Double Take* took a story for a thousand dollars. Well, you know, it's a nice piece of cash and it made me feel pretty good. Whenever *Harper's* takes a story it makes me feel good, and whenever *Best American Stories* takes a story I feel good about it.

But you don't need the validation like you did?

But I don't need the validation like I did. The older I grew the more I knew that the validation wasn't necessary, in fact, could be harmful, so I've made a strenuous effort not to be affected by any of the benefits that came from my writing and not to sort of celebrate it or anything quite like that.

Any idea what you spend a year on postage for manuscripts?

No, I don't. Probably a couple of hundred dollars. It's not so bad.

Not worth itemizing on your taxes?

Oh yeah. But I get it back. I earn about two thousand dollars a year from selling to little magazines.

What's the difference between being published by Henry Holt and the smaller presses that put out your earlier work?

It's obvious that I'm going to get more reviews because they have a bigger machine working for me. And I'll get a larger advance, which is still not very much. I still only get ten thousand dollars. I say only because a lot of writers would do it for nothing and I would too, but my students are getting a hundred thousand, two hundred thousand dollars. But there's a better chance that the book will be reviewed. Well, *Frog* got reviewed but only after it got the nomination.

The first National Book Award nomination was very exciting. The second was fine, but not as exciting as the first because the first was with a small press and it was a book that I'd spent five and a half years on, and also because the editor who called was crying on the phone when she told me, so she was sort of excited. It was also before the book even came out. I was still working on the galleys, so I knew that at least this book would have a chance to get reviewed.

But the difference with the smaller presses is that if I get one or two small reviews in small places, it's a lot.

Which stories are your favorites?

Stories that I think of are, let's say, "Milk Is Very Good for You," which is a one-of-a-kind story, or "Grace Calls," which is a one-of-a-kind story, though I did it again in a story called "Speak." It's more language than plot. A story like "Streets," to me, is one-of-a-kind. And it's also a breakthrough story. "Goodbye to Goodbye," which opened up a whole new way of writing for me, you know, telling the same story over and over again. Those are the kinds of stories that I like—the stories that sort of change my attitude toward what the possibilities are, that, rather than change, enlarge the possibilities of storytelling—and that's what those stories do, either stylistically or narratively.

What are your feelings about "Mac in Love?"

Oh, I love "Mac in Love." I love it because there's a leap, a real imaginative leap in that story, which goes through the voice, and it's like a metaphor for what the voice can do. His voice goes right into the apartment, and then the two women start speaking. A lot of people don't catch that, but that's what happens. I love that story because he becomes almost a prototypical character for me. That's where I started. It's my first book-published story. It really should've been the first story in *The Stories*, but then I wanted to make it an entire thirty years so I added "The Chess House" just to give a feeling of the past. I love "Mac in Love."

"Layaways."

"Layaways" I like because it's so emotionally deep. And it's also kind of a traditional story told not so much in an untraditional way, but the language isn't traditional. So you have a traditional story of a simple shopkeeper, almost a Bernard Malamud "The Assistant"-type situation, but there's a passage in that story which I think is among my very best, and that's when the shooting happens. It's like three-quarters of a page of just a single line, I believe, where everything happens. The clock is shot. A window is shot out. Somebody's killed and everything. And that story's a breakthrough in the sense of in that one moment I found a way of really getting style and story together in a way that I hadn't done before—where the style became the story and the story became the style. Something like that. So that, in a way, is another breakthrough story, but where the breakthrough came is just writing it. Of course, with "Milk Is Very Good for You," the intention was to write a breakthrough story.

What about "Love Has Its Own Actions?"

I love that story because that one also, in a way like "Goodbye to Goodbye," is such an absurdist story. You know, where man starts with woman and then ends with man. Of course, that was the only possible thing that could happen. There's kind of almost a moral to that story, that this is what will happen if you're so changeable in your relationships. It's sort of a whole bunch of little traditionally written stories to make an untraditional single story because the language is kind of banal, I think, in "Love Has Its Own Actions." It's an early story but it's a funny story, too. I really try to be funny first and then, if tragedy takes over, it has to happen.

Another one is "Said," which is a one-shot story where the point was to write a story where nothing is said and the reader imagines everything that is said. There are a lot of them. "A Sloppy Story" is, again, that recapitulation of events, each one getting longer and longer because he's recapitulating himself, recapitulating the event. That's another sort of breakthrough, one-shot story. That's what I tried to put in *The Stories*, as many of those as possible, to show the complete range, to show the sort of spectrum that I write in, the emotional and stylistic and narrative spectrum.

When we started off talking about the interview process, you said that you didn't like talking about your writing, but when I mention these stories your face lights up and the first thing out of your mouth is "Oh, I love that story." Maybe you just don't like being asked about how you come up with the idea.

Maybe I'm warming to the interview.

Steve Erickson
© Karan Rinaldo, 1996

Gordon Lish
© Richard Giles, 1996

Rick Moody
© *Richard Giles, 1996*

Robert Olen Butler
© *Richard Giles, 1996*

Charles Johnson
© *Richard Giles, 1998*

Stewart O'Nan
© *Richard Giles, 1997*

Stephen Dixon
© Richard Giles, 1997

Chris Offutt
© C. J. Hicks, 1997

A Conversation with Chris Offutt

In the summer of 1997, Chris Offutt is thirty-eight years old and the author of three published books: the story collection *Kentucky Straight*, *The Same River Twice*, a memoir, and a novel, *The Good Brother*. Another story collection, *Out of the Woods*, was published later that year.

Offutt grew up in eastern Kentucky before leaving home at the age of nineteen to ultimately drift through a series of odd jobs. This experience, along with his wife Rita's first pregnancy, provides the material for Offutt's memoir. *The Good Brother* begins in eastern Kentucky and ends in Montana where the writer and his family have recently moved. His fiction has appeared in such publications as *Esquire*, *GQ*, and *Best American Short Stories* and, in the year we met Offutt was recognized with a Whiting Award, a Guggenheim fellowship, and selected as one of *Granta*'s "Best Young American Fiction Writers."

We spoke on the campus of Wesleyan University in Middletown, Connecticut.

Setting is obviously an important element in your fiction and, on one level, The Good Brother *works as a comparison/contrast of two states. What are the similarities between Kentucky and Montana?*

Kentucky was the western frontier through the 1700s. At that point, all the land was settled and occupied, primarily by Scots-Irish. The rest of the country, in its westward expansion, went around Kentucky due to geography, so it stayed with the seventeenth-century mentality, in many ways, for almost two hundred years now, maintaining a frontier attitude about life, self-preservation, relationship with the land, relationship with animals, and relationship with people.

Montana was the genuine last frontier of the lower forty-eight so I, having grown up in Kentucky and being part of that mentality, wanted to see what it was like in another place. They're similar. They have mountains which, again, contributes to similarities in terms of people who are drawn to mountains, people who grow up in mountains. There's a certain independence. There's a desire to live closer to land, to be surrounded by natural beauty, and there's an understanding that the relationship with nature is important and precarious. When I went to Montana, I found a newer frontier mentality than eastern Kentucky and I enjoyed it.

Do the same things that drew you to Montana personally draw you fictionally as well, in terms of material?

I never intended to go to Montana. When I set up this story, Virgil was going to flee to Alaska because I thought Alaska was a genuine contemporary frontier, and I wanted to go there. I was exploring feud mentality in a contemporary time. I was exploring the relationship with land, and I thought Alaska would offer me what I wanted. My wife, with two children under six, utterly refused to go with me to Alaska, so we compromised on Montana.

I moved there to write the novel and went broke. My wife sold our couch for sixty dollars for grocery money. When your wife's selling furniture, you're pretty broke. I took a job in Albuquerque as a guest writer at the University of New Mexico and was there for three semesters. Then the University of Montana hired me for a one-year visiting gig.

Didn't you go through Montana and Idaho before you went to graduate school? I think there's a line in The Same River Twice *that says, "I would've loved to have stayed but there was no work."*

No work and no women. Someone told me when I was there the first time that if I came back I should bring a woman with me. So I did. They didn't tell me that I needed to bring more money.

It sometimes seems as if every Southern writer of the last thirty years has Faulkner hung around his or her neck, but I haven't seen his name appear in any of your reviews.

Yeah, I don't see that with me. Flannery O'Connor was a much bigger influence on me than Faulkner. In eastern Kentucky one out of every three people cannot read or write. There's few books. There are very few writers. It was easy for me to read the writers of my area and learn from them, and build upon them. It was very easy because they were so few. If you're an upper-class white guy in the Northeast, you've got a shit-load of books to read to get caught up. I don't have that problem.

I didn't like most depictions of eastern Kentucky. I especially didn't like the popular culture depictions: *Barney Google, Snuffy Smith, The Beverly Hillbillies, Dukes of Hazzard, Deliverance,* all that kind of crap. I wanted to present a version of Kentucky that was mine, that I grew up with. It was a post-Vietnam, post-VISTA world of Appalachia. I've never met a simple but happy mountaineer in my life. I've met incredibly complicated people, who are incredibly intelligent, in the hills.

In Same River *you say that your parents "moved very deep into the hills to drop a litter in private," and that "they discouraged both family branches from visiting." Where did your parents move from?*

My father grew up in a log cabin in Kentucky, and my mother was from a loose, lower-class Irish family affiliated with the gambling and saloon industry near Lexington. They moved east, essentially to get away from their families. I'm a little reluctant to discuss my family. I don't think it's fair to them.

The line in Same River *about your parents going off to "drop a litter" is one of several personal details. What was your family's reaction to the memoir?*

They all loved it, as far as I know. My family is very supportive of my writing, always have been, and I think they are pleased and surprised by the degree of success I'm having. They're glad. Hey, I was the fuck up, you know. I had a juvenile record and an adult record and dropped out of high school to join the Army. When I turned thirty, my father said to me, I'm glad, son. I never thought you'd make it. They thought I was headed for the prison or the grave and now I have a career, a wife, and two children.

Have you had any contact with any of the characters from The Same River *besides your family?*

I have real close contact with the guy who is Shadrack in the book. His real name is Jon Zaklikowski. He went by Zak. He just had his second baby. He was terrifically inspirational to me as a writer. He was an artist. He was older than me. He lived the way I sort of imagined artists would when I sat in Kentucky and read. He lived in a studio. He had no running water, no heat. He used a woodstove in his studio. It was an old chalk factory. He drank saki and drank tea and was into Chinese and Asian religions, and I'd never met anybody like that before. And he was brilliant. He was the smartest person I'd ever met. I thought he was a great painter. His example of how one can live and be devoted to art was enormously influential on me.

Speaking of Shadrack as an artistic inspiration, The Same River *traces the progression of your desire to be several different types of artist: a playwright, poet, painter. What was the genesis of your desire for artistic expression? Was it there before you left Kentucky?*

It was always there. I drew and wrote stories since the second grade. I constantly drew pictures in school. I was an A student who was bored out of my skull in school, and I would get in trouble a lot. I realized the way not to get in trouble was to draw. I drew all the time, and I wrote stories in grade school for spelling class.

You had to define twenty spelling words a week. So I wrote the definitions and the teacher said, Chris, this isn't right. And I said, Oh yes they are. She said, No, they have to be dictionary definitions. What she wanted me to do was open a dictionary and transcribe what was in there, which I thought was stupid. I said, Look, I know these words. I don't want to do that. And she said, Well, why don't you just write a story and use all the words to prove you know them. So I thought, Okay, great. I started writing a story a week in spelling class in the seventh grade. I wrote a story a week in seventh grade and eighth grade. I had her for two years' worth of spelling. I hated her guts.

What about now?

I still hate her guts. She gave me twelve licks with a paddle once. It was a school record. She gave me six for misbehaving, then six more for laughing. It was either laugh or cry. She beat the hell out of me. It's not one of those, Oh, she did me a favor. She didn't. That was not the favor I needed.

Do you still have any of those stories?

Yeah, I have them all. I have everything I ever wrote. The first story I wrote was in the second grade. It's about a guy named Kenny Clark, which is the reverse of Clark Kent, and the first line is, "Once upon a time in Bubbletown, there lived a man named Kenny Clark." A man ran into his house and said, "Some men are coming to kill you." So Kenny Clark goes out, gets in a car chase, gets in a fistfight, subdues the bad guys, throws them in the car, takes them and gives them to the police, goes home, cleans his car and the last line is, He lived happily ever after.

The Same River *mentions that your wife suggested that you write prose. How long of a break had it been from fiction?*

I wrote short stories in seventh and eighth grade. I did write in journals all through grade school and some in high school. In high school I worked for the school newspaper. I had a column called "The Cranny" where I could write whatever I wanted to write. That's when I realized the power of language. I could make grown-ups mad. I could make superintendents and school boards mad by what I wrote about. I thought, This is unbelievable. It's just me in my room, writing.

And I was a sports editor and I wrote all these sports stories, but it was boring to me. It was hard, too. It was kind of boring but it was hard. For one thing, you can't make stuff up, and for another thing, you have to write about what other people want you to write about. I didn't like the deadline much. I didn't have time to improve it.

In college I studied theater. I wanted to be an actor because I would go to the movies and I would see this ugly guy kissing a beautiful girl, and I thought, That's the job for me. So I studied theater in college. Theater provided me with a tremendous sense of group identity and security, because every misfit in the hills was studying theater and we worked together all the time. It was enormous work to put on a production. The university I went to, Morehead, in the hills, was very ambitious with its theater. It had a young teacher, who I still stay in touch with, who was the director of the program. We did a lot of plays and it was a lot of work. I had, for the first time, a group identity and a group belonging.

I wanted to be in this improv group which wrote its own stuff. In the meantime, in college, I'd started writing poetry to impress girls. Nothing else I did impressed them, you know, but all I did, really, was write poetry and smoke pot through most of college. There was this improv group that I wanted to get into in the theater department. Now, they wrote their own plays, and the year I got in there was a change in the structure, and one guy got to write the play. I think they let me in so I could drive the truck because nobody else could drive the truck in the hills.

I was furious because I wanted to write my own stuff, so I went to the director and I explained it to him and he said, Write your own play. Over Christmas I wrote a twelve-scene, one-act play which was "Punk Rock Oedipus Rex in the Future." And the motivation, again, like in grade school, was one of defiance and anger. And damned if it didn't get produced. I thought, Wow, this is great. I'll write plays. I wrote another play that had the misfortune to be produced, and I wrote three more and they were terrible, but I was writing.

In the meantime, at nineteen, when I had quit and gone to New York, I went to museums and bookstores for the first time. I'd never been in either. And I thought, Wow, this is great. I'm going to get books. I'd never seen either a new or a used bookstore before, and I'd never been to a gallery or a museum, and I went out and bought a bunch of paints. I was working as a truck driver and I started painting. I went back to college, switched my major to art, quit school again, and hitchhiked out to Arizona to be a dishwasher at the Grand Canyon and finally managed to graduate.

So you received an art degree?

No. It was theater. I had the most hours in it. I think I was a double major and a triple minor or something ridiculous.

I was also starting to write in journals in college. The journal was an arena of combat for me, and the combat was between acting and theater and painting—all my creative frustrations. I didn't know what to do. Also, relationships with girls went into the journal. Everything was going in there, and all of a sudden I was finished with college and I didn't know what to do, and that's when I sort of began traveling and having what turned out to be over fifty jobs, all part time. I've never worked full time except in college when I worked for the maintenance department during the summers.

It seems like the one creative pursuit that's missing is music.

Well, I love music.

Did you ever try it?

I'm no good. I can't hear. I can't sing. I'm tone deaf. I can't play a tune. I don't even like music that much. I like folk songs and the old blues. I like Bruce Springsteen because he tells a good story. Bob Dylan. I love the storytellers. But I like to work in silence and I prefer birds to music. I just was never musically inclined.

So you don't listen to music when you're writing.

No. I get the house clear and I listen to absolute silence when I write. I listen to my own head when I write. When I'm writing, the words that I write are just screaming inside my skull. They're just roaring in there.

What's the oldest of the stories that appear in Kentucky Straight?

"Horseweed." It was one of the stories I wrote to get into graduate school. What happened between leaving Kentucky and meeting Rita is I had all of these jobs, and I didn't write anything but journal entries. I would write twenty-page journal entries in a spiral-bound notebook, three times a day: in the morning, then I would write at lunch, and in the evening. I would carry it around with me all the time. I didn't have a car. I lived without a car or a phone for almost ten years. I had a bicycle and a backpack, you know, and I would just get around that way and live in really tiny, cheap rooms and write. When I first got some money, I bought a typewriter in Salem, Massachusetts. I was writing my journal entries in an astonishingly obsessive degree. And I really didn't know why I was doing it. I was just doing it. What it did was it developed the skill of putting my emotions and thoughts in very close contact to language, particularly how I felt and thought and how I perceived the world.

When I met Rita, we just fell in love and we were never apart. She was a friend, first, for a year. And she was the first woman that I became really good friends with after I left Kentucky, so I, you know, married her. She thought that I should try writing prose and urged me to go to graduate school, but I thought going to graduate school was the dumbest idea I'd ever heard in my life. However, by this time we'd gone back to Kentucky, living in a house with no insulation, a woodstove, and no plumbing. And we went broke. This was not what I'd planned for my new bride and me. She said, Let's go to graduate school, and it was like the Army to me. Fifteen years before I was in the same boat and I tried to join the Army. This time it was grad school. I wrote three short stories for the application process, one of which was "Horseweed," and got accepted and went. I like that story. It's one of my favorites.

Did "Horseweed" go through workshop at Iowa?

Yeah.

And what was the reception?

Poor. Poor to lousy. My teachers were supportive. I had Jim McPherson, Frank Conroy, and Jim Salter. I was writing about a lot of stuff that was very foreign to most of my fellow students. I spent more time with poets. They were most of my friends in graduate school. They cared about language. They talked about language, and they were spontaneous and they were fun.

How close was the workshop version to the published one?

You know, the basic structure was there. The basic story was there.

The fact that, in Same River, *you mention that Rita wanted to go to Arizona and you wanted to go to Montana is another reason I said there seems to be some kind of pull drawing you there.*

Yeah, that's true. I wanted to go to Montana all my life. I wanted to go to Alaska all my life. Those were the two places I wanted to go. I have no reason why. I read *Big Sky* by A. B. Guthrie and the book knocked me out. It was one of my favorite novels for a long time. It's about a guy from Kentucky whose name is Caudill who goes to Montana.

Is that where Virgil's name comes from?

Well, partly. There are a lot of Caudills in Kentucky. There's a writer named Harry Caudill in Kentucky, one of our few writers. It's a mix of names. All of my names are carefully chosen, but there's a lot of reasons that go into them. Like Boyd in *The Good Brother*, if you rearrange the letters, it's the word body. Well, he's dead the whole book. He's just a body.

You mentioned having to cut the epilogue that you'd written for The Good Brother. *What did it cover?*

Shit, they go up to Alaska and live happily ever after and homestead.

Joe and Botree and the two kids?

And Johnny and his girlfriend and their daughter. Coop is dead of a heart attack. There were some lawsuits. The ACLU was involved and they got charged with criminal syndicalism. They dusted it off, like this old prosecution charge I discovered. And then I thought, What are you doing, Chris? You can't have this book and then have people go off to Alaska. It just was me trying to not let Virgil face the music, and that's what got me so tore up over it. When I cut it, I started crying because I realized that Virgil couldn't just get off scot free, because for me to allow Virgil to run off to Alaska and live happily ever after was to condone homicide, which I don't.

In The Same River *you write, "More and more I depended on my journal. It was organic, I believed, even sentient. I came to regard the process of recording a lived life as the only material fit for writing." Tell me about your research for* The Good Brother. *How far did you take it?*

How far did I take it? I went to Kentucky. I flew my family to Montana. I started in Kentucky and made this drive, took notes all the way, stayed in the hotels I thought Virgil would stay in. During the course of writing, I acquired a variety of false identification including three birth certificates, a passport to British Honduras, a pilot's license, a military European driver's license, a private investigator's license, various library cards wherever I could, as many as I could, in order to sort of become him.

Virgil Caudill started out being based on my brother. He was the good brother in my family. All the memories that Virgil has of childhood and his brother are about my brother and me. But during the course of writing—it was a three-and-a-half-year project—it shifted over into much more being my perceptions instead of my brother's, and then, of course, Virgil became his own person to a certain extent.

In Montana we rented a house in town, and I rented a fishing cabin out in the woods up Rock Creek to write in because that's where Joe was going to live. Virgil changes his name to Joe Tiller in the novel.

I grew my hair long. I grew a big beard, as Joe did, played cards where he played cards, acted like he acted. I didn't talk much for a year and a half until we went broke, then I had to talk. I lived in that cabin for three or four days a week, then I'd go to live with my wife and kids three or four days a week. When I was in the cabin, I tried to be Joe Tiller. I tried to be my brother, who had become Virgil Caudill, who then became Joe Tiller. It was very hard. It was hardest on my wife. I was gone a lot, and she never knew who was going to walk in the door: Chris Offutt, Joe Tiller, or Virgil Caudill.

Virgil finds himself in a situation where, if he acts according to the code of the hills, he can no longer live there. And, of course, the irony is, this is the only place he knows so he's going to have to leave his home and family if he follows the code. Was that the primary motivation behind the novel?

My motivation for the book, really, had to do with identity. In two years, my identity changed. I went from a guy who had held fifty jobs, an unemployed graduate student in debt, and a guy who couldn't hold on to a relationship, to a husband, a father, and a writer. In two years. And it was overwhelming for me in every way. Utterly overwhelming. My behavior was very erratic. How I perceived myself was different. My role and roles were very different, how other people perceived me was very different, and I wanted to write about identity. That, to me, is what the whole book's all about.

In The Same River *you also write, "If riding a bicycle through a snowstorm sounded like good material for the journal, I borrowed a bike in a blizzard. The actual ride didn't matter. What I did was try to observe myself as carefully as possible, while simultaneously imagining myself writing everything down later."*

Right. I'm still doing that.

I know that you witnessed a bulldozer accident. I assume that contributed, in some way, to your story "House Raising," but obviously you didn't go out looking for a bulldozer accident. Did you do research like you did for the novel, living Joe's life, in either the stories of Kentucky Straight *or the new collection? By the way, do you have a title for the new book?*

Yeah. *Out of the Woods.* It's coming out next year.

How many stories?

Ten. With *Kentucky Straight,* I hadn't written about Kentucky for years. I knew that I would one day. I didn't have the courage. It took me a long time to get the courage up, and then ultimately I got the courage out of desperation. Most of the acts in my life have been motivated by desperation. And the things that ultimately have paid off for me have been acts of despair. People have often said to me, Oh boy, you're so courageous. You are so brave. But I'm not. I'm a desperate coward who takes action.

I got married and went back home with the hopes that I could fit in as the prodigal son. I had a little money and I could buy a house, and I had high hopes for that and it didn't work out. There was no work and we went broke. But that's what gave me the ability to write *Kentucky Straight,* ultimately—being gone for several years, returning, and realizing that I had to leave again. That's when I wrote *Kentucky Straight.* I was depressed and angry.

At Iowa I wrote that book, and most of those stories were written in a tornado cellar outside. You had to leave the house, go outside, lift up the hatch, go down those steps, close the door in the dark, find the light switch, and sit down there. Every house I've ever lived in, I've built an office in. I love to build my own office. I want to build my own and create my own space in which to work. So those stories were written in this tornado cellar, and then I moved outside of town to the river and a few were written out there.

Do you have a personal favorite among the stories?

I like "Nine Ball," Horseweed," and "Sawdust."

What's your weakest story?

Don't ask me. I have no idea. I don't think in terms like that. There's a couple of stories that were written in different periods of my life—

"Aunt Granny Lith" and "Old of the Moon," and "Leaving One"—that are sort of stylistically different, and those were written when my wife was pregnant. It was like a magical, mystical time. I had this pregnant wife and I couldn't believe it. It was wonderful. I was going in the woods all the time. She and I would go into the woods together, and I was existing in this zone of magic and joy and terror. Those stories came out of that experience, particularly "Old of the Moon."

I wrote "Old of the Moon" during the time when she was due and two weeks later when she had the baby. I wrote that story and revised it probably twelve to fifteen times. I revised it every single day of that two-week period waiting for her to go to the hospital. I mean, a drastic revision. Not just commas. Huge revisions. I have no idea what I threw away from that story. And that story is about my worse fear, the death of a baby. I wouldn't let Rita read it.

There's a lot of mysticism there. Those three stories all have that other-worldly quality.

Well, I think it's related to when Rita was pregnant, we were existing in another world. We really were. My wife called those stories my "mythistical" stories. She invented that word. I was reading mythology. I was reading legends and lore and folk stories and borrowing from them because I grew up hearing that sort of thing, and I was trying, in many ways, to create my own stories. But what you're talking about is really related to that time. I just can't describe the intensity of my feelings of being a part of an otherwordly experience and it was really, you know, that my wife was pregnant and it was amazing.

Did the process of the second child match the intensity of the first?

Oh yeah. When she was pregnant with the second child we were living in a three-room cabin on the Iowa River, and I was completing the final draft of *The Same River Twice*, so I was writing about the first child while living the second child and it was unbelievable, this little zone that I was in, of irreality, of otherworldliness. This three-room cabin had a porch on the back. Just poles to hold up the plastic, corrugated roof. I boxed it in and threw down a floor and my landlord gave me a window and I did all the work, built it in three days, and wrote in there. So I would write in there, go out, and there would be my wife who was pregnant, my little boy who was learning to walk, and the woods. It was just unbelievable. And I would go out and wander around these woods and go back into the house and it was the happiest two years of my life.

I'm a fairly superstitious person, you know. I come out of a culture that has a lot of superstitions and old folkways and this and that, but I invent stuff like that all the time, for myself. I have a lucky shirt. I have a lucky jacket. I wore one shirt for *The Good Brother*. I wore it every day I wrote. I had a chair. I have lucky stuff in my pockets right now, around my neck, two lucky objects in my briefcase. My room is filled with objects that I have imbued with powers.

What other lucky objects do you have?

The new one is a claw from an alligator that my wife gave me. There's a feather in my briefcase. There's a rock around my neck from "The Leaving One" that I've had ever since I was a kid. There's a belt balancer in my pocket like Virgil gets. I've carried it ever since the oldest man on the hill gave it to me. I didn't have any grandparents. My parents severed relations with both their families, so I didn't know my grandparents. My sisters were afraid of old people. Me? I was entranced by them. I still am. I would go up to this oldest man on the hill. I would go to his house in the summer when I was wandering around the woods, and I would ask him for water because it would be hot, and we would go around to the back where he had a well and he would give me this beautiful water, and I would just talk to him because I didn't have any old people in my life. Now the only reason he was old was because he didn't work in the mines. He was the gardener for the company town and was able to survive into old age as a result. All the other people who worked in the mines died. He then became the grade school janitor, so I saw him every day, and then he was the school bus driver for a little while, but he was a big part of my life. He was sort of a faux grandpa. His name was Sam, in fact, which I've named my first son, and he gave me this belt balancer when I went back to visit him, I don't know, ten years ago. I don't know how we got off on that.

Lucky stuff.

Oh yeah. Lucky stuff. I have all kinds of lucky stuff.

Do you have a stuffed possum?

I do have a stuffed possum. It was a gift. When I lived on the Iowa River, there was a man who was my neighbor who was fifty-eight, didn't finish grade school, one of the smartest people I'd ever met. He could do anything. Invented tools in order to do specific tasks. Would make a tool for a task. Would panel walls by holding a Skil saw in one hand and plywood in the other and just cut it in the air to fit. He was an amazing guy. I got to know him, and his wife, and he had lived on that river for years and had trapped it and fished it and paid the bills by sort of being a part-time carpet layer. I loved that guy, you know.

Well, he had a stuffed possum and I couldn't believe it. I would say, Jerry, who would stuff a possum? It's the ugliest animal in the hemisphere. Well, Jerry died. He went outside and sat on a stump and died. And I was living in Montana when that happened, and I got a call about it, and the next time I made a trip east I went to visit his widow and she gave me the possum.

You say that when you were at Iowa you hung around poets more than fiction writers because they were more concerned with language. Is there a difference between the attention to language in writing a short story and a novel?

In terms of language? No.

Are you more suited to writing one than the other?

I don't know. That's a tricky question. You know, I've written about ninety short stories and one novel, so I don't know yet. I don't see a difference on the level of language. There's a big difference in a lot of other ways, but as far as attention paid to language, I try to give as much attention to each word in each sentence with everything I write. That's the challenge, in general, for writing.

Did it scare you when you started writing the novel?

Yeah, I was scared. But I put myself in the position where I had to do it, see. I moved my family to Montana to write this novel. Well, goddammit, I better write it. I had failed in two attempts. My first novel was several years ago. I traveled around with a friend of mine and I was going to write down everything we said and did and turn it into a book at the end, and we did interesting things in order to have it in there, and I would transcribe our conversations as we were having them, which is an absurd and stupid thing to do. The novel went nowhere. It had a great beginning but then things changed.

The next time I tried to write a novel was after *The Same River Twice* was published. I got codlocked into it, really, through a contract, because it was a two-book contract so I had to write one. It was going to be a coming-of-age novel of a sensitive young man in eastern Kentucky. I wrote a seven-page prologue and became clinically depressed. Stayed on the couch for a long time and did not write another word for the longest period in years, probably ten months. The first thing I wrote after that was the story "Out of the Woods," so I thought, This is not the novel for me to write, and I came up with a one-page synopsis for *The Good Brother*. I thought it would be interesting and then proceeded from there.

Was the synopsis pretty much on track?

Oh yeah. Everything that happens in that book is on that page. I mean, not everything, but the major events.

When did you start writing The Good Brother?

The fall of 1993 but I'd been thinking about it and planning it for several months prior to the actual writing in January. And I wrote very little at that point. I just kind of got myself going to establish the fact that I felt like I could. That was before we moved to Montana. I started in

Iowa. I wrote the Work section and then I went back and wrote the big opening chapter and went from there.

Did you take any lengthy breaks?

Yeah. I took a few. In the summer of 1995 we started going broke and I had a hard time writing. Then we moved and I didn't write for about a month, so I didn't write for about three months. I really write best in the fall. I'm a real autumn writer. I just function great in the fall and I tend to get depressed in the spring, so that fall of 1995 I completed a draft and then didn't work on it for three months. Then we went broke again, and that's when we went to Albuquerque. We moved to Iowa for three months, hoping that my wife could get a job there, but it didn't work out. We went to Albuquerque in January of 1996 and I didn't write that spring. I'd finished a draft. Then I had reconstructive knee surgery and required nine months of rehab and I had to learn to walk again.

Was this before or after you wrote about Joe getting shot?

After. That's a very good question. It's scary, isn't it? My wife said, Next time you have to write about a guy who hits the lottery. I keep writing about this stuff and it happens.

I'd had a bad knee for a long time. I wrote about it in *The Same River Twice*, too. And in *Kentucky Straight* the guy hurts the shit out of his knee in "Smokehouse."

At least you didn't get run over by a bulldozer.

No, but it's the same leg. It's always that left leg.

Did you write any short stories while you were working on The Good Brother?

I decided not to write a single short story during the time I wrote this novel.

Were you ever tempted by a story idea?

No. I was utterly obsessed and consumed by the novel. It never entered my mind. I just lost the short story mentality. I took notes all the time.

There are things that didn't go into the novel that will go into short stories and all, but no, I never wrote a short story during that time.

What painters have influenced you? When you were going to museums in New York for the first time, what painters were you going to see?

Jasper Johns. I really admire his work. I like Kurt Schwitters. I think Picasso's a great painter. When I was heavily influenced by painters, I was actually under the influence of Zak, who was Shadrack in *The Same River Twice*. Zak was really, really interested in the abstract expressionists, so I was. Now this book, *The Same River Twice*, is structured based on the paintings of abstract expressionists, which is you can look at the picture anywhere, and your eye can move anywhere you want, and you take in the whole painting. *The Same River Twice* is designed to where you can start at any chapter in the book and read through to the end, and then begin at the beginning and read through. My idea is that there is no middle, there is no beginning or end to that book. You're forced into the beginning and end by the nature of narrative and by the structure of the physical creation of the book as object.

I'm with you except for the chronology of the pregnancy.

Well, she gets pregnant and then has the baby within chapters of each other. You can skip to the beginning. It's not going to work out perfectly, of course, but that was how I was trying to put it together. I was really influenced by visual art. I also wrote the sections of the past all in cities, in Boston and New York, and then the shorter piece about the pregnancy I wrote in the woods.

Were you living in Boston and New York or did you go there specifically to do the writing?

I was living in Boston and New York when I began it. I began *The Same River Twice* when I had been dumped by a woman and thrown out of an apartment, and I found myself in a rooming house. I had nothing to show for my life but a bunch of journals. I'd bought a typewriter and I'd tried to write some stories, but I'd failed at it. I thought I would try to write about the most dreadful circumstances of the past several years, which seemed to me like a sequence of errors. I was profoundly depressed. Nothing had worked out the way I wanted. I was alone in a rooming house, you know. I wasn't very happy, and I couldn't believe how I'd gotten there. It wasn't what I'd intended when I left Kentucky.

I thought I'd write about the worst experiences, and the ones that hurt me the most, and I'd try to understand how I went from a guy from Kentucky to a guy in a rooming house in eight years. I wound up with a six hundred-page manuscript and utterly no understanding of what had happened. I set it aside and several years passed. At one point my mother typed a draft of *The Same River Twice* before I went to Iowa because it was just a terrible mess and she typed it for me. I'd knocked it down from six hundred pages to like a hundred and thirty pages, and I took that with me.

So it was handwritten?

It was on all kinds of different papers that I could get for free. What I would do is I would go to copy shops and say, Look, give me your mistakes, because they always make mistakes on big projects. So I would get their mistakes for free.

Anyhow, it was never intended for print. It was intended for me to understand it. And then, after *Kentucky Straight*, all of a sudden I'm a writer. People said, What are you going to write next? Are you going to write another story collection next? And I thought, Goddamn, no. I'm sick of them. They said, Are you going to write a novel? And I thought, Goddamn, no. I'm scared to death of that. And they said, What then? And I said, Well, I have this manuscript, you know.

My aunt had given me a computer as a gift when I went to graduate school. Her husband had died and he had wanted to be a writer. I didn't know how to run a computer. I was always messing up, but I found, in the computer, two years after the fact, all these notes about Rita's pregnancy that I'd written and all of a sudden they just sort of appeared out of Computerworld. They just popped up on my screen.

By this time we were on the cabin by the river and I thought, My God. Here it is. Here's the structure I've been looking for for *The Same River Twice*. Prior to that it was a bad *On the Road*. It was just an anecdotal, bad picaresque book. It needed a structure. I tried a couple of different structures and they didn't work. I found those notes. My life had changed and it just came to me what I could do if I had the guts.

I wouldn't have discovered the abstract expressionism on my own, but the structure's great. It works.

Well, people have often commented on the structure. Let me tell you, that was a result of hundreds of hours of experimenting with chapters and sections and cutting and moving, and at one point I strung up clothespins in my office with pages of manuscript so I could see everything all at once, so I could see all the lines and I was utterly enveloped, then, in the pages of the manuscript. At one time the structure was only the last two weeks of her pregnancy. Then I realized that didn't work because it was winter and it sort of grew from there to all four seasons. In the meantime, she was pregnant again so I was able to reexperience what I had experienced, so I was living in two other worlds.

When you finish a story, can you put it in the mail right away, or do you have to put it in a drawer and come back in a week or so in order to be objective?

Oh, I don't send out a short story until I'm utterly sick of it. I revise them so much. I usually hang on to them for a year to two years, and I think about them six months to a year even before I start writing, so by the time I send one out I have them practically memorized. In the revision process, when I'm down to substituting a conjunction for a comma, and then the next day putting the comma back and taking out the conjunction, then I know I'm sick of the story and it's time to send it out.

Can you read when you're writing?

I read different material at different stages. If I'm writing fresh material, a first draft, I read nonfiction pertaining to the work with as flat and dull a prose as possible. When I'm revising I can read. When I was writing this novel, all I read was third-person novels. I didn't read short stories and I didn't read anything in first person. And I was very careful who I read. I didn't read Cormac's new book because his style is way too pervasive. I read Cormac and for two weeks, man, I'm writing bad Cormac McCarthy. But with Robert Stone, I could read him because I love his style. I could read Joseph Conrad and Graham Greene. I read writers who I thought were big, expansive storytellers, writers who were very ambitious within the project and achieved a genuine sense of reality on the page. And beautiful writers. Now I can return to short stories and first-person work.

Has any particular book had a significant impact on you?

Yeah. You'll like this little story. This is a good one. When I was a kid, my hero was Johnny Bench. He was a catcher for the Cincinnati Reds and they won the World Series in the late seventies and he was my hero, you know. I played Little League, but I was the shortest catcher in the league. I was tiny, but I wanted to be a catcher. Well, I was reading and reading and reading. In the meantime, they finally got a library in town and my mother would take me in. It was a very small library. You could only check out four books per card. Very small. So I got library cards in my name, my brother and sisters' name, and my dog's name. That's a fact. I would go in there with five library cards, check out twenty books a week, every Saturday. My mother would drop me off at the library, and she would go to the grocery, and come back to pick me up. She'd leave me a grocery sack. I'd fill it with twenty books and get out of there.

Finally I went to the librarian and I said, Look, I want a book on baseball. There are a lot of baseball books aimed at children that are sort of like, There's a new kid in town. He's great at baseball. Everybody likes him. That's all I wanted to be. Everybody would like me because I was good at something. So I said, I want a book on baseball. And she goes to the card catalog and she says, Is there anything you like? And I said, I like Johnny Bench. And she doesn't know who that is so I say, He's a catcher. So she looks up catcher and says, Oh, come here. I have a book for you. She takes me to this part of the library I'd never been in. She pulls out this book and hands it to me, and I say, Oh, great. I check it out. I go home. I start reading it. It's *Catcher in the Rye*. I stayed up all night and read that book when I was twelve years old. I could not believe it. I'm getting a funny feeling right now just remembering it. It tore me up. It just made my hair stand on end. I could not believe that you could write that way. That book probably had more influence than any single book I ever read. I never read another juvenile again. I couldn't believe you could write like that. I went from Hardy Boys to *Catcher in the Rye*.

What about people? Has any one person had a particular influence on your work as a writer?

My wife. Any success I achieve as a writer is due to her. She provides me with time, space, and support. She and I talk about everything all the time, all the people, all the stories. She's my first reader. If somebody sat and overheard us discussing *The Good Brother*, they would think we led the most unusual lives and knew the most interesting people. We talk about everything as if it's real, because in my imagination it is real.

A Conversation with Stewart O'Nan

Stewart O'Nan was born in Pittsburgh in 1961, majored in engineering at Boston University, and worked for Grumman Aerospace on Long Island before obtaining a graduate writing degree from Cornell. Beginning in 1991, he taught at Trinity College in Hartford, Connecticut, a job he left shortly after this interview took place in order to write full time. He lives in Connecticut with his wife, Trudy, and their two children.

Despite what he considers "a late start" into a writing career, O'Nan has been extremely productive. When we spoke in September of 1997, he had published three novels and a collection of short stories. Another novel was in production, and a second story collection and three more novels had been written and were awaiting publication. O'Nan also had written six screenplays and served as the editor of two books: *On Writers and Writing* and *The Vietnam Reader*.

This interview, however, concerns itself primarily with Stewart O'Nan's fiction. His first story collection, *In the Walled City*, won the Drue Heinz Prize. His first novel, *Snow Angels*, won the William Faulkner Prize, and in 1996 O'Nan was named one of Granta's "Best Young American Novelists."

We met near Union Square in Manhattan.

Let's start with a list of everything that has been written and edited. You've written five screenplays.

Six now. I just finished *Lie Down in Darkness*. There's *Poe, Clara, Angels, Violent Bear It Away, Going after Cacciato,* and now *Lie Down in Darkness*. Those are the six.

What does writing the screenplays give you that writing fiction doesn't?

Well, in the early work, especially the large, big books, possibly because I didn't know exactly where I was going, there were a lot of scenes where the characters were simply by themselves, the dreaded one-person scenes where they sit and sort of ruminate and I wanted to try and get away from that. And writing screenplays or just straight drama you've got to have something going on between two characters. I mean, this is not French film. You can't have Juliette Binoche looking out through the window. We're not going to buy it and say, Oh, isn't it soulful? Give us some people knocking into each other, talking to each other.

Do the screenplays serve as a break from fiction, or do they carry as much weight in terms of working on a project?

Usually they do because when I'm adapting stuff, I usually pick something I really, really love so I try to treat it with great care. Technically it's not as challenging because obviously it's a screenplay format. It's some sort of third omniscient, this omniscient eye of the camera throughout. And the language doesn't change quite as much across a screenplay. I usually do them after I finish a novel just to clear the head a little bit, do something else, but I think, and I argue with people about this, I think they use a lot of the same sort of brain muscles.

Besides the screenplays, there's the short story collection, In the Walled City, *three novels published, and at least two novels written that are waiting to be published.*

Four. Four novels waiting to go.

What are the names of the other two? I know of A Prayer for the Dying *and* A World Away.

Cuba Libre is one. It's more of an action thriller. There's less of an emphasis on character in that one, and *About a Girl,* which is a large, multinarrating consciousness. Big. Wide.

Is Cuba Libre *being shopped under your own name?*

So far, no. We may do it under a pseudonym. We'll see. Unfortunately, Elmore Leonard's next book is going to be called *Cuba Libre.* I had mine done a year and a half before he started writing his, but that's what happens when the publishing industry gets behind.

Have you come up with an alternate title?

Not really. It was a great title. It's a great, great title, and I thought it was mine alone. Leonard's doing something Spanish Civil War era. It doesn't quite fit but, you know.

You didn't make a distinction with About a Girl, *so I'm assuming that the book falls in line with* A World Away *and* Prayer for the Dying.

Yeah, it's a real good book. It may be my favorite book out of all of those.

In what order will they appear?

A World Away will come out next June and then it's a coin flip between *Prayer for the Dying* and *About a Girl,* two very different books.

There are two titles listed in Contemporary Authors *that you haven't mentioned:* End of Memory *and* Sentimental Journey.

End of Memory *is* About a Girl *and* Sentimental Journey *is* A World Away. I always start with an awful title and then move toward a less awful title. And let's not forget the Gardner book, *On Writers and Writing,* and *The Vietnam Reader,* which is coming out next September. I just delivered that this morning. Seven hundred and six pages.

Okay. So that does it, right? Six screenplays, two edited books, a short story collection, and seven novels.

I should have another short story collection done by the end of the month called *Twenty Burgers.*

Twenty Burgers?

Twenty Burgers. The title story is about a girl who, to get free food for a whole bus, eats twenty burgers. It's classic eighties American fiction.

Can we do a chronology? Snow Angels *was your first published novel. Is it the first novel you wrote?*

No. I wrote a book called *The Caretaker,* which is the dreaded drawer novel, the bad book.

What's it about?

It was a fictional response to Richard Ford's *The Sportswriter,* which, I believe, is a fictional response to Walker Percy's *The Moviegoer,* which is a fictional response to Jean Paul Sartre's *Nausea.* And so for my first large project after I'd written all the short stories, I took on the philosophical picaresque novel, which was not the way to go.

Not the way to go for you or not the way for you to go at that time?

Not the way to go for anybody. The philosophical novel is not the first thing one should start out with for a book-length project. It's a bad move.

I didn't have the tools or the intellect for it, and probably still don't, but it was sort of half comic, half romantic. It was very much after things like *The Moviegoer* with a bit of bitter and sophomoric philosophizing after someone like Sartre or Camus. That's how I first got interested in writing was reading people like Camus and Sartre, the existentialists, and I thought that this was my shot at the sort of post-Catholic, American urban, existentialist novel, and it didn't work at all.

Is The Caretaker *literally in a drawer or has it been disposed of in some fashion?*

No, there's a copy of it left. I think there's one copy. We got rid of all but one and my wife keeps telling me, Don't throw it away. That's my insurance policy.

I tried to revise it a few years ago. I'd just finished another book I'd been revising and I was so high on the other book I was like, Yeah, this is all working. This is all good. And then I picked up *The Caretaker*, figuring I'd just go in and finish in half a flash. I read about ten pages and I was like, There's nothing that can be done.

So Snow Angels *came after* Caretaker?

No. Actually, after *Caretaker* comes *End of Memory*, which is now titled *About a Girl*. It was my M.F.A. thesis at Cornell, and a very large, long book at the time. Now it's much cut down. Then comes *A World Away*, or *Sentimental Journey*, whichever, and that one I did in 1990 or 1991, I think, and then comes *Snow Angels*. So *Snow Angels* would be the fourth novel that I wrote.

Is there a reason that Snow Angels *was published first? Is there a particular reason that the novels have been published out of sequence?*

About a Girl got taken by an agent and we got real close at Farrar, Straus back in 1991. This was my first agent. He was, then, a very junior guy over at William Morris, and he loved the book. He was crazy about the book, and he shopped it and shopped it and shopped it, and he got everyone to say that I was a wonderful writer but no one would take it at the time. I showed him *A World Away*, and he liked it but he still wanted to get *About a Girl* sold. By that time I'd written *Snow Angels*, as well. It was a very quick book to write. He looked at that and said it was too violent, too grim, too much of a downer, that no one would want it. So at that point he had three of my books and he really only wanted to shop one. I said, One and two. That's not a good record. So at that time the stories won the Drue Heinz Prize, got picked up, and a few months later *Snow Angels* won the Faulkner Prize, and on the basis of that I got a new agent. That agent, of course, had seen *Snow Angels* and took me on for *Snow Angels* and sold *Snow Angels*.

So how did Names of the Dead *come next?*

That's what I was writing at the time when *Snow Angels* sold and my agent at the time had seen about a hundred pages of that and liked it a lot, and we decided to go with that one since it was hot.

Is your most recent novel Prayer for the Dying?

Right. I wrote that this spring. I finished it, I think, in April.

Okay. You finished it in April, but the last piece you finished was the screen-play for Lie Down in Darkness?

Well, I wrote a short story yesterday, but that doesn't count.

What a line. "I wrote a short story yesterday." That's what we have to talk about. Elizabeth McCracken told me that you once went on vacation and were disappointed that you only wrote three stories.

Yeah, that was this summer actually.

Most people don't write while they're on vacation, so the fact that you wrote three stories and were disappointed is a bit remarkable. Do you ever work on things concurrently, or do you strictly work on one thing at a time?

It's usually one at a time. Occasionally, a big project, something like *About a Girl*, will sit on the shelf for a while before I'll come back to it when I'm fresh and can hack at it again. Usually when I'm doing draft work, I try to go from Point A all the way to Point Z.

Can we use Prayer for the Dying *as an example since it's the most recent?*
Sure.

You finished in April. It's a hundred and fifty pages in manuscript. When did you start?

Yeah, it's very short. I started it about a year before. It took me about a year to write that book, mostly because I had difficulty with second person and doing some things technically in moving time in the second-person present tense. I was trying to do summary narration in second-person present tense, and no one else seems to have done that, so I'd look at my model to see how people move time in them, and I couldn't seem to find a model for it so I had to come up with some sort of solution.

What kind of second-person models are there available to use? Isn't Bright Lights, Big City *pretty much the most noted second-person novel?*

Well, that's the one and it's typical of a second-person present in that anytime he needs to do summary or backfill, it drops into a past tense, or it simply cuts to the end of the scene and starts at the beginning of the next scene in live, rendered action. The book that really inspired me to do it was Robert O'Connor's *Buffalo Soldiers*. I also used Lorrie Moore's *Self-Help*, and Charles Johnson has a short story called "Moving Pictures," which is kind of interesting.

Are these works models or inspirations for your book?

Well, I saw the capability of what second person could do by reading *Buffalo Soldiers*. I thought O'Connor used it very beautifully there.

Did the idea of using the second-person point of view come before the idea of the character or the idea of the story?

I had the idea of the story for a long time. The genesis, actually, was Michael Lesy's book, *Wisconsin Death Trip*. Lesy's book, which he did, I believe, for a master's thesis at the University of Wisconsin, was a compilation of memorial photographs from the late nineteenth century along with newspaper clippings and accounts of mental patients being admitted to the state hospital there. He did it in 1970, and it was all formatted in a way to make it seem as if the countryside—what we equate as the rural, bucolic countryside of the late nineteenth century—was going absolutely mad. Economic failure, breakdown in relationships, suicides, arsonists on the loose. He made it seem like this wild, crazed, gothic world. There's a really dark feel to the book. I decided then, If I can just get that into fiction, that's the kind of gothic horror novel that I'd like to write. Sunlit horror. So I had that feeling ever since reading that book, probably in the early nineties, and slowly the pieces of the puzzle of the narrative came to me.

So it took about a year to write. From the amount of work you've produced, I'm guessing that a hundred fifty pages in a year is slow for you.

Oh yeah. Very slow.

Did you take a break from it?

I did a few short stories during that time, probably about six or seven, but mostly I just moved very slowly on it. I wrote a page or two a day. I knew it was a book that wanted to be written at a very slow pace, and the book that I had written before that was *Cuba Libre* and I wrote that in forty-three days. Way too fast. I wrote *Speed Queen* in sixty-six days. Way too fast. At least in *Cuba Libre* I knew that I'd rushed the material so I wanted to slow down a little bit with *Prayer for the Dying*. Even though it's a gothic and it has this big sort of plot engine with the plague and the fire and all that stuff, it's a pastoral in a way, so I purposely tried to slow it down a little bit.

You mentioned writing a page or so a day. How about the actual process? Do you write in the same room when you're home?

Most of the time. Same room, same little word processor.

Do you write at the same time of day?

Nah, I can never get the time right, but I try to do three or four hours a day, two or three pages in a session. Two of them should be good. Two out of the three pages should be pretty good. I like to revise it in hard copy and then edit again the next day. I'll backtrack and revise everything I've written the day before, and that way it'll build me up enough steam to go into the new stuff.

So theoretically, by the time you've finished the rough draft of a novel, it's been through a rewrite.

I guess. I usually rewrite more than that because there'll be a time in the writing when it bogs down, like after, say, fifty pages. And then I'll obsess about the first fifty pages and I'll go over them a few times, and then I'll try to figure out where I am and if I suddenly veer off in one direction, which usually happens, then I'll have to re-outline.

So you do work from an outline?

Oh yeah. The last few books I have. It's gotten a lot easier and better if I work from an outline.

Do you start with an outline, or do you have a fragment or sample to work with and then try to map it out?

Usually I'll wait until I get two chapters or so, thirty or forty pages, until I know what my characters are sort of up to and how much space they're going to take. I mean, lately, in the last few books, I've been very project, or even product, oriented, which is probably not good, in that I will see the story, I will see what character needs to tell the story, what technical device I want to use, or try to use, this time—say the second person or the short chapter format—and I'll commit to that rather early.

You said that you've become more product oriented and that it's probably not a good thing. What does product oriented mean to you?

Well, it means that the last three novels that I've written have all been very short. I can see almost from the beginning to the end of them. I mean, there are parts in the middle that I can't see, but the earlier books—*Names of the Dead, About a Girl, A World Away*—were books where I really sort of felt my way through. I really didn't know where I was going. They're much heavier, much more based on language. They were also more generous in terms of the room that they gave the characters. *Names of the Dead* is only one narrating consciousness, but it's all of it. I mean, it's a good five hundred page manuscript of this guy. The other two large books spread out the narration. They give almost every character a shot at the narration, which is what I like to do usually.

So if we put this in track terminology, do you see yourself as more of a marathoner than a sprinter?

Well, I like to write a generous book, and I like to spread the narrative consciousness, the point of view duties, around, and lately I've been working on projects which only have one point-of-view character. I mean, *Prayer for the Dying* is a second-person novel. *Speed Queen* is a first-person novel, which is very quick, and *Cuba Libre* is a third-person limited novel. So I'd like to get back. The second book that I'll write, after the one this fall, I want to spread out again and do another five, six-hundred pager, and let everyone take a shot at it.

Do you see novels like Names of the Dead *and* World Away *as more of an accomplishment than* Speed Queen *or* Prayer for the Dying?

No, but they're more satisfying to work on, I think. You get a bigger cast. You get more people and you get to go into the lives of more people. What I really like about *About a Girl* is the original manuscript is like nine hundred pages long and I must have had like twenty-five point-of-view narrators and I'd get way, way away from the basic narrative, the central narrative line of it, and the further away I got, the more I liked it, because I was getting fascinated, more and more, by all these different people.

That's what I like about writing—going into the lives of these people I've never known before. That's interesting to me, but I don't know if that's valued by either the publishers or the readers. They like a nice, tight story. People want things to fit so perfectly.

You mentioned wanting to try different technical devices. Do you have a desire to write everything, or every way? You seem to place some priority on using different techniques. Is that what keeps you interested? Is it a challenge you present yourself?

Yeah. The challenge that I present to myself definitely keeps me interested but also, for certain books, for certain characters, for certain stories, by taking on what some people would think of as a very strange or even radical point of view, like second person, it adds a lot. It's the right point of view. Choosing exactly the right point of view and the right character at the right time is, I think, what's most effective about fiction writing. I mean, Tolstoy was a genius at that. If you look at something like *Anna Karenina,* he picks exactly the right person to narrate each event at exactly the right time, and that compulsion to narrate is built into certain characters. It needs to be taken advantage of.

But do you need to change things like point of view?

I don't think it's a need to write differently that I have. I think it's that the characters, the situation, the story, can be done more effectively in certain points of view, and I think that, as a writer, you should be able to do those points of view. You should be able to take those on. You should have the technical skill, the level of technical skill necessary, to take those on. I mean, I could've written, I think, *Prayer for the Dying* in first person but it probably wouldn't work nearly as well. This particular character has this overdeveloped sort of superego and it's always sort of accusing him. No matter how well he's doing it's always sort of saying, You're screwing up, you're screwing up, even though he wants to be this perfect, blameless person, so it fits him perfectly. Marjorie in *The Speed Queen.* That's definitely not a third-person book there. It's got to be a first-person book. Got to be unreliable, way unreliable.

You said that a writer should have the technical skill to write in different ways, but there are good writers out there who know they are stronger in the first person than they are in the third person, for example. Are they less of a writer by taking advantage of their strengths?

It doesn't matter what your style is. You're only as good as the characters, and you should do justice to your characters and the actions that they take. You're in service to those characters. You're not there to say, Oh look at me, I'm writing. Obviously there's a metafictional aspect to several of my works, but you're not there to say, Look, I'm writing beautifully, or Look what I can do. You're there in service of the character.

Let's go back to Speed Queen. *You wrote it in sixty-six days, but you said that that might've been too quick.*

Yeah, I think it might've been a little bit too quick. I think I could've slowed down on that. I mean, in the beginning I liked the idea of writing it fast, conceptually, because of Marjorie doing it all in one night, being on speed. Originally, I wanted to write it straight into a tape recorder and then play it back to myself.

I was wondering, with the breaks in the books—Side B, Tape Two, Side A— whether or not you'd read it aloud in order to time each section to the length of the tape.

No. Not at all. Originally I thought that I'd do something like that but, in the end, I didn't. It was a good book to work on, day by day, when I was teaching, because once I got the questionnaire together, I could just fall out of bed and get into character and answer the question. It gave me a chance to work in a way that I like to work, which I guess is more of a poet's way of juxtaposing things rather than following any sort of narrative line—just putting things up against each other and seeing how they fit. Working by feel, which is a lot more fun. I like that sort of method. A little bit here, a little bit there, a little collage. Some of the short stories are written that way, and this one seemed natural.

So Speed Queen *was written chronologically? You didn't answer question thirty-seven out of one hundred and forty-seven first?*

No. I got the questions in order. After about the first thirty or so I said, What am I doing? I better get that questionnaire together. So I looked at a lot of books of interviews. O. J. Simpson's book, which is written in Q and A from prison by someone who says they haven't committed multiple murder, helped me a lot.

So the questionnaire functioned as your outline?

Yeah.

What's the genesis of Speed Queen? *What made you want to write this book?*

That one came from a Vietnam veteran oral history, a very graphic oral history. It was Vietnam veterans who had been to prison for capital crimes talking about their experience. And this guy who had been in prison for a while was talking about what it was like kidnapping and almost killing this guy. He was talking about it as if it were a joke. He was absolutely gleeful, completely unapologetic. Then, about halfway through the interview, he realized this was the wrong way to be talking, so he started being very contrite and saying, Well, I've changed. I'm a different person. But then he'd break in again with, Oh man, you should've been there. And I said, That's really interesting. Maybe I should try to use this voice, because it was a great voice. So I put that away because I was working on the big Vietnam book, and after that was done I needed to sort of blow off some steam. I needed to write something really bizarre and sort of out there and very irresponsible after the Vietnam book being so responsible to all the vets.

So I sat down and came up with this idea of the killer writing from prison, the gallows broadside, a medieval form that John Gardner talks about in *The Art of Fiction*. I thought, That's an interesting one. Let me do something like that. And then I got the idea to do it with the tape recorder from *Double Indemnity*. I thought, Well, it's going to be kind of *noir*, a *noirish* gallows broadside. Perfect. A really easy form to do. I know it has to do with all these sort of murders. And then I got the idea of

Marjorie, the woman. I don't know where exactly I came up with her. And then she had to be talking to somebody. I remember *Lancelot,* Walker Percy's book, in which Lancelot, the condemned prisoner, is talking to a priest and I thought well, What do we have instead of a priest nowadays? I said, Maybe a gossip columnist, or maybe a writer, and then once I got the writer idea I said, Well, who would she confess her story to? Obviously Stephen King. He's the only one who could write it. And the only one who would have her respect. Once I had that I was just off to the races.

Tell me about Stephen King's involvement. At one point the book was called Dear Stephen King.

Well, throughout it was called *Dear Stephen King.* It was called *Dear Stephen King* until it appeared in front of the public.

What happened?

Well, I guess Stephen King was out in Hollywood doing the reshoot of *The Shining,* and I guess he caught wind of the novel because my Hollywood agent was shopping it around out there and he told his people to tell my people to cease and desist, so letters from Ralph Vicinanza appeared on my editor's desk, my agent's desk, and he said, You know, if this goes on we will certainly take legal action. And Doubleday, having already been King's publisher and having suffered the wrath of his legal action before, decided they didn't want to mess with him at all. And my agents were like, Well, you know, Stewart, are you sure you really need this title? At that point they said that no other publishing company would deal with the book with that title on it. Doubleday wouldn't sign a contract with that title on it. And, you know, we had meetings here in New York trying to convince me to take the title off and I was like, I'm the only one who's going to step up for the title. I can see where it might be in your best interest, monetarily, to say Take the title off, but it's completely not in my interest to take the title off. But eventually I signed the contract. I got the money. I got the book published with basically the wrong title on it.

I guess I'm surprised that King wanted the title gone and didn't ask for other changes. There are so many King references throughout the book that there's no mistaking who Marjorie is addressing.

Well, the thing is, the title is supposed to do two things. One is it's supposed to be a frame for the tale and so obviously going in and being informed by the title, *Dear Stephen King*, is different than going in with the title *The Speed Queen*.

But it takes the reader almost no time to catch up.

No, but it's also a total difference in terms of the book as a whole, the identity of the book as a whole. After writing a book of short stories and two novels, which are basically realistic tragedies—I mean, sure, *Names of the Dead* is truly a gothic but no one took it that way—people were expecting yet another straight-ahead, realistic tragedy. The title *Dear Stephen King* is enough of a sign, I would hope, to say, Look, this is going to be something a little stranger, a little crazier. This is not the regular Stewart O'Nan novel that you've seen before. So it seemed to me to be very important, but it may simply be an author's conceit. I don't know.

Marjorie has read all of Stephen King's novels. Have you?

I've read everything up through *Christine*, I think was the last one. My wife has read all of them, and I picked her brain for all the other stuff.

Are Marjorie's opinions of King's work the same as your wife's opinions?

Not quite, actually. We argued about that a little bit. Most of them are, but not all of them.

Marjorie's much more impressed with movies than she is with the written word, and you have a wonderful line in the novel when she turns a question around. She says, "But what about you, what are you afraid of? No one reading your books after you're dead, I bet. Hey, it's okay, they'll still watch your movies, and that's what's counts." Speed Queen *contains innumerable movie references. Badlands, in particular, is mentioned a few times. Was that the main part of your research?*

Oh yeah, *Badlands* is a great, great film.

    I figured that the mass media and their love affair with the road movie and that type of life is partly what influenced her to go ahead and take on this life. Throughout my novels there are characters in search of models, ways to live, and Marjorie has found those models in the most unlikely places, but are they really that unlikely?

Well, she says, after mentioning Janis Joplin and John Belushi, "We respected people like that, who'd killed themselves having a big time. We were like them except we weren't famous yet, or dead."

"We were like them except we weren't famous yet." Yeah, she's looking for common ground in the people that the mass media gives us. And of course we're going to look for ourselves in there, but the reflection that it gives back has nothing to do with real life and that's part of the book. Its metafictional aspect is the tearing down of escapist fiction, or fake fiction, for not having anything to do with real life. Marjorie's real life is living in her shitty apartment, getting the crappy food out of the re-frigerator, but she says, That's not my life. My life is not like that. My life is *Badlands*. My life is *Bonnie and Clyde*. I'm going to be famous. This is somehow going to lift me out of this life and into this big media life, which is supposedly larger than life, and King, of course, is supposed to help her do that.

Natural Born Killers *is almost conspicuous by its absence. There seems to be a shared amoral desire among the characters to be famous at any cost. Is* Natural Born Killers *missing for a reason other than the time frame?*

It's missing for two reasons. One is it's exactly what *Speed Queen* is against, and second is it's simply inept. It's a sort of bumbling piece of pseudo art. It's one of the most annoying and stupid films ever made, I think.

But we're in Marjorie's voice. Does Marjorie feel the same way?

In Marjorie's opinion? I think Marjorie's much more complex than the Juliette Lewis character in *Natural Born Killers*, who's conspicuous because I can't remember her damn name. She's not really a character. She's more like a chess piece. I think Marjorie has a great complexity to her. She's not stupid. She's not completely amoral. She knows that what she's done is wrong and is trying her best to cover it up and to paint herself as the innocent. She's like everybody else in these tell-all memoirs. Everyone else was wrong and they're against me and I may have done some bad things but here's who's really to blame. So in that sense it's a parody of the memoir as an exercise of an unreliable narrator.

Marjorie denies almost everything. She says that she didn't smoke, drink, or do drugs during her pregnancy, yet we learn that she smokes, drinks, and when she goes into labor she initially refuses medication because she's afraid the doctor will see her needle tracks. Is Marjorie innocent of anything?

Almost all of her denials are empty.

She's completely unreliable?

Oh yeah. She's pretty much completely unreliable, and yet in terms of emotions she's utterly reliable. I think some of the emotions she has for other people are absolutely true, at least instantaneously. She does care for Gainey. She does care for Lamont. She does care for Natalie, at times. She's really slippery, I think. She's a typical death row con. You can't believe a single word she says.

You mentioned obtaining models, Buffalo Soldiers *for* Prayer for the Dying *and O. J. Simpson's memoirs for* Speed Queen. *It seems as if Lish's* Dear Mr. Capote *is a more obvious model. How much, if any, reference was that book?*

Oh, it's definitely a conscious allusion to *Dear Mr. Capote* and of the comparison of, Why would anyone write to Truman Capote anymore? First, he's dead and second, he's nowhere near as big as King. So yeah, it's there. The sort of obsessive narrator that Lish has in that book, as well as in *Peru*. I don't have that sort of spiral around, but I've always wanted to play with that, that spiraling narrative that goes over and over, obsessively, this stuff, but I'd do that probably rather in a short story, I think. I don't think it's strong enough to hold up to an entire novel.

Robert Pinget's *Inquisitory* was also one of the frames for this book. It has that kind of narrator. He's a great French writer, a "new" novelist. In fact, my rap on this book is it's basically a French "new" novel except it's got super octane characters and action that make it read incredibly fast, even though the form it takes is incredibly slow. It spirals around the little tiny things like, What did you do all day when you were living with Lamont? The exact mode of how it operates is not confused but it's conflicted, I guess.

We've talked about a lot of different references that inform your fiction. Is there any book or writer that affects your writing across the board, or are you simply looking for the best model for the particular project?

Definitely the best model for the project. I mean, any time that you're going to take on a certain character or situation or format, you look and see what other people have done in that situation. Like writing the big Vietnam book. Obviously I can't write the things that have already been written. Obviously I don't want to write a *Paco's Story* all over again. So you look at what has been done, how well it's been done, and what you can do that's different or better somehow. Same thing with the road movie. Basically everything that I've written so far has been done by other people, but maybe not as sharply or with not the same sort of spin.

Does the word "derivative" scare you at all?

No, it doesn't because I'm doing something different. Certainly *The Names of the Dead* talks about what a Vietnam story is and what it means to the Vietnam veteran, the general public, the sons and daughters of Vietnam vets. *Snow Angels* is a story within a story. It's a narrator hidden within so, again, it's about the story itself. It's not just the raw material of, say, the Vietnam novel. Certainly *Speed Queen* is incredibly, not merely, self-reflective, but bounces off of all sorts of American culture and how America sees itself. So derivative doesn't really scare me. Some of the short stories perhaps are, in that I was learning from some of the masters that I really enjoyed like Flannery O'Connor, John Cheever, and, of course, Carver.

Do you look for models for the short stories in the same way that you look for models for the novels?

No. The short stories are very early stuff. They're like '86, '87, '88 and I was just learning how to simply put sentences together, to put stories together, to have characters, to believe in my characters, and to care about my characters deeply enough to take them all the way through a believable dramatic action, whereas the novels, especially everything that has been published so far, have been very consciously worked and very carefully put together. I mean, certainly *Snow Angels* has an interesting form or structure to it. *Names of the Dead*, again, has a challenging crosscutting element to it. *Speed Queen* has a completely unconventional format.

You used the word "quick" in reference to Speed Queen. *Do you write first person more quickly? With* Speed Queen *you talked about coming up with the questionnaire and getting into character. Is it a matter of role-playing?*

Maybe, but it also may be that they were smaller projects, too. *The Names of the Dead* took fucking forever, or it seemed to me at least. I thought I knew what I was doing with it, but it still took me two and a half years and then a shitload of research and then rewriting when the research proved to be not always accurate.

It seems I work in two basic sizes. One is around four fifty and one is around two hundred, even though *Prayer* is a little tinier than that. *Cuba Libre* is a small book as well, about that size. And the smaller projects it seems, I can see basically what they are and they're relatively fast paced no matter what form they take. Even though the form may traditionally not be a fast-paced form like the French new novel or the crosscutting between times or the changing first and third, they're relatively quick, whereas the longer books are heavy, the line writing is larger, longer, heavier.

About a Girl opens up and it's basically Faulknerian. The sentences are big and rambling and gusty and rhetorical, whereas something like *Snow Angels* is obviously very spare, very stripped down. *Speed Queen* is even more stripped down. You probably can't get fifteen adjectives out of that book that aren't colors. It is real spare. *A World Away* is a slower voice, very Salter like, very precise, almost self-consciously, so it may be the type of prose that I'm using as well as the number of characters I'm dealing with.

Which book has been the most satisfying for you? Which one comes closest to what you wanted or what you thought it could be?

That's hard to say because the books do different things. *Speed Queen* is real satisfying because it does things I didn't think it could do at first and because technically, I think it's pretty much exactly what I wanted to do. You have an ideal book, and I got that all the way onto the page and I was pretty amazed at that.

Names of the Dead has got some problems in it, I think, and yet it goes deeper into character and into the feeling of this character than any of the other books. That may be just a function of the third-person subjective narrator. *A World Away* is easily the prettiest book I've done. It's what I wanted to do with the book. It may lag in parts.

Snow Angels? Everyone seems to love it. I think it could use some cutting here and there. It's not always "on" as much as I think it could be. And *Prayer for the Dying?* It seems like I got what I want out of it. It's a scary, weird, sort of trippy, dark, gothic book so in that sense, all of them except for *Cuba Libre*, I think I'm satisfied with. *About a Girl*, since I've cut it so far back from what it was, I'm a little disappointed that it isn't the big monster that it used to be, but otherwise I'm pretty satisfied with it.

Just listening to you talk, you seem to be fairly well satisfied, happy, almost excited that Speed Queen *came close to the ideal, but earlier you said that you probably wrote it too quickly. If that's true, what did it cost?*

It may not have cost anything and it may have even ended up better for the book, but for how I felt about writing the book, it probably just went straight past me. It was too fast. It's nice when something, you know, writes itself, but you feel like it's getting a little bit out of control.

Is it any less of a book because of the short amount of time?

No. Probably not. It just seems to you, as a writer, that maybe it's not. I think it's an accomplishment, but perhaps if I'd taken another three months I could've fit even more into that basket.

So why didn't you, if that's the way you feel?

Well, that's all in retrospect. I guess after I finished it up, after I got it exactly where I wanted it, I probably looked back and said, There's probably more room in that book. I probably could've done a little more in that book because I've got this big sort of engine of the killings, you know, that lets me work under an umbrella of suspense, if not drama, and I could fit things underneath that umbrella. I could fit in all the sort of niceties of the home life and Marjorie's unreliability and all the weird stuff, the weird sex and all of that, because I've got that big engine of the bloodbath at the end. And I probably think, or thought, after I'd finished it, that I could've done a little bit more.

Two things: What determines "finished"? And aren't you kind of arguing with your own conception of the piece once it's complete?

Oh yeah. Oh yeah. You never stop arguing with yourself over the conception of the piece. I mean, even yesterday I was thinking, How would I rewrite *Names of the Dead*? How would I go in and rewrite that to make it more satisfying to myself?

You won't do that, will you?

Who knows?

Have you ever gone back to something after it's been placed between hard covers?

Oh yeah. Actually the stories. Look at *Snow Angels*. Especially when you go out on a reading tour and start reading this stuff you think, Well, this could be better. That could be better. It's just a different way that your ears are hearing the stuff now. I could reconceptualize the end of the *Names of the Dead*.

Next year we're publishing the original last chapter of *Snow Angels* in a limited edition just because it was the way I wanted the book to be, and it didn't turn out to be the way the book was. I had already finished that book before I wrote what became the final chapter. It was like a year between finishing the book and writing the new final chapter.

What happened to the original final chapter?

My new agent and my two main readers, Paul Cody and Manette Ansay, both said, You take the pressure off Arthur. In the original ending there's the frame of the present, then you go into the past. In the original, the frame is completed on the back end like any other nested book. But supposedly I didn't get enough pressure on Arthur there because I end with the killing chapter and then I go into Arthur in the present again. And they said, You should really keep the pressure on Arthur, back in the past there, in that last chapter. And after a while I kind of grudgingly agreed with them that I'd taken it easy on Arthur. So a year after I'd delivered the book, already won the Faulkner Prize and all that stuff, I went back and I wrote a last chapter to the book. So that reconceptualizing goes on well after the book is done.

So the word "finished" is loosely defined?

Very loosely.

How about Snow Angels? *The novel grew from your short story "Finding Amy," but where did the short story come from?*

The short story was sparked by something that happened in Ithaca, New York, when I was there as a grad student. A girl had wandered away from her house, supposedly, and the mother called the police, frantic, in the middle of a snowstorm, and about half the town turned out to go search these snowy fields to find the kid. And the newspaper article about what happened—they hadn't found the kid yet—said the mother found the mitten at the foot of the driveway, and I thought, What a great line. So I cut that out and put it on my refrigerator, and I underlined the part about the mother finding the mitten at the foot of the driveway. It turned out later that the woman had, in fact, killed the child and buried her back in a meadow. This came out several weeks later. It was very much like the Susan Smith thing.

From that beginning I thought, What if I start at that point? Finding the mitten and talking about the search for the child. Let me see if I can get inside the head of that woman and find out what would cause a mother to kill her child, because it sounds cruel, but it's a rather common thing. Parents kill their children, although it's something that we can't quite grasp. So I tried to write a story about this mother that would kill her child and about halfway through, maybe perhaps I was too sentimental, I couldn't quite get to that point. I just couldn't get there. I could not find a mother that would do that. Not in my head, not in any head. So I wrote a story about the town showing its heart by going out and trying to find the kid. I had to end it somehow and there's two ways you can end that story: find the kid or don't find the kid. And because they had not really found the kid in time, I wrote it so that they didn't find the kid in time. They found the kid, but the kid was dead. It was a tough short story. It's too small for what it's trying to do. There are too many characters in it. There's too many scenes.

At what point do you realize something like there are too many characters?

Well, that's what everybody said about it. Everybody. Everyone who's ever read that story has said there's just too much going on.

Did it go through workshop at Cornell?

It went through workshop, it went through editors, it went through friends, it went through other writers, it went through Trudy, my wife, it went through everybody. And they were like, There's just too much going on in here.

But the story was still published.

Yeah. I like the story. I don't think there's too much going on. I like the story. It's a damn good story. What the fuck do other people know? I'm not changing a goddamn word.

So after I'd finished *A World Away*, back then, I wanted to start on a new project and I figured I'd write a short novel because I'd just written three very, very large novels, so I wanted a smaller project that I could see pretty much all of. And I looked at that story and I said, I'm not really done finishing the stories of all the different people. I know they've got lives going on after this. Basically I changed the setting, the time, and I had to come up with a way to make it warmer. The short story is very cold. Very cold. Very distant. It was third person, which is almost like hovering in a helicopter over this town. It's a frigid story, in a way, so I had to find a way to bring it closer and the obvious, immediate answer to that is to go first person. So I said, Well, who in this story is my first-person narrator? So I looked throughout the story at all the different people and the only one that was really intriguing was the kid who shows up in the last line and finds the body. And I said, Wow, that's kind of interesting. What if that had happened to some kid who was fourteen years old? What would that do to a kid, you know? How would that affect a kid? And I said, Okay, he's my first-person narrator, but what's his connection with Annie, the other major character? And for some reason, I don't know exactly how I got it, the baby-sitter connection seemed to make sense. And then once I got the baby-sitter connection, I said, Well, what's Arthur's story? What's his line? And I thought, Well, it's obvious. His parents are breaking up. That lack of security and the family sort of falling apart. And once I came up with those, then that's when I had to say, Well, I better look for a model, because I was basically looking at a third- and first-person novel, which really isn't done that much. And the one that I found that I really love is William Maxwell's *So Long, See You Tomorrow*.

Back up with me a step. You said that you looked for a model, and this is the one that you found. How does that search take place?

It's not even something that's conscious at that point. You don't say, Well, I've got to get a model. I need to base this on something. You just go through all the possible different ways of narrating this story and you think, Well, I could do first first, I could do first and multiple first, I could do third first, I could do multiple third, multiple firsts, you know, I could do *As I Lay Dying,* I could do something completely stream of conscious. You look at all of the possibilities and then you say, Which is the one that will really do this novel justice?

But So Long, See You Tomorrow *is something that you'd already read when you decided that this was the way to go?*

Yeah. I'd already read it, liked it, enjoyed the effect, and the effect is kind of the same effect that I wanted. And I thought, Well, maybe that will work. *So Long, See You Tomorrow* is this first person who's looking back on this time in his life when things went wrong, as a child, then he drops from that first, into the past, and suddenly he's third omniscient except we know he's not omniscient. We know this is some sort of subjective narration even though it has that veneer of being semiobjective, semiomniscient. So I'd read Maxwell before that and I thought, That could kind of work, even though it'd be damn tricky to do it.

So do you reread at that point?

Sometimes I'll look at it again, but usually whatever feeling I have of how the thing works doesn't appear again. Usually it's internalized somehow. It's basically a choice that you make in the writing or in the brainstorming process. It's almost like improvising in a way. There's this phrase you heard that Sonny Rollins was blowing three weeks ago, and suddenly you're there onstage and you see a place for it and you step in with it and it fits. And you're like, Holy shit, it fits. So William Maxwell's book was the semiconscious model there in the third to first combination.

Tim O'Brien's *The Things They Carried* also was a bit of one. I wanted to work a little bit more with Arthur's unreliability in the third person, but that never really happened.

Arthur's parents are separated. There are several sets of separated couples in In the Walled City.

Names of the Dead, *as well.*

Is that a personal comment on the state of the family or do families waiting for divorce carry more dramatic possibility?

I think, you know, starting from those existential roots of Camus and Sartre and Percy, and even Flannery O'Connor, that I tend, at least in these works so far, to look at, unfortunately, the typical individual, to look at how people are separated, how people are both separate and one, and how they're looking to combine and no longer be just one, and yet they're stuck with that condition. That's certainly probably a cultural hangover from, you know, the existentialism of the fifties and sixties and the age of anxiety crap.

When you wrote "Finding Amy," were you working at Grumman?

No. I was at Cornell at that point.

You went to Cornell in 1988. Were any of the stories in In the Walled City *written before graduate school?*

Yeah. "Third of July," "Calling," "Mr. Wu Thinks," "Doctor's Sickness," "Steak," and "Econoline." About half.

So in graduate school you were working on a novel?

Yeah. I was working on *About a Girl* and then later *A World Away*.

Most people, I believe, would probably think that working as a test engineer at Grumman and being a graduate writing student are just about diametrically opposed. Are there similarities?

Well, my usual rap on that is that both the engineer and the writer do the same basic thing, and that is they solve seemingly insoluble problems that have never been solved before within the constraints of some controlling reality. You make assumptions. You make hypotheses, and you follow them out and if they do not fly in the real world, then they don't work at all.

What was your major in college?

Aerospace.

Were you reading in college? Were you writing in college?

Reading, not writing.

When did you start writing?

I started the year after I was out of college. I was working in a muffler warehouse in Brighton, Massachusetts, and then I'd come home and I'd try to write. I'd just try to write every day. I'd write a few sentences and I was reading like Theodore Sturgeon and Thomas Wolfe, Harlan Ellison and James Joyce, and I was just trying to steal sentences from different kinds of writers to try them out. I'd find a sentence that I knew that I wouldn't naturally write, and I'd copy it down and I'd see how it worked and I'd sort of take it apart, so a lot of those engineering traits, you know, seeing how technically things operate, helped me, I think, with a lot of the nuts and bolts of writing.

Did you have a writing schedule when you were working at Grumman? Did you feel like you were stealing the time?

Oh yeah, you're always stealing time. You're always stealing the time.

But you weren't getting in the three- and four-hour shifts of writing, were you?

No, maybe two hours tops, and I'd read a lot, too. That was the major thing back then—maybe '84, '85, '86—was just reading a lot and trying to figure out what stories were and what writing was. At some point, probably around '86 or so, I decided, Let me see if I can cross the line from being a very committed and enthusiastic reader into actually trying to create something.

At what point did you decide to go from employed engineer to graduate writing student?

Well, I was starting to commit almost all of my time outside of engineering to writing and reading—I mean, an obsessive amount of time. I was doing it all the time. Nothing but. My mind was on it all the time and when I was working in engineering, I wasn't happy. I wanted to be doing something else, which was writing or reading. I won the Ascent Fiction Prize for "Econoline" in '87 and I was getting published all along. You know, a lot of stories got published that never made *In the Walled City*. They weren't terribly good. Some of them were very strange. Very Robbe-Grilletesque or surreal or bizarre. I was trying all sorts of different techniques. I was getting very excited about technique at the time, and I was getting published and winning some awards. I took a trip out to the University of Illinois to receive an award there and they were all talking like, Yeah, you can do it. You're a real writer. You can do it. And I was like, Well, I don't know about that. But then I had a chance to go to grad school and my wife was like, Yeah, you ought to go. It's what you want to do. Why don't you just do it? And I was sort of against that, but she said, Yeah, give it a shot. Give it a try.

Why grad school? If you're already getting published and winning awards, what was the need for graduate school?

Two things. First and most important was time—time to actually spend with the work and make it my primary work. Second was that feeling of, Yes, this is your work. You get some kind of standard set. Now, you may be a writer. You know you're already a writer by that point because you're getting published and stuff like that, but here someone is saying, Here, he's a writer, and that always feels good. Time is really what I wanted. What I got was way more than that. It was really important to go to grad school, I think, to get turned on to a lot of writers that I otherwise wouldn't have found.

Like who?

James Salter, for one. Don DeLillo. Living in my basement in Long Island no one's telling me, Hey, you should be reading Don DeLillo. It's 1988 and I haven't read Don DeLillo yet? Hello?

In the way that I write and the way that I think about fiction, the way that I try to incorporate everything that I've read into possibly being a way of writing a story or thinking about a story, that just blew the doors open. So that was good. Plus I got two and a half, almost three years to just concentrate on writing. The teaching stuff didn't take up too much time. But I wrote at least three books up there. A lot of pages.

Did the career change cause you to value the time more?

I don't know if it's a switch in career but the fact that I waited until my mid twenties just to start doing this, and finding in my mid twenties that this is the one thing I wanted to do. I mean, this is exactly what I want to do. I don't want to do anything else. I don't want to go direct Hollywood movies. I don't want to be a race car driver. This is it. When I'm sitting at my computer and writing, that's it. That is the peak experience. It doesn't get tiring. It just gets more and more interesting and challenging and fun.

Is there an aspect of trying to play catch-up for the time lost?

I don't know if it's catch-up. It may be a case of the kid who doesn't get to eat any candy and suddenly the shop is free. You stuff yourself, but I guess I'm not full yet.

A Conversation with Barry Hannah

Barry Hannah, born five months after the bombing of Pearl Harbor, published eleven books of fiction between 1972 and 1997, beginning with *Geronimo Rex* (which was nominated for the National Book Award) and ending with two story collections, *Bats Out of Hell* and *High Lonesome*. Since 1982, Hannah has lived in the land of Faulkner, serving as writer-in-residence at the University of Mississippi. The author has also taught at Clemson University, Middlebury College, the University of Montana, the University of Iowa, and the University of Alabama. Hannah's time in Tuscaloosa, though troubled by drinking and divorce, yielded some of his most appreciated fiction. Many of the stories in his collection *Airships*, published in 1978, were written in Tuscaloosa, and the book won the Arnold Gingrich Award for Short Fiction from *Esquire* magazine, where nine of the stories originally appeared. *Ray*, the short novel that followed, was similarly lauded. The *New York Times'* Benjamin DeMott wrote that *Ray* was "the funniest, weirdest, soul-happiest work by a genuinely young American writer that I've read in a long while, ordinary reviewerese is no help in explaining why. You need a fresh lingo to do justice to this much magic, mystery and hilarity. You need new strategies, new arguments, new adjectives, new everything."

By the time Hannah left Alabama in 1980, his reputation was already established. Philip Roth called him "the real thing, a young writer as true and original as any writing fiction anywhere."

I spoke with Barry Hannah at his Mississippi home in October of 1997.

***

Let me get the requisite Oxford literary history out of the way. Faulkner was known to stretch the truth in interviews. Are you a threat to do that? Have you done that before?

No, not particularly. He didn't like interviews and I don't either, but that isn't a way I evade them. No, I'm fairly truthful.

Then I'll start with a big question. In both Ray *and* Airships, *the reader is faced with narrators who have just turned thirty-three. In "Water Liars" the narrator goes as far as to draw the Christ allusion for us. Did you go through a similar crisis at thirty-three, or is the age just a convenient literary reference?*

I was conscious of being thirty-three, since I was raised Baptist. Like John Barth once said in a book, "Everything's significant and nothing's important." It just felt significant, and it should be when you realize that the founder of an entire religion is dead when you're carrying on. It's a good time to pause and reflect about final things or about who you are. It's just a natural age, I think. A lot of people do that right about thirty-three. They decide, I've been a bum too long. I've been drinking too much too long. I need to get my work on the road. Some people drop out around in there. What they've been doing is no good to them, so it's not an unusual time for people to change directions.

Did you have a change in direction?

Later, for me. Later. I haven't changed in direction much since, as far as my writing's gone. I live much healthier now, but I've had no change in direction since I first wrote a decent sentence. It's been about the same. I'm not even certain I've gotten any better; I just do different things. I just love to write and to tell stories. The art and the music have never changed for me. There's been no big conversion toward anything except lately, more than ever, I have more distrust of fiction. I don't get as much out of fiction as I used to. I have some suspicion that a great deal of it is too close to camera work and documentary, and it does less for me than when I just kind of scarfed down everything.

Are you talking about other people's writing or is this true even with your own?

It means I've set an extremely high mark for those things that do move me, like Cormac McCarthy's work does. There's less plodding realism, fewer decent stories told that get to me. I've seen competence too long. I'm looking for what's really sterling and deep. I often get to the middle of a novel, like this quite fine book by DeLillo, and DeLillo's one of the best, but there are moments when I say, Well, this is about a few things, but I'm not sure it's worth the marching band to say it. Maybe I'm closer to poetry now, where it shouldn't take this much time. That you can get more with expression than in long, lingering themes. I've also been reading much more history and biography in the last five, seven years. I think this is just quite natural when you get older. You're closer to the actual. You want to see the music of truth.

You said, It shouldn't take as much time as it does, but you're talking about the number of pages rather than actual time, right? You want it more quickly than a book like Underworld *delivers?*

There's still too much banality in the ordinary American novel. There's just too much conversation, husband and wife, guys at work. It may be accurate, but it doesn't stir me. It's just seems like chat, just talk. I want more Faulkner. I want more art. I want more sweep and power as in Cormac McCarthy. I'm not interested in people chatting about ideas that much.

So it doesn't have to do with line length or novel length?

It has more to do with vision, who has a vision and who doesn't. I quite frankly find the novel to be very plodding and pedestrian, a very talky, almost artificial bulk to get to some fairly interesting conclusions, but not worth a two-week trip.

In previous interviews you've always upheld the story above the novel, but aren't you working on a novel now? Is rationalization required to promote the story above the novel and then go back to the novel?

There's too much rationalization in the novel, I think, is my big point. I'm a romanticist. I don't care that much about unified theories of existence. I'm responsive to novels that howl. I'm much more akin to the work of Miles Davis, Jimi Hendrix. There just is power. There just is existence. Cormac McCarthy just simply is. It doesn't imitate. It is. That's what I'm attempting, you see? Because I go to any number of readings and often, nowadays, wonder why I'm there. I'm listening to another conversation between a man and his wife that has a few bright little mots, but I don't know why I'm listening. These novels win prizes. I'm not jumping on mediocre student work. What I'm talking about is what's accepted as good as an old convention, the novel. I don't think it's dead, but its power to lift and to shock and to reveal unknown territory has been given over to discursive and ruminative books that we don't particularly need.

I read that Blood Meridian *is your favorite of McCarthy's.*

Yeah, it probably is despite the huge carnival of violence. It's got more poetry. *Blood Meridian* is just more true to what he was always writing about and that is the ruthless march of fascism through nature, regardless of anything you ever really think or anything you ever really do. It's just that in *Blood Meridian* people are more agents of it. They enjoy it.

One of the silliest comments I ever read was by this British fellow who writes military history, teaches at Sandhurst, and he was listing the good American writers. In one volume of his after another he talks about how soldiers feel, how World War II went on. He wrote one book about American wars. And he said he couldn't read *Blood Meridian* because it was just too violent. My God, here's a guy who's made a career of war. Does he think that it's going to be a discussion in a tearoom on the edge of Sandhurst Military Academy? This man has never been a soldier, by the way, but you might have a lot less interest in dedicating your life to military history if you read *Blood Meridian*. Like Robert E. Lee said, "The worst choice I ever made was a military education." This is a regenerative novel because of its fierce awfulness.

I've heard it called the bloodiest novel since The Odyssey.

It may be. I don't know. But there's also the fine poetry of nature and the stars and this allied existence that we as people just crawling across the plains have. It's an affirmative book that puts you in the world. This is what people lack, if Cormac has any message. There is no world anymore. People have made an artifice of everything. There are no makers. There are no real doers. I think that's why he has no interest in writing about the present.

Tom McGuane had a great line in one of his rare short stories where a guy's lost an expensive bird dog somewhere in Mississippi. His dogs run off and he feels forlorn and stupid, and he's sitting down to fret by a Confederate cemetery and it occurs to him that these people went to their grave with more happiness than he has in his life now.

It's about vitality, too. Counting the bodies is horrible, but the thing about it is, it's very true. You better look at it if you're an American because we ain't nice. We haven't been that nice. American niceness is often very artificial and so comfortable that it's obscene. So you better know these things.

Do you find the achievement of Blood Meridian, *the fact that McCarthy does live up to the possibilities of the form, daunting or inspiring?*

Inspiring. Inspiring. His story is very good. His current editor at Knopf told me that he had sold twelve hundred copies of many of his earlier books. Twelve hundred. It makes me sound like a commercial star for selling twenty thousand. I love the way he was ignored, ignored and kept plugging away.

Actually a few people did pay attention to him. He got great grants, but it's inspiring to know that a single vision like that can win through. However, the vision that wins through is the lesser, chattier books, the ones that are closer to Hemingway, the more accessible.

You're referring to the novels that form The Border Trilogy?

Yeah. They've got more horses, and more girls and more standard love themes. They're the ones that finally got close to folks. Not the more awesome, pitiless books, which the public, I suppose, is never really going to accept widely. Just like Faulkner. The mark is high. Even my students here who don't like Faulkner, the town is good because the mark is so high. I mean, it's better to fail here trying big stuff. There's a high experiment in Faulkner, a high risk. He's good for young people. A little man from an obscure state, mocked by his neighbors. It sounds like a Noah who wins through. That story lifts people.

Your favorite Faulkner is As I Lay Dying?

Still is, yeah. For its voices and for its clarity and for its high poetry.

Was As I Lay Dying *in your mind, was it in any way a model when you were working on* Nightwatchmen?

No. I don't think I was familiar with that book that much then. No, it wasn't. I'd forgotten I wrote that book. That's right. That has different people on tape recorders.

 No, they talk too long. I like the economy of *As I Lay Dying*. It's sort of like somebody handing the camera off to another person. It winds up in the hands of a loony, of a dead person. It's not just a gathered, sensitive group at Bennington, you know. It is really perverse. Somebody holds the camera upside down. Another guy's got it at the ground. One guy's got it in the air. Faulkner uses the technique of cinema vérité except it's the directors who change. It's like one director after another and yet there's a wholeness. These disparate parts come through to something on the edge of lunacy, but they're also full of pathos and real human feelings.

I want to get back to Nightwatchmen *for a minute.*

I haven't read that in twenty-five years and I have not let it be released in paperback. Norton wanted to do it in paperback years ago, and I don't think I like it that much.

That was my question. The University Press of Mississippi recently released Never Die *and* Boomerang *together in paperback, and so I assume that if you wanted* Nightwatchmen *to come out in paperback you could have it done.*

Oh yeah. If I pushed for it, it would be done. I wrote that book in a hurry, some of it in New York, which wasn't very good for me. New York's too fascinating for somebody like me to write in. There are too many people, too many events.

It probably needs to be thinned down. I think there are too many people in it and too much event but, like I say, I haven't read it in twenty-five years. I don't know what it's like.

Isn't there a certain mystique around the book because that's the only one that hasn't been released in paperback? Nightwatchmen *is, in a sense, Barry Hannah's lost novel. How many copies were printed?*

Five thousand, but it didn't sell out the first edition and my editor went off to write herself. It never even had a paperback sale. It didn't get good reviews. Hell yes, lost, but it might deserve to be lost. I don't know how I feel about it. Maybe one day I'll read it again and somebody will do it. I don't know. I haven't worried about it.

My God, that book is twenty-three years old and I'm trying so hard to write the kind of novel I was telling you about right now. It's hard enough to write a novel that glistens and that has that power. It takes everything I got. No fudging. No hobbying around. I've not written anything for about six or seven months because I've been thinking about this book so much. I haven't even written a short story, which is strange for me because I love stories.

I want to go two ways here. First I want to ask one more Nightwatchmen *question.*

Fine. I'm not opposed to talking about that book.

You've made apologies for the novel in the past by saying you delivered it more quickly than you should have in order to capitalize on the success of Geronimo Rex. *Are there other books that you felt like you let go before they were ready or was* Nightwatchmen *a lesson learned?*

That's the only one. The lesson learned is that authors need good editors. I didn't really have one on that book. Nobody in America much has a good editor anymore. They're letting more and more books go as they are. They don't care to brighten them up. The built-in critical instinct is a whole other thing from the creation instinct sometimes, so that a friend or somebody needs to read this thing. You'll pass judgment on it because you're simply fatigued or you don't want to see it again. People need editors, especially the more they shoot for. They need editors to tell them when it's coherent, when it's precise.

You've been more generous toward editors, more willing to both acknowledge and share the accomplishment, than many writers who sometimes pretend that editors don't exist. You started working with Gordon Lish on Airships, *correct?*

Yes, that's correct.

There's a distinctive shift toward the experimental that occurs with the appearance of that book. How much did having Lish as an editor contribute to that change? What did he bring that was lacking in Nightwatchmen, *or had the change been made before Lish got hold of the work?*

Well, Lish, for the purposes of the short story especially, loves the echo, and sometimes the ambiguous echo more than I did as a younger writer. He went more for tone, more toward poetry, the unresolved, the echoing so, sure, he had an influence.

I learned a lot of great lessons from Lish, about what you don't have to say and what you shouldn't say. Sometimes I would insist on a line and it would stay. But yes, the *Airships* stories are much more clipped and the writing less dense than in *Geronimo*. They probably should be for the stories. The kind of stories which are kind of an inhale and then just blast it out and then stop. They have more to do with body rhythms than they do with ordinary literary structure.

I know that there was a five-year lull between the publication of Nightwatchmen *and* Airships *and that break was the longest in your career. I'm not trying to suggest that Lish found the voice in your writing, but what happened between those books that would cause such a radical shift in style? Anything conscious?*

I can't recall much conscious going on except that I was gearing up for short stories more. I was writing long stories, "Testimony of a Pilot" and "Return to Return." I think I was just thinking more story suddenly. Lish started taking about everything that I wrote at *Esquire* when I moved to Tuscaloosa, and I had always admired *Esquire*, grew up with it as sort of totem in my world, so I tended to write stories because he would print them and so that's the big change. And for magazine space and Lish's own aesthetic.

By the way, this works two ways. Many people say that some of Lish's work sounds like mine, so I think we shared aesthetics during that time. I learned some things and Lish learned some things.

Also, it was the period in my life when I drank the heaviest. I think that your concentration goes. You tend to want to do shorter things when you're drinking heavily. I have much more endurance now for the long vision. I think Bukowski's poems, for instance, are necessary for him. You can write them even when you feel horrible, you know. You can't keep that single vision up even though he has about two very fine novels. I think that has a lot to do with it.

Do any of the stories in Airships *precede the publication of* Nightwatchmen?

The entire collection was written after *Nightwatchmen,* many of them up at Middlebury and some at Clemson and several in Tuscaloosa. The more despairing, wilder stuff was at Tuscaloosa, like "Constant Pain in Tuscaloosa" and "Coming Close to Donna." They're short; they're violent. I was going for a kind of *Wasteland* edge. More ruthless, quick stories. There are four or five of those like that. But I couldn't keep it up forever. It can't be continued indefinitely.

Where was "Water Liars" written?

In Tuscaloosa. That's a mournful story, too. Pretty mournful.

You mentioned that in both your reading and your writing, you're looking for power. You mentioned the burst you had when you were drinking. Does being sober in any way cost you that burst, that power, or does the experience now offset the loss?

No. You are incapacitated to do anything much else when you're drinking, but you can do that also when you're straight and pretty healthy. I mean, I still think in bursts and maybe I think more as a poet than I do as a novelist, so I have done those things lately. I do the short bursts and the more lyrical, unfinished pieces. You can do both.

Even Ray Carver, whom I knew fairly well, claimed, which I thought was phenomenal, that he never wrote when he was drinking. It was always done afterwards, which meant when he was writing that he was hungover. He didn't even feel good when he wrote the stories that are acclaimed all over America now. Because if you're an alcoholic, you're either drunk or you're sick. You're wanting there. So I think it's phenomenal, if it's true, that he didn't drink at all when he wrote the stories.

I don't know that this is a question that can be answered, but do you think the fact that Carver was an alcoholic had anything to do with his not writing a novel?

It probably had a great deal to do with it. He just blamed it on attention span, but attention span increases when you're off the juice. Ray did start a kind of novel. You can't think about what he would've done as a novelist though. You just take people as they are. He did what he could and there's some fate in everything. I don't wish that he'd written novels. I don't think much of what he had would've gone as novels. The power of those stories is better than most novels that cost twenty-seven dollars. Scholars are always good at wishing people had gone ahead and lived to eighty and written five more huge books but hell, that's forgetting humanity. They wish their lives, essentially, onto others, and their lives couldn't have created these things in the first place.

When you said earlier that you haven't written in six or seven months, I'm not supposed to take that literally, am I?

No. I've written about fifty pages, but I'm not certain of them. These feelings that I get when I read the work of the best Americans now even are not settling to me. I'm just not getting out of fiction what I used to, and I want to write books that will matter and count and just won't be filed along with late-century knowledge and facts, you know. I want to lift readers. I want a certain power all the way through a book. I don't want there to be much chat at all.

You don't think there's much chance that your books will be filed away though, do you? I would think that if there's any adjective you can place on the work of Barry Hannah, it would be "distinctive."

Maybe, but I'm writing for a much blander universe than when I first started writing. I'm writing for people who are less patient with the word, who don't give a damn about English, who find it just a vehicle. I mean, I started out in the days when Jim Dickey was hitting the road and lighting up audiences with his poetry. I believed in that stuff and still do. And now you've got a much lazier, more passive reader who has to be fed more. In fact, the novel has gotten more conventional since I started writing, you know. The old-fashioned writers are the ones who are succeeding more. The ones who are just kind of blocky and chatty. There are no experimental successes unless they're over there at City Lights. There's always some guy in a basement doing a tome, but you never hear of him until he dies. Or usually there is, but I don't hear about these wild, undercover guys anymore. They never make it anywhere. They don't even make it into print with little presses.

What about Pynchon? Would you term him as experimental?

Yeah, and he's wonderful. He's like a Leonardo da Vinci. He can do so much. He's like the James Joyce of our day.

And I'm not interested, by the way, in there being any more *Finnegans Wakes* because I couldn't read it. I don't think you ought to push and bludgeon the reader that much. And I don't think we're decadent because we can't understand it, as Beckett said. I think it's an act of insanity. There are a few highly sensitized sorts that love that it's inaccessible to the unwashed, and they're the only ones who are subscribing to that book now. It gives them a profession. But even among the partisans of Faulkner and McCarthy, I don't think it has much movement. It doesn't make an impression on them. It's just too far away from us.

Let me ask about your own writing. You've talked a lot about who you're reading and your disappointment with contemporary fiction. When you're in the groove, writing-wise, does your reading drop off?

It's just the modern novel that my complaint is about. It's too close to information. I like Virginia Woolf. Her interiors, I really think, are very wonderful. I love the power of Flannery O'Connor.

But I don't read anything when I'm working. I even resent reading my students' manuscripts at that time. I won't read a damn thing when I'm working well. Maybe a few poems by Richard Hugo late, late at night when I'm done and I'm just fatigued. A little Hugo, a little Eliot, but never whole fiction much.

And you write in the mornings?

Yeah. When I'm working well, some days I'll get up about five and work until about two, and then go play tennis or something. That's what I love. That's when I feel like a man, a whole man. When I'm working and loving to get up. Just seeing a tablet and a pencil in there. It looks exciting.

So you write longhand?

I write with a pencil on lined paper.

I'm assuming that at some point you were not an early morning writer. I can't imagine, for example, Ray being written in daylight hours.

Probably it wasn't. There's not much daylight writing in there. No, I was much more of a night person until the late eighties.

What's the difference between writing in the morning and writing at night?

I think that it doesn't matter. I just want to stay away from expository writing. I don't think there's much expository in *Ray*. I wouldn't write *Ray* again, but I like the book where there's not much explanation at all. There's too much explanation in daylight writing often because you feel too much in control sometimes. I don't think it's good for a writer to feel totally in control of his material. I think there has to be something bigger, that he's just like a court reporter. He can't quite get it down and he makes some errors getting it down. I like that feeling in writing.

I read where you once said that you listened to music very, very loudly so you could clear your head to write.

I used to. I can't deal with it now—with earphones maybe. The music really helps, still. I can be absolutely stuck and I can hear certain old voices, Dylan for example. I've got his new album. The simplicity of about three of those tunes. People are raving about that new Dylan but hell, it's not different. It could be a little darker, but I think what it is is the critics are afraid he's going to die on them and they're rushing now to give him praise. This new album is no less remarkable than many of his that have been jeered at, you know. They have simply missed the boat often. He's always had this in him. I don't see it as a great breakthrough.

There's nothing about a near-death experience to get people to talk nicely about you.

Right. It was a good career move, as a cynical hack would say.

I give my students books. You can't really use music in class, but a little Camus, a little *Stranger*, or Hemingway or Flannery O'Connor.

Kids have told me, You know, I didn't think I could write the stuff I wanted to until I read this story. They rumble up something the way that Hendrix or Miles Davis or Dylan would do for me. That's what I'm after.

You mentioned once in an interview that if Ray *had a model, it was Camus's* The Stranger.

I did?

Yeah.

That's right. It makes sense now. I forgot saying that. The model would be the length more than anything else, the tighter structure. *The Stranger* is an even-toned book about a curious man, whereas *Ray* is much more manic-depressive. There are bursts. There are remembrances of history. There are acts. It is more back and forth tonally whereas *The Stranger*, which I think is one of the best books ever written, is a wholeness. I think it's the shortness and what he got from it, a heightened sense of alienation, disconnectedness.

Can you remember starting Ray?

I can barely remember how the book came into existence. I wrote that first part, and I remember Lish loved it so much that somebody in his office or my agent sent it off on its own to the *Kenyon Review* and they printed it. I got into something that I thought was really delightful with Ray opening the book and then going over to the Hooches'. Something that I hadn't felt that good about since maybe *Geronimo Rex*. You know, just a good patch. I guess that would've been around '77, '78 in Tuscaloosa.

You begin with "Ray is thirty-three" and you get him as far as the Hooches' house and you feel good about it. When did you know you were working on a novel?

I never did. I never did. I just knew I was working on a piece of writing, and this is what I'm getting at. When I'm in there sweating it out in there, trying to write, I'm not thinking about how Ned gets across campus or how Ned gets into a plane or how to line it up chronologically or when to introduce somebody. That ain't the way I think at all anyway. I mean, I'm thinking about what follows. What piece of experience should go here? What does it need? It's more musical than chronology. Much more musical. Much more instinctual.

That's why many people don't need writing school. Larry Brown, for instance, just had good instincts about what made a story, and if you've got good instincts you don't need any tutelage about form, structure. You just feel stuff like you would feel a tune. Now, that's why I never have any books about creative writing to teach. They're all bad.

Even The Triggering Town?

Well, there are some wonderful thoughts in there, but that's not a text for writing.

I think it tells you what to avoid more than it tells you what to do which, I think, is why I'm fond of it.

Right. I don't think Hugo ever wrote a bad book. It's just got deep, wonderful thoughts in it. I don't mind that, but instructive books by people you've never heard of. My God, who's buying those? I mean, why should I buy it or teach it? You don't want to pull out characters, atmosphere, setting, dialogue. When you start pulling them out separately, it's over. You've got to think whole all the time or you're no good at all.

Despite the fact that it's been edited and revised, Ray *seems spontaneous. How mistaken a notion would it be to look at the chapters and view them as separate writing sessions? Could you sit down with the pad and write a J. E. B. Stuart section and then come back to the Hooches' house in one session, or did you need breaks in order to change subject matter and locale?*

The breaks, I think, are for me and the reader. I can't remember. I don't know how the book was finally separated into chapters. Me and Lish working together or something when it was done. I don't really recall, Rob.

But it was a much longer manuscript when you turned it over, right?

Yeah, but it wasn't ever like six hundred pages. I heard somebody suggest that. As I recall it was fifty or sixty pages longer. It was always short. I may have given that false information because I wrote a hell of a lot on it, but a lot of it wasn't useful.

You once said it was three hundred pages.

Right. That's the reason I'm clearing that up. It doesn't matter, but it wasn't that much longer. It was always conceived as a short book. In fact, I was amazed at how short it was when it printed out. I thought that I had about three hundred or that it would print to about two fifty. I was amazed that it had been whittled to this.

But the editing was more of the line edit variety?

There was no internal editing. Only line editing.

Let's get back to music. Am I understanding correctly that when you sit down with pencil and lined paper that you've got music on while you're doing the actual writing?

Sometimes. Sometimes I forget music. I work in the quiet now. I just think I got all I could out of loudness. I can't even walk into a bar now with a band going anymore. My ears are just oversensitive. I think you've got to have three whiskeys to really bear many small places today, like my son played in. I couldn't attend those things. I would have to stay about fifty yards out and listen to the band. But I'm still just as attuned to music as I ever was, it's just that it's more useful in incremental bursts than as a scheduled thing now.

Is it dangerous or risky in any way to listen to music with lyrics, say Dylan rather than Miles Davis, while you're working on a first draft?

No. No, it's not dangerous at all. Sometimes it'll give you a line or half a line or a thought.

By the way, people who try to make a direct connection between prose lines and music are fools. You can't write music. Those who try to get it on the page are idiots. It's a whole different thing, but the motive is much the same.

Well, because your books are so dependent on voice and language, the rhythm is a necessity and rhythm is what music brings.

Right, but it's much different to read something on the page. In fact, if some kid in a creative writing workshop at Iowa where I'm going— I'm going up to be the acting director at Iowa for a semester in January. Can you believe it? If some kid in there wrote the latest Dylan song on the page and handed it in, he would be hooted at by his intellectual brethren and maybe deservedly. It doesn't make it at all without the tunes.

I'll agree with you but you are writing music. There's a built-in rhythm to your language, like poetry.

What you're talking about is the reason I buy books. I get a lot of them free, but the reason I buy one and put like twenty-seven or twenty-eight bucks down is I read that first page, and if it doesn't have what you're talking about, the rhythm, the ear, I won't buy it. It's got to have rhythm and ear, as well as vision, but that matters less to audiences now. There are many millionaire writers in America who have no ear at all now, and I don't see how people get through the books. It's just a kind of cluttered, pedestrian, factual prose. I've got to be taken in by that rhythm originally to love it. The thing about it is, a lot of people like Jim Thompson would never confess that they had rhythm like that, that it's aesthetic at all, but they did. They just simply did and it invites you into it.

Do you ever read your prose aloud before you let it go?

Yeah, I'm always reading, probably like some dumb person who's learning to read and moving his lips. I read it like that. I can hear it.

Tell me about "Even Greenland." That story seems especially dependent on rhythm.

That story's about the only good thing I did in Hollywood. I worked on that in the studio in California. It's the one that has my heart in it, whereas the film work was Altman's idea, and he was very sweet to give me money. I didn't accomplish that much. I just wasn't a good screenwriter.

Anyway, I wrote that in the studios out there and it went through many, many revisions, although it's not all that marvelous a story. It's just one that occupied me a long time. I wanted to get it exactly right, with the breaths and all. I wanted to put a woman in it. It originally didn't have a woman in it. The guy kills himself and then that's about it. He just buys it. And then I wanted Celeste in the end, you know. It was really kind of saying hello to what I loved again, because I hadn't written anything in about a year. I'd been messed up, in a hospital, and gotten straight. I haven't read that book in a long time, but many of those stories are very sedulously slow-going stories because I was making words, hearing them again, and putting them in the right order, and "Greenland" is one of those.

It might've inspired a *Wasteland* feeling or a suicide notion, but for me it was high aesthetics. It was as good as I could do to get back in the game, you know, at that time.

"Power and Light" is okay, but I wrote that for an audience after I'd written the screenplay. There were some good things in it, I thought. I liked some of the writing. It's an odd bastard form that's never going to be seriously a genre, but there are other pieces in *Captain Maximus* that I like. It's very slight. It may be even shorter than *Ray,* I don't know, but it was the example of what I could do for about three years. It was almost like a cripple taking his first steps back in to what he loved.

They're some pretty good steps.

Well, I think they're pretty good. They're pretty good. They're chiseled, slow going, chiseled stories, you know. I like that one about "I'm Shaking to Death." And "Fans." I wrote that in that little green house down by the tracks in Tuscaloosa, and it got me to Hollywood. This guy drove over from Atlanta, from the *Atlanta Weekly*, said he wanted me to write a story. I was too screwed up to give it to him. I wrote that story on a Sunday afternoon with about two six-packs of those tall Budweisers. He was very much the gentleman. He was in the other room just reading the Tuscaloosa sports, waiting on me to finish the story, and then I gave it to him and in a couple of days I got my five hundred dollars which was a good deal of money in the seventies. It was like fifteen hundred or two thousand now. It just tells you that you can do what you want to do, or have to do. I still like that story.

Have you been approached or have you thought about a Selected Stories of Barry Hannah?

No, I haven't brought that up. Maybe when I'm older I'll suggest it.

I don't mean that we're at the end of a career, but maybe this is a segue into a question. If you had to put one together, which stories would hold up as your best work?

I really do like all of my stories except for about two, and I will stand behind every one of them right now. They were delivered, finally, with confidence after sometimes no revision and sometimes much revision. Today I can't tell the difference between the ones that were worked hard. I didn't let them go until I and at least a couple of other people that I believe in passed on them. There wouldn't be many that I would say, This doesn't speak for me. For one thing, you change through the decades. That's why young people often write better than older people. There's something you can't duplicate about being twenty-eight— things that a forty-year-old doesn't know anymore, or has lost. So I wouldn't change things now. I wouldn't edit for smoothness or anything because they're testimonies of you in that decade and as you were. But I'm proud of my stories, yeah.

You were talking about your particular fondness for "Even Greenland," and I would assume that "Water Liars" would be another of your favorites, since you made the effort to update it.

It's all right. Yeah. I like "Water Liars." I'm a little shocked that it keeps getting anthologized. I think it's because editors have had trouble with their wives. Everybody has had trouble with his wife in regards to this. It just speaks to something that nobody wants to talk about. And maybe the scene on the lake, that certainly started something good for me. I'll still probably write about some more old men at the pier. I like that scene. It's kind of the end of things. They may quit lying, but I like the old guys at the pier.

Susan wants me to write a whole book of the pier changing through the years. That's the alternative. If I don't get anywhere more with this novel, I think I'm going to the men at the end of the pier and what's happened in the last thirty years.

Well, you've got "High-Water Railers," an update of "Water Liars," leading off Bats out of Hell. *You've got "All the Old Harkening Faces at the Rail," another one from* Airships, *which is, in a sense, a companion piece. I apologize for getting into the criticism, but I see "Water Liars" as an almost protypical Barry Hannah work. There are a lot of Hannah elements in that story: the poignancy, the hit and hurt of the ending line, "We were both crucified by the truth."*

Well, I'm glad you like it. I think I like it, it's just I've seen it too much. I like the old liars at the rail. The one where the guy's trying to have a sweetheart in a one-man boat. I'm fond of that one. I've always been attracted to water, old men, dogs. In that, I'm pretty traditional Southern. I love water, old men, the fishermen or would-be fishermen, the lies, the desperate lies to have a little dignity that everybody tells.

In fact, in almost every story I've ever done, I try to catch whole lives. I try to do what would've been novels. Whole guys. Whole women. That's the difference. I don't care about psychological moments outside of Kroger's like they do in a lot of workshop stories. I never have. That's why I don't like much modern fiction. There's too much of this insight in the Kroger parking lot, you know. I like whole lives delivered over to something. Sometimes people don't even know what.

I'm not trying to beat "Water Liars" to death, but in it you've got the juxta-position of the truth versus lying. In one interview you said that you started with autobiography in order "to get to the lying" because that's where you felt like the best fiction is. In your work, the truth is damn painful.

It's almost always painful. The truth is what you think of yourself at 3 A.M. It's not encouraging. Every guilt, every indolence attacks you then. Your worthlessness. I'm nothing. I've done very little. Loss. Despair. I don't know how we can get up, frankly. I think we're very tough folks to get up and get this social veneer like it matters, like it's worth a shit. But with caffeine sometimes we just do it. We get up and act. We wing it. We act like it matters. I'm almost staggered by this fact.

You said you would stand behind all your stories except maybe two. Do you know, offhand, which two you're speaking of?

You know, I really don't have them in mind right now, but I remember I taught *Airships* here a couple of years ago at Ole Miss.

Really?

I've done it twice. I finally got up the nerve to teach my own stuff sim-ply because the stories have been around and people knew them, and I thought I could be helpful in how they were formed. And I remember seeing a couple in there that I just thought I could pitch, you know? I would have to go back. I haven't read it since. They just weren't strong and up to the others, but God, I don't know a writer around who doesn't think that way.

Oh sure. Everybody. Well, actually I do know a couple of writers who say they would stand behind every single word, but those are people you wouldn't want to spend a lot of time with.

Why does that happen so much and why don't people recognize that? Why is there this blindness to how dull the novel generally is? And some by very fine writers. They just keep going along with that rather tired form. I just read yet another sterling review of John Updike. He doesn't take me any new direction. He seems content to still describe things exquisitely.

Isn't the novel seen as a greater pursuit? It pays better than short stories or poetry, and people have to pay the bills.

But this one book every two years syndrome, writing about dull things. Fictional people who have lost a daughter. I mean, that's the point, that they have lost a daughter. It comes close to Oprah. They don't take you anywhere with the loss of the daughter.

Do you think that certain writers are more adaptable to a particular form, that some writers are short story writers and some are novelists? Maybe they don't realize their own strengths and weaknesses.

Yeah. Faulkner could do both, and very beautifully. There are not many who can do both exquisitely, but Faulkner could.

Are writing short stories and writing novels two different sports?

In a way, yes. America is a short story. People live as short stories. I don't think it's all the public's fault that fiction is disregarded. I think there's too much reality in fiction they can get in the newspapers. I think it's redundant to what they already know. I don't think the writers are giving them great vision, great insight. So why not read the sports page? Hell, you can get a better vision out of a good run from an Alabama back than you do from some supersensitive guy in a Kroger parking lot, thinking, Gee, I have been unkind to blacks. Or, I never knew what the black man was. It's because fiction has degenerated also. It doesn't excite folks. It hasn't found a new excitement. On the other hand, neither has rock and roll. Rock and roll has degenerated terribly. It doesn't have that excitement and exploring and kick ass.

So you don't buy into Nirvana?

No, not at all. I think it's phony angst, a lot of it. I don't know what these white kids are yelling about. I don't know what they're yelling about.

Let me ask you about setting in your fiction. Some places seem to almost rise to the level of character. There's a distinct personality to cities like Houston, Atlanta, Mobile. Did you ever live in Mobile?

No. I know the eastern shore much more than I know Mobile.

I think the University of South Alabama shows up in your fiction more than any other educational institution.

Really? I don't even know where it is.

Yeah. Like when Ray sends Sister to South Alabama.

Well, she went there. It was a known thing when I was in Tuscaloosa, but I don't even know where it is.

Houston, for instance. I grew up in the South and through the late sixties and early seventies, especially, if you had cancer, you had to go to Houston for treatment.

Yeah, well my Dad's life was saved at M. D. Anderson in Houston. At least it gave him eight more years.

I hate to tell you that I'm this easy a mark, but I think because of where I grew up, if you put cancer and Houston in the same sentence, then I'm there. I understand. My grandmother and my great aunt. If you had cancer, then you were on a plane to Houston.

Sure. Right. They're the best. I couldn't exist without the South. My voice couldn't start without the South that I adore. It's wretched. I know almost everything wrong with the South, and I also know everything glorious that's really never spoken in *Southern Living*. Just the familiar ease with the earth is never spoken of. I mean, I think Southerners don't have any philosophy because they are philosophers. They move with the earth better than other people, but they don't need to write it.

   Look at *Ray*. I mean, Tuscaloosa is a jumbled little city with outbursts of great beauty and then ugly hovels and crack rings. It's elegant,

Old World, with great gestures toward old liberal America. I mean, Alabama supported itself during the Depression by advertising to Yankee students who could afford the tuition. It is *Ray*. It's start, stop, ugly, beautiful. It's a very confused town, and a lot of people go to pieces in Tuscaloosa. I guarantee you it's like Scandinavia in depression, suicide, and divorce. I bet you. And I haven't seen a study, but a lot of people are torn up by that little place. They have bad affairs. Their marriages go to hell. They drink themselves into trouble. Drugs. There's something built in about Tuscaloosa that is not in Oxford, which is like Chapel Hill in the sixties. It's a distinct, little pretty place without the sort of cosmopolitan complexities of Tuscaloosa.

Looking back, of course, setting. *Ray* is like Tuscaloosa. The hospitals, the ugly hospital emergency room, right next to glorious nature out at Lake Tuscaloosa, you know. The sand gulleys, the beautiful fields, the Sipsey River. I just love it there, but it also has some of the most stone-mean rednecks I've ever run into out around Shiloh and Northport. So I think it's a very interesting town and a lot of people, somehow, go bonkers and sink over there.

Some cities—Houston, Mobile, and Atlanta, for example—come across, over the years, consistently, almost like supporting characters. Tuscaloosa, though, changes like a protagonist. It seems to represent the "contrarieties in their heart" that Ray talks about. It's almost like there's a love-hate relationship.

Yeah, it is. Deep love hate.

You get pissed off at the potential Tuscaloosa has yet never realizes.

True. I saw more writers over there, for some reason, sink. They just disappeared into what was there. Much unrealized talent. There's a great deal of unrealized talent in Tuscaloosa. That was my major complaint. Even my friend Brad Watson. He was writing that well twenty years ago when I was there. I don't know why it took him twenty years to get the confidence. I had confidence in him. I cheered him. I don't know why it took him twenty years to put that book together. The kid had it. Long ago. Now he's up at Harvard and he's doing really well, but there's a horrible delaying or something that happens to folks over there. I don't understand it.

It has a large population of losers who can't disattach. Also there's an inflated opinion of themselves without content, I noticed. It's a smugness. They see it as the center of the universe for some damn reason. I don't get it. My children are there and I care about them deeply.

Ray and Airships *are two of the most critically acclaimed books in your repertoire. Do you share the critics' affinity for* Airships *and* Ray? *I know that they were written during a time of personal turmoil, but both have those bursts, the power you were talking about. What was the cost of those books and was it worth it?*

Yeah, it was worth it but there are different ways to tell stories and I thought *Bats out of Hell* was the best book I ever did, but it's much more discursive than the others. I like the last thing I did. *High Lonesome* has some power that I'm trying to get to in narrative. So, God knows, Rob, what's better, the critical attention? It depends on the critic. There's not a uniform voice. The critics have gotten worse since I've been writing. The *New York Times* has gotten worse. I see a good review of my work in the *New York Times*, but it's so blandly stated I wonder why it was written. I expect my future work to have not only acceptance but some celebration from these people, but who knows? You just do your best. I have affection for everything I've written so far, I think, except for *Nightwatchmen*. I just don't know how to feel about it.

I guess the heart of the question was answered. You did say Bats out of Hell *is your favorite.*

Well, I think it's as strong as *Airships* in many ways.

You know, writers are often wrong about their work. That's why I'm so tentative here. Writers are wrong about their work.

One thing you've got to realize is that the *Airships* stories hit at a time when there had not been writing like that before. I'm not saying that I'm a genius at improvising or experimentation, but once it's done it's done.

As a reader and as a fellow writer of Ray Carver's, let me use this as an example. The critics celebrated *Cathedral* as if it were a major opus and a great step forward, but I remember the very first book of Carver's that really made the powerful inroads, *Will You Please Be Quiet, Please?* There were no stories like that in the world when that book came out, and I like it better. *Cathedral* is more thoughtful, it's kinder, it's more humane, it's longer, but who are you satisfying? Like when I was in Tuscaloosa, I saw *Will You Please Be Quiet, Please?* I said, My God, what a singular, distinctive voice. Nobody's ever done this before. So I liked it when it first happened. I'm not as interested in the longer, more humane Ray Carver, and my stories in *Bats out of Hell* are longer and possibly more humane. There may be others who possibly say that same thing.

Sometimes a band never gets better than its first album, when it's raw and there are a lot of errors. The Rolling Stones have never actually gotten better than their second or third album. They've just done it so well over and over. So that's going to happen when you come out with your own voice anyway. If you're distinct, you'll be remembered for that first distinctness.

Well, you talked about taking the risk. That McCarthy took the risk and Faulkner took the risk and that you would rather read early Ray Carver than Cathedral, *the kinder, more thoughtful Ray Carver. In a sense, isn't that an argument on behalf of* Airships?

That's what I'm saying.

To not only take the risk, but to take the risk and succeed. It seems like that would make you bow your chest up a little bit.

Well, yeah, I'm proud, but I tell you, the older you get as a writer, the more modest you get and the more you should shut up. You're less arrogant, with good reason. There's just a hell of a lot going on in the world. You've not penetrated too many consciousnesses. When I was twenty-one, I thought that you wrote a book and the world paid attention, man. There was no doubt. Then you grow up and you see that

that's not it at all. That you have to love it itself. And that you're working for about the top 3 percent, max, of America. And they're literary.
That's not the nuclear scientists, who ain't going to read you. You're
working with literary folks, 3 percent of the reading public, and it becomes a tiny club and you should have some modesty.

But Cormac McCarthy, Faulkner, Flannery O'Connor, Virginia
Woolf, that's what you should shoot for. Beckett. The best of Beckett's
prose, you know. If you can get that close to the heart, and that honesty,
with some music, why write the other kind of books that many people
can agree with and not be disturbed by? I don't like the books where
everybody shakes their heads and says, How true, how true. I want to be
in a region that's beyond good and evil. Where it's just like fireworks or
Mozart. Where there's just no explanation. That's what McCarthy and
Faulkner do for me. It's better than any review. That's what I'm after.

A Conversation with Russell Banks

Between 1975 and 1998, Russell Banks published thirteen works of fiction including *Trailerpark, Continental Drift, Affliction, The Sweet Hereafter,* and *Rule of the Bone.* The most recent novel to this conversation, *Cloudsplitter,* is also his most ambitious. Seven years in the making and weighing in at 758 pages, *Cloudsplitter* is the story of the abolitionist John Brown, as narrated by his son Owen fifty years after the raid on Harper's Ferry. That Banks would commit so much time and energy to John Brown's tale is not at all surprising. Much of the author's fiction is centered on the relationship between blacks and whites in America, and the legendary abolitionist is buried less than ten miles from Banks's home in upstate New York.

The book's publication makes demands on the writer's schedule. At the time of this interview, Banks had slept one night at home in the last three weeks and would leave again in less than forty-eight hours to begin a series of readings in Canada. In the prior week alone, he had celebrated his fifty-eighth birthday, given five readings and attended the Academy Awards. Yes, Banks's work also has drawn the attention of Hollywood, a development that has not only increased the demands on his time but his visibility, as well. An adaptation of the 1991 novel,

The Sweet Hereafter, earned director Atom Egoyan two Oscar nominations, and the subsequent release of Paul Schrader's adaption of *Affliction* (starring Nick Nolte and Willem Dafoe) earned James Coburn an Academy Award for Best Supporting Actor.

I spoke with Russell Banks in Princeton, New Jersey in late March of 1998.

I guess with the recent publication of Cloudsplitter, *the most obvious question to start with is, Why John Brown?*

Well, I think that's a question you can ask about any novel in a way. Why a school bus accident? Why a fourteen-year-old mall rat? Or, Why a white whale, Mr. Melville? And you're going to get a similar answer from most writers, because there's a braid of reasons. There's rarely, if ever, just one reason, if you look at it honestly and try to understand it, or try to speak about it honestly.

I can say that, on a personal level—this is one strand in the braid—Brown was in my life in a vivid way when I was in my twenties in college in Chapel Hill in the middle sixties, because he was sort of an emblematic figure like Che Guevara, very much like Che Guevara. He was a man of action whose ideals one could identify with. And his picture would be up on the wall of the SDS office or the SCLC office, and he crossed those racial lines that a lot of us white kids were trying to cross during that period, trying to do it in a thoughtful and respectful and committed political way. He was also, at the same time, uniquely connected to the literary figures that meant a great deal to me then and still do, which is to say the mid-nineteenth century New England writers— the Transcendentalists, Thoreau and Emerson, and so on. I loved Melville's poem about him, and even lesser poets like John Greenleaf Whittier wrote about him, so he was a figure who was a part of my literary constellation, too. In addition to being a part of my political and social constellation, he was part of my literary constellation, and unique in that regard. So Brown was there at the beginning, but I was a kid and I couldn't have imagined writing about him, although at the time I couldn't have imagined but did write about Simon Bolivar and other historical figures without much hesitation. But somehow I couldn't imagine him. I couldn't get to him.

And then he kind of faded from my conscious mind, but in 1987 Chase and I bought a house that was going to be a summer house, and it's turned out to be our year-round house now, up in the Adirondacks in the northeast corner of New York State, just south of Canada a little ways, south of Quebec, and it turned out he was buried up there. Not just that he was buried there, but so were eleven others who were killed at Harper's Ferry or executed afterwards. And he had lived there longer than he had lived anywhere else and had run an underground railroad stop there, and there had been a settlement of black families, of freed slaves and escaped slaves, living on land grants that they'd been given by a wealthy New York abolitionist.

So his presence—in this ghostly way all of a sudden, I mean, really, it was almost like his ghost was in the woods, and also physically, because that area, since most of it is state forest, is not that different from the way it was in the 1840s and '50s visually, and I could walk through the woods and over those hills and even alongside many of those old roads and know I was in John Brown territory. So he was physically present, and it didn't take me very long to begin to imagine his life there in that period. And I had been doing some local history research anyhow. I was kind of getting the background, really, of what turned out to be Brown's life. So it wasn't a very complicated move for me. That's the personal linkup.

Then, as I got into the material, sort of superficially and tentatively, of his life and the era and the whole abolitionist movement, pretty soon I began to see that he's a really mythical figure and his story is a major American myth, a historical myth, and I really wanted to understand that and see it freshly. I mean, this is why so many poets and novelists and dramatists and even moviemakers have gone back to that story. It isn't because of the personality of the man. It's really the arc of his life, and the end of it and the obsessive quality of it, the fix that his life has on race, that drives people back to it again and again. As long as race is a central part of our historical narrative, and it is and will continue to be for a long, long time, then you go back to Brown and you try to reconnect with him and reunderstand that.

So there was that, which is a kind of a literary and maybe even social or historical connection to Brown, and then also I realized that for nearly twenty years in one way or the other, certainly in at least four books, I had been writing about the African diaspora from the white point of view. That's another great and continuously retold story, but it's been told almost exclusively from the African-American perspective, yet it's a big white story, too. It's a big part of white history on this continent, in this hemisphere, the African diaspora, because we white folks obviously participated in it, to the greatest degree caused it, benefited from it, and have suffered from it as well, and I realized that I've had this sort of obsession with it over the years. I've come back to that story, have been fascinated by that story. You know, the Caribbean in *The Book of Jamaica*, and the Haitian extension of it in *Continental Drift*, and certainly a big chunk of *Rule of the Bone* deals with it from another angle, and Brown is central to that story because that deals with the most dramatic episode in it, in a way, outside of the actual fact of slavery itself, the commencement of slavery itself. So for literary reasons, I suppose, looking at the body of my own work, I thought this was a necessary thing for me to do.

There's a been a recent trend toward the large, historical work. Thomas Pynchon, Don DeLillo, and yourself—three white male Northeastern writers in their fifties—have all published large, historical novels in the past couple of years. Cloudsplitter *is twice as long as any of your previous works, and it took you at least twice as long to write it. Was there something in your mind where you needed or wanted to write "the big book" and John Brown was the proper topic, or did Brown come first and necessitate a sizable effort?*

I think the latter. I felt the desire to write this particular book about John Brown, or a novel based on the life of Brown, more accurately, and—of necessity—it would be a long, dense book. The historical narrative, for me anyhow, at least to do it in a realistic way, required a great deal of space, and I didn't want to just focus on one episode or aspect of

Brown's life. I felt that I needed to cover quite a bit of time, at least twenty years, and that required me to fill out a lot of space. And also just the density of detail and background and material that would not be familiar to most readers and its being a historical fiction and displacing the story by a hundred and fifty years from the time of its composition required me to explain a lot. I needed a lot of space, so I think those are all factors.

Actually, you've put your finger on an interesting phenomenon, really. A number of novelists in their fifties are writing ambitious, historical novels, and that's of some interest to me, and I think that it probably has to do with a couple of factors. Something that's true, certainly, for the three you named, but you could add another half dozen— Charles Johnson, Jane Smiley's got a novel coming out right now that's about the Kansas wars. John Wideman had a historical novel a year or two ago set in Philadelphia, the antebellum era. You could come up with a number of writers in my generation who are writing historical fiction, and I have a feeling this is in response to a culturewide mindset, or a culturewide confusion might be a better way to say it, a culturewide confusion about what it means to be American. And for a novelist, that question will send you back in time.

In the late twentieth century, we are extremely conscious of ourselves, as a people, of being hyphenated. We're Asian-Americans, African-Americans, Euro-Americans, Native Americans. We're hyphenated. To the left of the hyphen we know what we are—Euro, Afro, Asian, or whatever. What we don't know is what really is embodied to the right of the hyphen. What does that mean? What do we share? Why bother to call ourselves something-American anyhow? It's historically true, at least for Americans, that when people are unsure about what it is to be themselves, their novelists start writing historical fiction. In the 1830s and '40s it was not that clear what it meant to be American. Fifty years after the revolution you could ask, Why aren't we British? Well, politically we're not, but really, Why aren't we British? And so Hawthorne writes *The Scarlet Letter*, and you have Cooper and you have Irving and the major novelists, both South and North, of that era writing historical fiction. And I think there's something like that going on now. There's a certain kind of confusion and lack of confidence in what it means to be American, and novelists are essentially, at bottom, mythmakers—mythmakers with regard to social identity, the tribe's identity. I mean a storyteller, basically, is creating, always, a myth about what it is to be whoever you are in this tribe. Why are we in this tribe and living in this corner of the planet instead of some other?

Your fiction of the past seven or eight years has been told with a more conventional narrative than your earlier work. I'm thinking in terms of form and structure. Hamilton Stark, *for example, has a unique form, a unique structure. Does the historical fiction, as a form, dictate in any way the structure of the novel that you have to write?*

Well, *Cloudsplitter* is basically an epistolary novel, that's the form, and the structure of it is the arc of the life of John Brown. See, I think of form and structure as two different things, almost as if one is exterior—form—and one is interior—structure—which grows out of the material that you're writing, the necessary pressures that the material puts on the narrative structure, the narrative itself. The novel is in some ways a sum of or a record of the tension between the interior—structure—and the exterior—form—and the limits of both. And I had the structure of it, because I had the material of Brown's life in hand. I could have put a different form on it. It could've been a bildungsroman told by Owen Brown about growing up in episodic ways. I could have used the same form basically that I used with *Rule of the Bone*, or I could have done it with four different narratives as I did with *The Sweet Hereafter*, that form, that choral form. But it seemed to me that a more intimate, and yet formalized in terms of rhetoric, mode for telling the story was the epistolary, so I elected to use that. I made that choice for lots of different reasons, but in some sense it just kind of happened. It just was there and seemed to feel good and feel right and so I used it. It wasn't all that conscious a process.

But to go back to the early part of the question, it is true that one reads my earlier work with greater awareness of the artifices of fiction. They're worn almost on their sleeves. You're very aware of it. But I don't think that I've had any particularly dramatic shift in my writing life over the years from that early work, whether it's *Hamilton Stark* or *Relation of My Imprisonment*, particularly. It's just that I think I've become more skillful at hiding the form and less insecure about it and so what was an exoderm has in some ways been absorbed into the text and made invisible, or less visible, to a more scrutinizing, analytical eye maybe.

When I was a younger writer, I was acting out of some insecurity and therefore tended to need to prove to myself and my reader that I understood the traditions and the forms and the formats of fiction, of modernist and post-modernist fiction, and so I was asserting it more than I feel the need to do now. But in some ways, you know, an awful lot of the overt aspects of any work of art are telling. They tell us what the artist is insecure about, in a way. What you push in the reader's face is very often what you're least secure about. And as you grow more secure about it, you think about it less and you have less necessity to assert it. Your trust is there and you don't have to worry about that.

Do you feel any insecurity looking back on those books?

Well, not particularly. I mean, obviously I would write them differently today, but I think they have their own essential identity and qualities; they're just different qualities than the work I'm writing now. I don't think they're less or more, necessarily. I have a sense that all my books are failures and that none of them are finished; they're just abandoned. That's a commonplace, almost. Most writers say that, one way or another, and mean it, too. But what that means is that you can't then put your work in a hierarchy. You can't value one more than the other, because they're all failures in that essential sense and you have to look at them that way and forgive them.

So there's no particular work that maintains a softer spot?

Oh yeah, but that's for reasons outside the text itself. Like, I have a great sentimental affection for *The Relation of My Imprisonment*, and it has a lot to do with the fact that nobody wanted to publish it. At the time I wrote it, I was publishing at Houghton Mifflin, and they didn't even

want to look at it or think about it, and then later at Harper Collins, after I had published *Continental Drift*, they didn't want to deal with it.
They said, Well, if you want to go ahead and do it with a small press,
you can do it. You won't be violating your contract, and so on. Like it
was a big favor. Like, You want to go and play around on the side? Go
ahead. And they condescended to it, so it was published first, serially,
in about six issues of a wonderful, mimeographed, stapled together,
Lower East Side magazine called *United Artists*. Bernadette Mayer and
Louis Warsh were the editors. And then an editor at a small, wonderful
press in Los Angeles who had followed the serialization picked it up and
published it in a small, very handsome edition. And then it was a different thing. Later, when Ballantine brought all the paperbacks out in
a uniform edition, they picked it up so it came out as a nice trade paperback, and now it's in the Harper Collins Perennial Library, their
trade paperback. So it's had a nice history, you know. It's sort of like the
outcast that managed to come in from the cold, so I have an affection
for it for those reasons if no other.

While we're on the subject of The Relation of My Imprisonment, *do you
feel any pressure to write commercially viable fiction? Would someone at
Harper Collins hemorrhage if you wrote* Relation, *Part Two?*

They'd publish it, but they'd hate the idea, and they wouldn't offer me
a big advance, that's for sure. But any pressure I have to write commercial fiction, or fiction other than that which is driven by a personal obsession, comes from me, myself. I put it on myself or would have to put
it on myself, because my own personal, obsession fiction gets published.
I mean, it's a different position for a younger writer who's just sort of
worried and trying hard to get his or her work in print. They may think,
Well, maybe if I just shade it this way or shade it that way then I can
get it published, but there are no assurances that it's going to reach
print. I mean, I have at least that assurance that it's going to reach print.
I don't have assurance it's going to sell, or be popular, or that critics are
going to like it or anything else, but at least I'm pretty sure I can get over
that first hurdle. I can get it into print in any number of ways, and that's

been true, you know, for a long time. So that doesn't put pressure on me. After that it becomes a desire to be loved by as many people as possible. You never know the degree to which you're immune from that desire. And you need an immunity, because it's like a sickness, that desire. It's a sneaky sickness, and it gets sneakier as you get older and more popular. In a way, it becomes more insidious. It can really creep in without your being aware of it, because other people, they're stroking you.

How conscious are you of the reader when you're writing? A few reviews of Cloudsplitter *have been one-sided arguments about what the novel should have been. One reviewer even suggested that Owen wasn't the character who should've been telling the story.*

Michiko Kakutani said, Well, if this is history it would be a bad book. Well, if it were poetry it would be a bad book. If it were a play it would be a bad book. It's not. It's a novel.

Are you conscious of the reader? Were you more conscious with this book?

I'm not conscious of the reader particularly. When I'm not writing, I'm conscious of the reader certainly, and conscious of my career, as we call it, but I'm not conscious of the reader when I'm working. I've worked very hard since I was young to separate my career from my work because the career is the part that I have no control over or very, very little control over, and it's got nothing to do with the work. It's like managing, you know, a mutual stock fund or something like that. I don't know enough about it to do it, so I don't. Let somebody else do it. But the work I know a lot about. I'm the only one who knows about it. Nobody else knows about my work but me. Not even my wife knows what I really want to do or what I really want to say or what I really feel or intuit. I don't even know what it is half the time until it's there. But that's where I can do something and can control things, and so when I'm there I don't think about audience at all. When I'm not there, I do think about audience. Sure, I think about it. I'm not going to play some kind of faux naive. I think about it, and I think I've been reasonably cautious and careful and knowledgeable in my handling of my career, but I can say with confidence that I don't think about my reader at all when I'm writing. That would be death to the writing, for me.

I write books that have an effect on me, and that's the main reason why I write, for how they will affect me. Not thrill me, although I hope that will happen, nor move me, but so that it will make me a more intelligent person and maybe even, if possible, a more decent person. Writing *Cloudsplitter*, for instance, made me more intelligent about a number of things: about race, about relations between fathers and sons, about sex—Owen, after all, has a sexual identity that plays a significant role—about the interweaving between sex and race in America, about American history. It just made me more intelligent about those things, because I put myself at open-ended risk in the writing of the book and that's what the book's about. That I'm working within the disciplines of an art means it may connect with other human beings in a way that resembles the way the writing of it connected to me.

But after the book is done and out, then you look around. I mean, I can take a look at it. I'm a somewhat educated reader of this book, and I can look at it somewhat from the outside and I can see, Yes, this will appeal to certain people. Or not. If you don't already know something about American history, for instance, this book is going to be troublesome. I have a French publisher and an Italian publisher and so on, and they look at this manuscript and they say, Well, I don't know. Maybe we need a glossary. We don't know a lot of this stuff and who a lot of these people are. And that's a way of considering your reader. I think in those terms I do consider my reader, after the fact, in a kind of demographic or sociological way. And I suppose, naturally, I want the book to be popular. I want the book to reach as many readers as possible, for various reasons, some of them venal and some of them not so.

But you read your reviews.

I read them quickly, just to catch the tone of them. I don't pore over them or study them or remember them very well. And I don't remember who wrote the bad ones unless it was really a cheap shot and then I wait.

You've never found a review instructive?

No, I never have. Not about the work. I've found them instructive about the audience. What we were just saying here. Like, Oh, this isn't as obvious to everybody as it is to me. That sort of thing. And that's instructive about the audience.

Do you know which of your books has sold the most?

Over the years *Continental Drift*, because it's taught the most, but with the initial publication it didn't sell very much. It's just that over the years it kind of settled into a comfortable role within the culture, generally, so that an awful lot of people under twenty-five have read it, because they read it in school or their friends told them to read it or something like that. But the initial publication didn't sell very well. In terms of initial publication, then, I would say probably the most recent, *Cloudsplitter*, but before that it was *Rule of the Bone*. Each book has sold more on initial publication than the previous, but some have greater staying power. Some are stronger as backlist books.

I know there's not a direct relationship between sales and quality, but do you find any significance in those numbers in terms of learning about your audience? Do you understand why each book has done what it has in terms of sales? Are you comfortable with Continental Drift *being your best-selling work? I would imagine that* The Sweet Hereafter *is quickly catching up.*

Well, actually, I was just about to say, my agent called me earlier and she had some sales figures over the last few months for *The Sweet Hereafter*, and it's gone through the roof, but that's obviously because of the film tie-in. It happened to be Oscar week and it got a tremendous amount of publicity for the previous couple of months and Fine Line was advertising the film, but they were advertising it in terms of the book often enough and sometimes playing my name up as big as they were playing up the director's name. What's that got to do with quality? That's just the luck of the draw, the accident of a film being made, so I don't think there's any correlation between quality and numbers. There may be a correlation between the quality of a book and its staying power, its ability to continue to be read for no reason other than it continues to speak to people's lives in an ongoing way. People continue to read *Rule of the Bone*. That seems to be largely because younger readers talk to each other and pass it on. It has a real life with kids now.

Do you think the primary audience for Bone *is younger readers? I did find a copy in the Young Adult section of the New York Public Library.*

That's great. I think the New York State Education Board has just approved it for being taught in public high schools, which pleases me immensely. Probably it's natural, and a continuing audience would be younger readers who would connect to Bone and would feel that their lives, in many ways, are validated by the book and affirmed by the book. That would be great.

How conscious were you of Huck Finn *when you were writing* Rule of the Bone?

Totally.

What term would you be comfortable with? Is it an homage?

It's an homage and a critique. There's an intertextual dialogue that I was trying to set up and participate in with *Huck Finn*. Definitely it was there.

Well, I know the connection wasn't accidental. I mean, the words "light out" do appear at the end.

Absolutely. It's throughout. I want to not only bow down before *Huck Finn* but also to argue with it and to point out, by similarities, the differences between Twain's world and Banks's world, the 1870s and 1990s. He's a middle-aged man writing about a teenaged kid, obviously an adolescent version of himself, and I was doing something very similar these many years later. It would be absurd for me to even begin to write a book about a kid like that without first giving more than a passing nod in the direction of *Huckleberry Finn*, and then going on, by noting the similarities, by seeding the book with plenty of similarities to note that there's a big difference in our worlds. I mean, the world has changed in dramatic and frightening ways in the intervening years.

In what sense are you arguing with Huckleberry Finn?

I only mean that figuratively. I think that basically what I mean is, not arguing with it, but adding to it. That's a better way to think about it. That book establishes a tradition in American literature that most writers participate in, consciously or not, and I was conscious of participating in it and wanted to extend the tradition into the late twentieth century, because there's so much in the book that's still valid and applicable. It's a great, classic work of art. But all the best stories, *The Odyssey*, *The Iliad*, have to constantly be retold, can be constantly retold. That's what we mean by classics. They can be retold. Not just updated but retold so we can hear again and recycle, apply again to our lives with fresh eyes and ears, the essential insights and power that that tradition holds.

This certainly wasn't the first time that you worked from a specific literary reference. I'm thinking that Trailerpark *is a response to* Winesburg, Ohio, *and that the short story from* Trailerpark *"Black Man and White Woman in Dark Green Rowboat" came from Dreiser's* An American Tragedy.

Naturally those are important points of reference for me in the writing of the story and of that book, but there are others, as well. *Trailerpark* is in some ways a response to my reading of *The Canterbury Tales*, too, and *Dubliners*. There are various levels of response in, I think, any work of literature. You don't write in a vacuum. You participate. That's one of the great, satisfying things about being a fiction writer or a poet, an artist of any kind. Nobody's dead. You participate in the tradition. You become one with these books, and these texts become part of your immediate daily life, and so you enter into that conversation and hope you become part of the chorus in the course of writing the book. It's inevitable. It's inescapable for me. I've been a compulsive reader since my

youth, since adolescence, so how could I not end up having a conversation of that sort—having my work be a response to the works, the
books that I've read?

Can we go to either a short story or a novel and talk about the particular process?

Actually, there's a double source for the short story you mentioned,
"Black Man and White Woman in Dark Green Rowboat." Well, not
source. It responds to Dreiser, certainly, in terms of the psychology of
the characters, but it reverses and plays with it so that the victim is the
man, in a sense. But also it's a response to a Hemingway story in how
it's structured, so the psychology, in a way, and the erotic component of
it comes out of Dreiser, but certainly the form of the story and the
arrangement, one might even say the architecture of the story, comes
out of "Hills Like White Elephants." The physical positioning of the
characters and the movement of the boat, when they turn and so forth,
is very much learned from Hemingway. I mean, I learned how to do that
from Hemingway, how to dramatize by moving the characters around
physically in relation to each other and in relation to the landscape.
Where they are in the lake and in the boat is all very carefully orchestrated or choreographed, and I didn't know how to do that until I read
Hemingway's stories.

*When you sit down in front of the keyboard, have you just finished reading
the Hemingway story or are you working from some distant memory?*

Usually I'm working from memory and what's retained. I read like a
writer, and what stays with me is often what has resonance for me as a
writer. It might be a false memory, too. It often is. If I go back and reread
it, I say, Well, it wasn't like I remembered it at all.

But if it gets you the story . . .

Right. It's what I needed from it. So it isn't necessarily a close reading
by any means. It's associational and sometimes it's intuited and it's
strong enough or raises questions for what I really was responding to
that I'll go back to the text. I did that with *Cloudsplitter*. As I was nearing

the end of it, I was hearing certain tones, you know. I'd orchestrated these various pieces and I was starting to hear tones that were reminding me of tones at the end of *Moby Dick*. And I wanted to get it right and I remembered that there's a beautiful diminuendo ending to *Moby Dick*. That was how I remembered it. I didn't remember it as like the great, cataclysmic ending. There is a cataclysm and then there is a diminuendo, and I was remembering that and that's what I was reaching for. I was starting to hear the necessity for that. Coming down from Harper's Ferry I thought, There has to be a diminuendo. It can't just sort of be like, That's all, folks. There has to be a follow-through. I was orchestrating it almost musically in my mind, so I went back and read the last forty, fifty pages of *Moby Dick* to see how he did that. Really, it was pacing I was looking at, and the rhetoric, to see how the rhetoric kind of cooled down, and how the narrative became more direct at the end and how the whole voice was lowered, and I studied it consciously, but I was led there by what I deeply remembered, not having read *Moby Dick* in twenty-five years, so I think it operates that way, too. Sometimes you will go directly back to the text and see how it's done, but you're led there because you have this memory of it. You're led there because what's unfolding on the page is leading you there. It's in response to what's unfolding on the page.

Was "The Guinea Pig Lady" the first story written for Trailerpark?

Yeah. Actually, they were pretty much written in the order they appear. That book is more orchestrated than it looks. It's more formal than it looks. I remember planning it out very carefully, the order in which the stories would be written.

You knew it was going to be a book before you wrote the stories?

Yeah. That one I definitely did. I had a cast of characters, and I was trying to structure it, in some ways, like an opera. All of the characters appear in the first story. All of the characters appear in the end story. Also, each of the characters assumed a role in my mind as a member of the tribe—the warrior, the magician, the fool, and so on, the mother, the virgin, the initiate. Merle Ring, the fisherman at the end, is the magician. And the guinea pig lady is the fool, and they're both at the extreme outside of the community, but they have the greatest power over the community, too. So those pieces and those relationships were worked out in my mind. I don't remember, at this point, what the exact details were, but I do know that they all had roles and I was trying to write a novel that wasn't a novel but that was, in an important way to me, a portrait of a community.

Which is not all that dissimilar to your attempt with The Sweet Hereafter.

Exactly. I think it's much more successful in *The Sweet Hereafter*. I was trying to avoid having a hero. I was really playing with the whole idea of having a hero by avoidance. Can you write a novel without a hero?

Can you use the term "protagonist" in the same sense as "hero" or do you have to stay with the classical term?

I think you can say protagonist—a single, central figure. What James called the emotional center of the narrative. A single person where all values are tested. Any action which occurs is important insofar as it affects that character. And so *Trailerpark* is kind of a crude attempt to do what I think I did much more successfully in *The Sweet Hereafter*, but in *The Sweet Hereafter* I gave up the ambition of making each of the separate parts stand alone and satisfy the needs of drama in the short story. *Trailerpark* is a very schematic book in a way. Sometimes maybe too schematic.

What do you see as the book's shortcomings? What makes The Sweet Hereafter *more of an accomplishment?*

Well, I don't know that it's more of an accomplishment. I think it more successfully meets my intentions. One ambition I had with *Trailerpark* was to write a narrative that was a continuing narrative that used the same cast of characters throughout but was absent a single protagonist, and that in some way was a dramatization of tribal life.

So the structure came before the characters?

Well, the form came before the characters. And then the individual stories and characters provided the structure. Anyway, I had the characters before I wrote any of the stories. I knew what each one was supposed to be about and I had the order, too, that they were supposed to be in. But I didn't write the individual stories until I got to that place in the book and then I wrote them. I didn't write them in any old order and then put them in that order. I wrote it from page one until the end.

The first and last stories, especially, feel that way.

There are small references back and forth to different stories and characters.

Yes, it's wonderfully interlocked.

And the reason why they are is because I did write them as you would write a novel.

You use an unnamed, omniscient narrator in that book. Of course, there's almost no way for me to discuss point of view with you since, throughout your fiction, it's never as simple as first, second and third person, but you have, in a sense, an outside narrator in Trailerpark. *Even though he lives on the grounds, the reader knows nothing about him.*

That's right. In fact, if you count the stories and go against the number of the trailers which are identified in the park, you know where he lives. He's a member of the community.

But the outside narrator is a point-of-view technique that you've used several times. Is there anything particularly telling about your use of first person, because outside of Bone, *its use is not what most would term as standard?*

In *Trailerpark*, because that was published before *Continental Drift*, that kind of narrator made it possible for me to imagine the narrator of *Continental Drift*, because I got to imagine, in a fairly literal way, the narrator of that story by inventing a character who wasn't there, and that let me understand the narrator as a character. Even when it's third-person omniscient, it's still a character in the story. It's a part of the story and has a responsibility then as one of the actors, and it was sort of overt there and then it became a little more subtle, though it's a *loa* speaking, in *Continental Drift*. Or at least it's a narrator who's inspired by a *loa*, who invokes a *loa*, is taken over by a *loa*, in order to tell the story, so it's maybe a long, ongoing process of inventing myself as storyteller, and creating a role for myself in the work as a storyteller. I never want to write about myself in any pointed or obvious way. I mine myself. I pillage myself as much as I pillage the newspapers.

And that gives you distance?

Sure. And it also gives me a kind of freedom, too. I just use myself as raw material, the same way I use history or dreams or literature. It's just raw material.

Was Continental Drift *written sequentially?*

Yes.

You wrote a Bob chapter and then followed it with a Vanise chapter?

Right. I wrote that in that order. I think I had to, because I had to control the pacing of those episodes very carefully. I couldn't go on too long, on the one hand, or I would have forgotten the other story. I'd lose track of the other story, and this is true for the reader as well. There had to be a point where it was just right, where I could get into this story yet it wouldn't be so long that I lost track of the other story, so when I then jumped to the other story it was immediately familiar to me, so therefore I had to write it in sequence. I couldn't do it consciously after the fact.

This question probably puts too much pressure on memory, but when you talk about writing the story sequentially so it's still familiar, there's a certain amount of time that it takes to write each chapter. Was there a relationship in the time it took to write each of the chapters?

There's literal time and then there's writing time, and they're different. They really have different clocks.

Is that still true today after writing for so many years? Some days it's just not there?

Oh yeah. Absolutely. And however long it takes me to write a certain section of a book is no indication of how long that section of the book is. It's the same thing with *Continental Drift*. All of those sections are approximately the same length, but some of them may have taken me a week to write and others may have taken two months, but for me that's the same amount of time. It's the same amount of imaginative time.

You took a break when you were writing Cloudsplitter. *Is that the first time it's ever happened? That you put something aside?*

Yeah. I think so. I think I probably have stopped before in the middle of a novel to write a short story now and then.

How far were you into Cloudsplitter *before you took a break?*

I think I was probably two-thirds through *Cloudsplitter* when I pulled away from it and wrote *Rule of the Bone*, and then I went back to *Cloudsplitter*, and then the last third I went through pretty fast. I did a lot of revising and changing after that, but just getting it down went pretty fast.

I think I got bogged down and scared of *Cloudsplitter* in some ways, because there was just so much material to organize and to structure into a coherent and compelling story. What to leave out, what to put in, how much to allow myself to digress, controlling the pacing. It was hard work. Harder work than anything I'd tried before. It's as good as I can do now. I learned a lot and maybe I can do better next time, but I was certainly working as hard as I could.

It wasn't a choice to pull away from it? It was something that had to be done?

Well, you know, it didn't work quite like that. I didn't want to go away from it, but it was just as well and wise that I did. Sometimes your sleeping self is a lot smarter than your waking self, and I just thought, Well, I'll stop and write a short story about this kid, because I was really getting into these kids and the kid's voice, and I was getting into that world, being seduced by it, and I said, Well, I'd love to tell this funny story about this kid stealing his grandmother's coins and using it for dope and then he doesn't know it until they're all gone because he stole one or two at a time. The story appealed to me, the setup with the kid, the kid's voice. I could hear that, because I really like kidspeak. So I wrote the story, what became the first chapter of the book, as a story and I said, Wait a minute. This is more than that. This is opening up a whole world here. This is just a door. This is just a way in. It's not a very good short story, but it's really a way in to a larger world that I'm fascinated by and a character I really, already, love. I've only been with him for ten or fifteen pages and I already love him, so that's when I decided to go ahead and see how long it would take me. John Brown was going to be around a long, long time anyhow.

There was never any doubt that you would go back to Cloudsplitter?

No. Never. I never thought of abandoning it. I just knew it would be there, and I'd already done too much work and I was too committed to it to fear that I wouldn't finish it. But then when I got into the other book I realized, Boy, it's a good thing I'm doing this because I didn't know what the fuck I was doing for a while there, for the last six months, on that book. And maybe I'll know when I go back, freshened by this, and it was true. It was the case. When I got back, I was freshened by it. But I didn't deliberately pause and look around, put down *Cloudsplitter* and say, Now what do I really want to write while I'm waiting around? Really, I just got kind of seduced. It was like a little love affair or something.

And how long of a break was that for Rule of the Bone?

About a year and a half.

And how quickly did the thought of Huck Finn *come? You seemed to have some kind of conscious thought ten or fifteen pages in. Or can you write about a teenaged boy in America and not think about* Huck Finn?

I would say almost immediately. I know I went back and rewrote that earlier part to consciously shape it to evoke echoes of *Huck Finn*, the opening paragraph and so forth. I guess I was thirty or forty pages into it and

I realized I better reconsider the sources here, the tradition that I'm working in, and I did go back and reread *Huck Finn* and *Catcher in the Rye*.

How about Augie March?

I didn't go back to *Augie March*, although I love that book. I read *To Kill a Mockingbird*, though, which is obviously in the same tradition, and then just rethought that whole tradition a little bit and realized what I was working in. You don't have to reinvent the wheel.

Did you have pages on John Brown written before you had Owen's voice, or did you have Owen from the beginning?

No, I had Owen from page one. Oh, absolutely. And the setup, I had the epistolary setup, the letters to Katharine Mayo I had from the start. I knew that. I didn't have to write a page to get that. In fact, I couldn't write a page until I had that. I had no entry, no point of view, until I had that.

You've been involved with several film projects recently, and that obviously takes a lot of time and energy and attention. Is it a distraction? A welcome opportunity? How does it fit in with your fiction?

Well, I think of it as a temporary engagement and not a distraction at the moment. I realized when I finished *Cloudsplitter* last May that I'd been really working hard for a decade, without a break, and that I needed a break. I was tired. I was kind of bone weary. So I decided just to try a few different things, and I had the opportunity to get involved in these film projects, to write the script for *Continental Drift* and to help produce *Book of Jamaica* and *Continental Drift*, and I've learned a lot over the last couple of years, over the making of *The Sweet Hereafter* and *Affliction*, about how a movie gets made, and I liked it. I was interested. I am interested in how a movie gets made. It's also one of the few ways a writer can keep some control over what the movie ends up being. I certainly plan to do that this year up to a certain point. I mean, I don't think this is a continuing thing.

But you've been on a fiction break since last May?

Yeah, I wrote a text for a book of photographs by a man named Arturo Patton, who does the author's headshot for *Cloudsplitter*, but he's mainly known as a portrait artist in Europe. He's not known here, although he is becoming better known. His work is being exhibited now more. Anyway, he did a collection of photographs of all the citizens of a small town in Maine, and I loved them. They're just real formal, renaissance style portraits of these country people, and they're just beautiful. It turned these people into universal types without condescending, without sentimentalizing them. They're just beautiful portraits, so my French publisher wanted to do a book of them and asked me if I'd write the text and I got into the pictures, and now HarperCollins is going to do it here and it'll be out next year.

And then I'm doing an opera libretto. I've done most of the background work and blocked it out and I'll try to write that over the next few months, once I come in off the road, but the movie stuff, you know, if you sit around worrying about the movie stuff, you go crazy. It basically takes time in fits and starts, so it'll be like two or three days where I'll work and be all involved in it and then there won't be anything going on for a week or ten days.

Is that easily controlled, where you know when the breaks will happen?

Well, sometimes the work comes unexpectedly, but most of the time I know about it in advance. A lot of it's just yak yak phones and stuff, and meetings and bullshit. I don't want to direct a movie. I had fun writing *Continental Drift*. I might write another one along the way somewhere. Egoyan and I are talking about doing something together, an original screenplay that he would direct. It's an interesting thing for me to do. I love films and I take them very seriously. I grew up in the era when it was clear that films were capable of being high art.

Do you expect the same satisfaction with your participation in these film projects as you get with fiction, or does the fact that film is a collaborative effort diminish it in any way?

It doesn't diminish it, but it certainly alters it, and I'm probably not temperamentally suited to collaborate, except as a temporary engagement.

In a continuing and permanent way, I can't imagine it satisfying me enough. I need to be in control of everything as much as possible.

Do you know when your fiction break will be over, or will the film projects dictate that?

I'll probably go for another year at most. I've already got a novel that's starting to boil up in my mind, and I imagine that'll put everything else on the back burner. There'll be a point in which I just say, Okay, enough of this shit. Now I've got to write fiction. I need to get this story told.

I know it goes against all sorts of rules and superstitions, but can you tell me anything about that novel you have in your mind?

Oh yeah, I don't have those superstitions. I want to write a novel about the Liberian Civil War of 1991. I want to follow the diaspora to its logical conclusion, which is Liberia in the 1990s, the last chapter in the African diaspora. I want to write that, and then I have in my mind a fifth novel, if you think of these as a cycle of novels about the diaspora from the white point of view, which would be the first chapter, a historical novel dealing with the slave trade set in West Africa in the seventeenth century. I'd love to write about the slave trade, the beginnings of the diaspora, and then I could put together, in my own mind, *Book of Jamaica, Continental Drift, Rule of the Bone, Cloudsplitter*, and the Liberian novel. I could just see a sequence of them that would make sense to me and that would probably exhaust the subject for me.

Will this be a large book?

I don't think so. I don't think so. I don't imagine it that way. I can't imagine it that way. It'll be a very personal book, a white woman telling the story. The story of a white woman, a nice white liberal, who goes to Africa as a Peace Corps worker in the seventies. A woman my age.

You love the research, don't you?

Yeah. The research is the most fun. That's other worlds.

A Conversation with Charles Johnson

$\mathbf{N}$ ovelist, short story writer, essayist, screenwriter, and cartoonist Charles Johnson received his bachelor's degree in journalism and his master's in philosophy from Southern Illinois University before studying with the legendary John Gardner at SUNY-Stony Brook. Johnson has published two books of cartoons, a book-length essay entitled *Being & Race: Black Writing since 1970*, and serves as coeditor of a collection of essays, *Black Men Speaking*. His published fiction includes *Faith and the Good Thing*, *Oxherding Tale*, *The Sorcerer's Apprentice*, and *Middle Passage*, a novel that garnered the National Book Award, making Johnson the first African-American male to capture the prize since Ralph Ellison won for *Invisible Man* in 1953.

Johnson is currently the Pollack Professor in the Department of English at the University of Washington and is the recipient of a MacArthur Fellowship.

I interviewed Charles Johnson three days before his fiftieth birthday in his Manhattan hotel room as he toured in support of his novel *Dreamer*.

I got tired just reading over your list of accomplishments. It almost doesn't seem fair that you're still alive.

Well, you have to take one day at a time, man. I've been working since I was seventeen years old, as a publishing artist. I've worked steadily.

I'm amazed that you find time to breathe. My point in bringing this up is, Do you ever feel pressure in your work, whether fiction or nonfiction, to please more than Charles Johnson and his immediate family?

No, actually I think I just write to satisfy myself. My friend August Wilson, you know, he's got these rules for writers. There are four of them. One of them is: There are no rules for writing. That's one. The second one is: The first statement is a lie so pay attention. The third one is: You can't write for an audience. The writer's first job is to survive. And the fourth one is: You can do no wrong but anything can be made better. As simple as those are, I think they make a lot of sense. You have to write to satisfy yourself, first and foremost. Who else could you possibly write for? The audience? What is that exactly? You see people who come into bookstores and they're from all walks of life, all backgrounds, and all ethnic groups, all religions and races. So are you going to target one group as opposed to another? No, you're going to write for yourself.

When I write, I think about people who I've worked with in the past, or known. I'll say to myself, Now if John Gardner were alive, he'd like that line. If my wife reads this, she's going to like it. Or if my buddy over there looks at this little passage on martial arts, since he's a martial artist, he's going to like it. That's about as big as the audience gets for me, because you can't know all these invisible people out there who you've never met. So you have to work for yourself to satisfy yourself.

I'm trying to figure a way to ask this next question without sounding like I'm fawning.

Well, it's not even about that. Here's why I'm a Buddhist, man. None of this is about ego. None of this is about career for me. It never has been. I have no interest in that. I've just loved to create ever since I was a kid. First with drawings, and then later on I discovered I could write. And there's specific things that I do want to write, particularly philosophical fictions, for a number of different reasons. Because that's my training and background, in terms of formal education, and also because we didn't have a whole lot of that in African-American literature, except for Jean Toomer, Richard Wright, and Ralph Ellison. So I figured there was a gap. There was a void. I could fill that void. And that's what it was about, enriching our literature through, I hope, books like *Dreamer* and the previous ones.

Now I also do other assignments and those were, primarily, to see if I could do them, in fact. Like public television and other kinds of things. To see if I could write a different kind of thing, just to challenge myself. You can also make some money that way, too.

You hit on a couple of points there. The assignments like Black Men Speaking *and* Being & Race. *Maybe when I say institution, I'm asking if you feel any kind of responsibility other than to yourself.*

Responsibility? Keep going. What do you mean by responsibility?

When you say that you've done assignments for the challenge, to see if you could do them, it seems like that might have been a concern early on, but not now. It seems like the motivation to create Black Men Speaking *has to come from another place than just "to see if you could do it." Does the nonfiction provide as much enjoyment as fiction?*

Being & Race is actually one of the most enjoyable things that I think I've done, primarily because that was going to be my dissertation at Stony Brook. I did all but the dissertation. I got hired by a writing program and they said, You know, you're publishing. You don't need to finish the Ph.D. because the M.F.A. is a terminal degree. And I said, Okay, fine. That gives me free time to write, literary fiction and other things, but I still wanted that dissertation on phenomenology in respect to black American literature. And also, not as a dissertation, but something a bit more readable than a dissertation is. So that's why I went back and did *Being & Race*. The third reason was because I thought some of the reviews of earlier books were just abysmal. I thought that the book reviewers were, aesthetically, just totally at sea with an original work of art. So it's a manifesto of sorts.

When you say "earlier books," you're referring to your earlier books?

Faith and the Good Thing in particular. *Oxherding Tale* threw a lot of people because they didn't know what to do with it. They didn't understand it. People seem to think ideologically, very often, about black art, and they have presuppositions in their mind, and all kinds of sociological clichés. Ellison addresses this very eloquently, and other writers as well. But that's what *Being & Race* is largely about, the first half of it. It's an aesthetic in the first half, and then in the second half I talk about writers and assess various texts, in a capsule kind of way in some cases, for people who may not know who those writers are. Or those times. Or those books. So that book was something I enjoyed doing and I still like it, very much, among all the books that I've done.

Black Men Speaking was another matter. That was requested by my friend John Gallman, at Indiana, and came from his desire to do that kind of book, and my desire to deal with the plight of young black men in the eighties. Again, my son had just entered that critical age group, sixteen to thirty-four, at the time, that's been labeled an endangered species. I wanted to work through all that mess, all those statistics that were so bad, and then get other writers to address those same questions, but in a fresh way. And not the usual kind of writers.

I owe the way that book looks to John McCluskey, who was able to put more time into it than I was, because I was busy with other things, like *Dreamer*. John was very interested in not getting academics, and not getting published writers, because those are the voices you usually hear in an anthology on black men. He wanted grass roots people. He wanted people who were not writers and that meant that we, he and I, all had to work very carefully with the writers to bring the prose up to speed, because they didn't have a literary background.

I think some of the pieces are really quite fine. My colleague Joe Scott's first piece in there, on growing up in Detroit in the thirties, called "Making a Way Out of No Way," is really fine. Everybody loves that piece. And David Nicholson's piece is really good. Of course, David is a *Washington Post* reporter so it's going to be good. John got some good people to participate in this particular project, and to tell the truth. Basically a lot of people don't want to deal with those statistics. They want to deny them, or skip around them, but they're real. And until somebody just looks at it and accepts it as being the case, nobody can move forward so, to me, that's a different kind of a book, but I feel very strongly about it. I feel a certain passion about it.

You said a few minutes ago that one of the things being a Buddhist helped with was not having an ego.

Well, you work at it. It's an illusion anyway.

Do you ever feel competitive with your fiction?

Competitive in what sense?

I'm thinking of a particular section from the introduction to Oxherding Tale *paperback: "The 1980s began as a decade when the work of Black male writers was systematically downplayed and ignored in commercial, New York publishing. For example,* Oxherding Tale *appeared the same year as Alice Walker's* The Color Purple. *I leave it to readers to decide which book pushes harder at the boundaries of invention, and inhabits most confidently the space where fiction and philosophy meet."*

The reason I've never felt competitive with other writers is because I know exactly what I showed up to do, and it's basically philosophical fiction. That's my background. And, once again, everything I've done in the way of my own, self-generated projects, novels, and short stories, have always been, I hope, in that area where fiction and philosophy meet. I don't even write a story unless it's philosophically engaging to me or addresses some perennial question in Eastern or Western philosophy. I'm not going to write my own stories unless they do that.

But if there's anybody that I'm competitive with, then that's me, and that's it. To say that writers are competitive, what does that really mean? Are they doing the same thing? Is that what they mean? And so they're competing with each other? If that's the case, then you have two writers doing the same thing and you don't need one of them.

But you seem to have a special pride for Oxherding Tale.

Definitely. If I had not done that book, I would not have gone on to do
the other books. I know that. That's a very special book for me for a lot
of reasons. That is the book I wanted to write when I became a writer.
That is to say, I wrote six novels in two years prior to *Faith and the Good
Thing*. They weren't the books I wanted to write because I hadn't figured out how to write out of a philosophical sensibility.

I met John Gardner while I was writing *Faith and the Good Thing*, and
I was beginning to understand what that could be—this place where fiction and philosophy merge. Because we divide things, I think. This is this
and this is that and that thing's over there. And that's bullshit, because
everything really is one whole, one unit. I hadn't figured out, exactly, how
to carve at that until *Faith and the Good Thing*, but that still didn't satisfy
me. John didn't really understand Eastern philosophy. He was actually
kind of opposed to it. In fact, he was a lot opposed to it, at the time, though
he changed later on, in his writing, and even wrote a piece called "Medi-
tational Fiction" for a book he translated by a Japanese writer by the name
of Kikuo Itaya, a book of short stories. John brought his work back here,
had SIU Press publish him, did the introduction, mainly to say he didn't
understand these stories, which were very anchored in Buddhism, but he
loved them. That's the kind of human being he was.

But at the time I was working with John, he didn't really understand and I didn't go that far, philosophically, in *Faith and the Good
Thing*. For me, whenever I write a book, and this is probably a very difficult thing for some people to understand, I don't write a book just to
be writing a book. I write a book as if it's the last thing in this world I'm
ever going to do, the last statement I'm ever going to make. I take this
final manuscript, when it's done, and I put it in the mail, and it's my Last
Will and Testament in language. That's what this is. For me, it's got to
be total when I do a book. I mean, total. Every emotion, thought. The
best emotion. The best thought. The best technique. I'm going to have
to learn something new from it and draw off of everything I ever knew.
Pull up emotions I haven't felt before. I'm going to have to feel differently. I'm going to come out of this process different when I do a novel.
It's a total thing. And one of the things dearest to me in my life, since

my teens, ever since I got into martial arts, has been Eastern thought, Eastern philosophy. And I'm thinking about all kinds of things in respect to Eastern philosophy and its emphasis on personal liberation. And all the things that go into Buddhism, and then I'm thinking about the slave narrative, which had never been the form used for a novel. You know what I'm saying? And how you go about updating that and go philosophically deeper into it and focus on questions of freedom in a deeper way. Other kinds of slavery, such as psychological, sexual, metaphysical. All of that is something I just really had to deal with, in some book, somewhere, and that's *Oxherding Tale*.

I was looking at the "Ten Oxherding Pictures" from my late teens, when I was a cartoonist. I'd look at all kinds of art and that one is a seminal Buddhist text. That was important to me in grappling with this subject. So all of that went into *Oxherding Tale*, and why doing this book as opposed to something else.

My editor at the time, whose name I won't mention, I pitched the idea to him that maybe I could do a family drama, a black family drama, and he was like, Oh yeah, I can sell that idea. And then I told him I never intended to do that. I just wanted to see what you would say. I'm doing this book. I said, It's this book or nothing. If you stick with something, fortunately somebody will understand it. That's why I have this long relationship now with John Gallman at Indiana University Press. I feel indebted to John for making that book a reality because I really would not have written anything else, in the way of a novel, unless I had gotten that book done. Everything I do refers to that in some way, if not to the novel then to the complex themes of Eastern philosophies, Taoism and Buddhism, that animate the book.

So that's sort of, basically, the story of that novel. I threw away 2,400 pages as I wrote it. It had to be this book in our literature or I wasn't going to be happy.

Compared to most writers, your novels have long gestation periods.

It depends on the novel. I used to write novels one every ten weeks when I first started writing fiction. *Faith and the Good Thing* took me nine months.

Maybe I should follow that lead. What's the difference between the first six novels that you wrote and the seventh, Faith and the Good Thing, *which was the first novel published?*

The first six are easier. They're not philosophical novels. That's one thing. When I wrote *Oxherding Tale,* I sped read every book on slavery in the State University of New York at Stony Brook's library, just because I wanted to immerse myself in that, in all the slave narratives. I spent six years just reading stuff on the sea, reading literature on the sea for *Middle Passage,* everything from Appolonius to *Voyage of Argo* forward to Conrad. All of Melville I looked at again, nautical dictionaries. Everything about the sea, because I didn't know that stuff. That was '83 to '86, but, prior to that, going all the way back to 1971, I'd been collecting stuff on the slave trade from the time I was a discussion group leader in Black Studies at Southern Illinois University, when Black Studies first started there. There was a big lecture class, and we divided the students up and some of us undergraduates were discussion group leaders when I first saw the image of a slave ship projected on an overhead projector, a cross section of a ship with those silhouetted figures. So one of the first six novels I did was on the slave trade. It's like number two, so it would be like 1971 or something like that, and I wasn't ready to write it. It was just too early. But I had the research. Anything related to the slave trade I collected or took notes on, from '71 all the way to '83, and I began *Middle Passage* in '83. So, again, a lot of history.

Dreamer, I hope, embodies a great deal of history and biography. Every take on the life of the spirit is in this book. The Christian tradition as well as Moslem, as well as Hinduism, Buddhism, Taoism, and so forth. Because I like to learn, that's one thing, as I'm doing something. I mean, I come out with far more knowledge on a particular subject than I can get in that book. And that's just very enriching. I don't know if the next novel I do will have so much history as its foundation, as one of its conditions for coming into being. If that's the case, then give me maybe two years.

Usually I don't write autobiographically. I don't do that because it just doesn't interest me. I'm interested in other things. This novel,

Dreamer, oddly enough, does have a couple autobiographical things in it. The sketch of my hometown in the fifties.

Your great-uncle makes an appearance.

My great-uncle's in there. And that trip that the character makes with his mother, down South, that was actually a trip that my parents made. I usually don't pull out stuff like that because I'm interested in other subjects. I don't think the gestation period for a nonhistory-based novel would be too long.

But I'm very demanding about other things, too. As Sartre once said, Every sentence is a risk. I think everything needs to be compressed. I tell my students all the time, the French have a term, *remplissage*. It means "literary padding." I don't want any of that in my book. I want this compression that happens when you have a lot of material presented poetically, distilled. It's like philosophy. You don't have a line in philosophy that doesn't advance the argument or, in this case, the aesthetic feeling. It's got to justify itself in some way. Every paragraph has to do that, and not just in one way, in two or three ways. So I tend to throw out a lot of stuff. Probably about three thousand pages for *Dreamer*. I know it was about three thousand pages for *Middle Passage*. Scenes, approaches that just didn't really fit. Characters that didn't develop. Who knows? Out of one page you might have one sentence or one paragraph that's really useful, for this fiction or for something else. I mean, I got to the point in this novel where I'm following this character, this Kinglike character, Chaym Smith, and he starts shooting up. I didn't know he was going to do that. Where did I learn about shooting up? Well, that's in a novel, one of the first six I did in those first two years. I remembered that. I did the research before. I pulled out the drawer of my filing cabinet and there it was, everything I needed just for that one description. So I never throw stuff away, because it might be one little thing on a page. One image, one idea that'll make a lot of sense.

You know, there's a phrase in *Dreamer*, "isomers of the divine presence," that King uses when he's thinking about spiritual immanence. That was actually the title of the last three books of the six novels I wrote between 1970 and '72. It was a trilogy that ran 958 pages. That was the last three of the six I did in two years, and it was called *Isomers of God* because I was thinking about isomerization and spiritual things all at the same time. But that trilogy is in my filing cabinet. All I got out of it is that one little phrase in that particular chapter of *Dreamer*.

But the second of the six unpublished novels became Middle Passage?

Yes. The first one was actually called *The Last Liberation*. It was about a young black man, studying at a martial arts school like the one I was in when I was nineteen, and this whole other universe that opens up to him. You start with practice and you train the body, then you train the mind, train the spirit. And it was a first novel that just didn't work although I've returned to that subject, really, in short stories.

Like "China"?

"China" and a couple of other things that've moved beyond the original premise. It didn't work, but I do revisit some of the earlier subjects and themes with different characters. But I'm sure I'll never go back to the trilogy. It was about the childhood, adulthood, and middle age of a black musician. That's what that was about. Again, I used to write ten pages a day so I could do a novel in ten weeks, and they would go through three drafts. I didn't know how to really revise until I met Gardner, though. I'd just go back over the whole book again, from the start to the end. But the second book in that series was accepted by some little publisher here in New York, and I asked Gardner, while I was working on *Faith and the Good Thing*, Should I publish this book? I'd found a publisher. And the book was very different from *Faith and the Good Thing*. And he said, You know, if you think you'll ever have to climb over it, then you shouldn't do it. So I asked for it back. The reason that they liked it was because it sounded like James Baldwin. It was very Baldwinesque. Those were just sort of my models in the back of my mind—Baldwin, Richard Wright, John A. Williams, and so forth. And I took it back and I'm glad I did. It doesn't fit. It doesn't fit within the body of work that I want to develop. It was a good training novel, teaching me how to write. Do this and do that. But I didn't know enough about music to write something like that.

It seems extraordinarily patient for a young author to turn down an offer to publish.

Everybody's got this hunger to publish, as a writer, but I don't. I don't have a hunger to publish. I have a hunger to create certain things along the lines that I've been telling you about, but not just to publish for the sake of publishing.

Now, I was like that when I was a cartoonist. I was panting, as a teenager, to publish. Anything anywhere. And that's really why I started so early. I used to come here to New York and stay with my relatives in Brooklyn, and take my portfolio of drawings all around to the cartoon editors and comic book companies, but I couldn't really do much assignment work because I didn't live here and, again, I was fifteen, sixteen years old. But I had a hunger to publish as a cartoonist. Anywhere and everywhere. I did a lot of that. I published a thousand drawings, two books, and had a TV series by the time I was twenty-two, so basically the thrill was gone in terms of seeing my name in print. It's fine but you have to ask yourself, What am I publishing? What is it that my name is attached to? Is it something that I can hand to my kids and say, Well, this is about the best your dad has been able to make out of his journey through existence? That's the kind of book that means something to me. That's the only kind of book that I would want to put my name on and release to other people. So it's not about the hunger to publish. That doesn't mean much.

With *Dreamer*, I made a promise to Lee Goerner, my late editor, who passed away before the book was finished. I made a promise to Lee. I said, Lee, I'm going to do the best book I can for you, so my feeling now is, Okay, I think I did that.

All my duties are discharged. All my promises are kept. I don't owe anybody anything, for the first time in my life. Nobody, nothing, nowhere. Not to former teachers, not to parents, not to colleagues, not to students. Nobody, nowhere. It's a clean slate, so fifty, for me, basically means all my debts are discharged and I can do what I want. I've always done what I wanted to do, but I can do it a little bit differently now. Something may get moved to the side. It may be teaching. It just might be one of the balls I've been keeping up in the air for twenty-something years.

I noticed that writing wasn't one of those things that might get moved.

Oh no, never.

Do you know what the next novel will be?

No, I don't.

I read a piece on you that was written around the time of Middle Passage, *and you were already talking about King.*

I was. I was. This is how it happened. Lee said, What do you want to do next? I told him I'd been thinking about this short story I did on King and the issues that affect black people in America today, and looking back thirty years to recapture what the last few years of this man's life were like. So he called up the head of the company, whoever he was, and got an advance, and then we were rolling. But then I had to do the research. I didn't know the man. I just needed to immerse myself in King, while I was doing a bunch of other stuff right after the National Book Award. I was ready to start writing around '93. So the composition really took from '93 until September of 1997.

Is there a stage during the research when you're tempted to try and put words down or do you tell yourself, No, this is the research stage?

Well, all of '92 I just was reading King. I was going off to do promotion for *Middle Passage*, lectures and stuff, and I would take the King books with me, so it was all going on continuously. I was accumulating. Going to the King birth house. I'd been to the Lorraine before, in the eighties, so I didn't need to go back, but I was just sort of gathering things. Documents, film stuff on the Civil Rights movement. Letting all of that stuff come together until I was ready to write, and the first thing I was ready to write was the Prologue. I just sat down and wrote it. Unlike with other books, I was basically working from the seat of my pants. I had a model for everything else. *Faith and the Good Thing* was a folktale, *Oxherding Tale* was a slave narrative, and *Middle Passage* was a classic sea story. I had no model for this book, but the first thing that came to me was just that Prologue, just the feeling, and the feeling led me to where I needed to go.

I thought about this book, once, in terms of it being a classic gospel. You know, we have a whole tradition of literature written by monks writing to other monks about what you're doing with your life and how you should be a monk. I thought about that as a possible model, but finally I decided on this structure, the alternating first and third persons. But maybe it still is a gospel. It has a structure that resembles one long prayer, you know, ending with Amen. And so that's the form it took, but I really didn't have a literal model for this particular novel. I kind of like to play with forms, literary forms, because you learn so much from doing that. You bring in another aesthetic dimension from the nineteenth or eighteenth century and that's just a lot of fun. But I didn't really have that for this particular book.

It's not nearly as cut and dried a process as two years of research followed by five years of writing, is it?

No. I just finished a piece for a magazine called *Commonquest*, and there's stuff in there that's not in the novel because I was still thinking about King. I'm still thinking about the guy. I still read about him. I still try to improve my knowledge about who he was and what he represented. He really was a philosopher. In the past, you know, I might have a problem I'm writing about and I'd ask, What would Kant have to say about this, or What would Hegel say, but now it's pretty easy for me to say, What would King say about this? I have a sense now. Why did he say a particular thing? Well, I know why he said it. I think I understand a bit more about his intellectual foundation. That is now part of my literary repertoire. And I want to improve that understanding, to sharpen it. On this book tour, a guy gave me his Ph.D. dissertation and it's a philosophical analysis of "Letter from a Birmingham Jail." King is a philosopher and we should be talking about him in those terms, not just as a Civil Rights leader.

When you first started writing Dreamer, *you had King and you had the dop-
pelgänger, but didn't the story change? I read that with at least one of your
books you submitted an outline, but then the book changed.*

They all do. But the only book where I've submitted an outline is *Oxherding Tale*. It changed, over the years, from its original incarnations,
because you live with something for five years, it evolves as you evolve.
You start with one interest and three years later you may have a different interest, so the book has got to be capacious enough to contain your
own changing perceptions and emotions and desires.

*I guess maybe I'm having a hard time understanding the patience that allows
you to go through eight or nine drafts of a novel and still feel something's missing, that something's not exactly right. With* Oxherding Tale, *you went from
a black protagonist to a mulatto protagonist and then from a more or less
stereotypical slave owner to Flo Hatfield. I'm interested in that moment of
change. Whether it's measured by length of time or number of pages or emotional investment, how far are you into* Oxherding Tale *when you realize
the protagonist isn't black, he's mulatto?*

Oh, there was a point where I was ready to leave it alone and just move
on to something else. It was around Christmas. I didn't want another year
to begin with me looking at this book. I literally sat down, this is between
Christmas and New Year's, to give myself reasons for why this book was
impossible. I said, First of all, to me, the narrator is boring. He's a typical
black in the typical situation that a slave is in. As soon as I thought of
that—because this is the way imagination usually works, I try to tell my
students this a lot—I thought of a variation. Suppose he's mulatto? Ah.
All of sudden he belongs to both the white and the black world. He's
walking down this tightrope. He could fall either way, or be attacked from
either side. Okay. That's interesting. But no, no, no. I still don't like the
slavemaster. His name was Colonel Woofter, or something like that, and
he was just predictable. He did everything you ever thought a slavemaster should do from Simon Legree forward. But what if, I thought, he's a
woman? It's just a little thing, but all of a sudden a door opens up. So I
talked myself out of abandoning the novel. It was really the first of the

year, January, and I said, Okay, I'm going to go back over this novel and I'm going to look at these new possibilities and chase them.

And, I tell you, much the same thing happened with *Dreamer*, because you're right: At the very beginning I had the double and I had King. The last layer of this novel went on early last year. Sometimes things just happen serendipitously. They're just pure chance. You know, I did that Bill Moyers show called "Genesis," where a bunch of writers came in to talk about Cain and Abel. A little before I did that there was a Black Writers Conference at Claremont McKenna College, and Dr. Ricardo Quinones, who was the host, invited a bunch of people there. Shelby Steele was there and Walter Mosley, Ishmael Reed, and a few others, but as we were leaving he gave me a copy of his book, *The Changes of Cain*. It's the history of the character of Cain for two thousand years. And I said, I can't believe you gave me this. I've got a show to do and I don't know anything about the subject. This will help me.

I read a third of the book before the show and as we're sitting there, talking about Cain and Abel, I'm really getting interested in this story. I think I probably knew more than anybody else on that show because nobody else had time to do the research, or to prepare. So we're just kicking around ideas, but I'm really getting interested and thinking, What the hell does it mean that the first two brothers are characterized by envy and murder? Cain brings murder into the world. Well, I still hadn't connected the dots. The show was over and I went back to work on this book, and my agent saw the show and she had seen the drafts of *Dreamer* along the way, and she said, What about Cain and Abel? And I thought, Oh my God.

So Cain and Abel weren't there until a year ago?

Early last year. I said, Oh my God. And then I went back and finished Quinones's book. I looked at his sources. I went and read all these other stories about Cain and Abel, and it provided the *gestalt*, the glue between all the other elements. Chaym becomes Cain to King's Abel. It's all there. It's just all there. You know, sometimes writing is almost like the philosophical process. You're looking for that one last piece that will snap everything into focus so you've got a unified, organic whole.

Otherwise, I was basically developing the double as a kind of unedu-
cated guy, poor, from the south side of Chicago. I was having a really
hard time with the double learning so much about King. Well, Chaym
is way different. His problem is something else. It's a problem deep inside, one of faith. He's a mythic character. That gave me what I like to
have in the novel, which is a kind of myth dimension. Because the
other novels do have that as well.

I want to know, before the answer comes, before the change of protagonist in
Oxherding Tale *or before you get the Cain and Abel connection in* Dreamer,
do you feel dissatisfied? Do you feel like something's missing? Are you physi-
cally writing or are you taking a break, waiting for some kind of intervention?

I think doing both. On the one hand, you're working with the idea
you've got at the moment, to make it as good as you can, and the writing can actually be very elegant, but it's still not what you want and you
can feel that. Or, the other thing is, you just want to take a break for a
while and work on some other assignment. One thing that's nice about
having lots of assignments to work on is it's like being a poet. A poet
works on a poem, hits the wall, puts it in the drawer, writes another
poem, hits the wall, then puts that in the drawer and takes the first one
out, working on it with fresh eyes.

So the nonfiction does give you a break, a release?

It's like painters who work on several canvases. Ray Carver used to do
the same thing with short stories. He'd put one away for a little while
and work on a second one, and then six months later he'd pull the first
one out, because now he's got an idea for where it should go. So moving from one idea to the other can be very refreshing. A nonfiction
piece can do that, or an essay or a screenplay. It allows you to back off,
for a moment, from the intensity.

Now, when I got back on this book, I worked on it night and day
from July 1st to September 16th. That was it. I just told my family, Look,
I'm going to go into one of these phases. I'll be here but I won't really
be here, because I was just living it every day, because I wanted it done
for my fiftieth birthday. People say, Well, why is the book coming out

now? On the thirtieth anniversary of King's death? Well, that wasn't the reason. I wanted it done by my fiftieth birthday so I could say, Okay, the slate is clear. This is no longer on my "to do" board. That was the reason, so I worked on nothing else. I told people I couldn't work on anything else. I couldn't talk to them. Even friends. Actually, sometimes when I have a deadline on a screenplay, it has to be that way, too. I'll just sort of go into that mode. Night and day. Work on the book until I'm exhausted. Sleep. Work on the book. It's just all day long like that. But when it's a long project, like a novel of this sort, I think you have to have time where you back away and then come back to it. Where you have something else to refresh yourself. And there's a lot of things you do that people can't understand exactly why you're doing it.

I remember Lee called me one time as I was studying social Darwinism and he said, Why the hell are you studying social Darwinism? You're still working on the King book, right? And I said, Believe me. It's got something to do with it. I read five books on acting because I was thinking, The double. He's got to be trained. So I got to learn some stuff about that. That may amount to half a paragraph in what remains in the book.

I was talking to my friend and former student David Guterson about this when he dropped by over Christmas. He showed me what was in the trunk of his car. And it was some monograph, some academic paper from the forties on nursing that he needed for the book he was finishing up. We both started talking about how this is where the real fun is. You learn so much more than you're going to put in a project because you don't know what you're going to need to know. Then finally it just gets winnowed out and scaled down. Yeah, there's stuff that gets left on the side that you find very enriching, but I personally believe that, even though a reader may be enriched by a book, nobody's enriched like the writer is from having done it. All the things that you feel and have gone through and learn. That's the process. It's always intimidating with a novel, at least the way I like to do it, because I never know exactly what it's going to look like. I've often contradicted, at the end, everything I thought at the time I started it. It should be a process of discovery. If I don't learn, discover something that I didn't know before, I don't think the reader's going to have a sense of discovery. If there are no surprises for me, there won't be surprises for the reader. I'm convinced of that.

Let me ask you to do a comparison/contrast of the process of writing Oxherding Tale *and the process of writing* Dreamer. *I assume that you possessed a certain amount of faith, given your experience, while writing*
Dreamer, *that the answer's going to come. Did you have the same confidence
while you were writing* Oxherding Tale?

Well, there's a faith in the material. There's a belief in what you're doing.

What about faith in yourself?

Oh yeah, faith in yourself. Absolutely. The person I studied with, John
Gardner, was the most incredible writing teacher anybody could have.
The one thing that everybody I know who worked with John got from
John was the sense that, if you're willing to sweat, then you can write
greatly. You can write as greatly as the great literature of the past. And
he could get you excited about the great literature of the past as well. If
you were willing to work hard, and long enough, then you will achieve
what you want to do. So it's not a matter of ever doubting yourself,
because the wonderful thing about writing is you can rewrite. That's
90 percent of it. That's where the real joy is, as far as I'm concerned, going over something again and again. It's like sculpture. It gets more refined. It gets tighter. It's more precise. There's a greater fusion between
sound and sense. The cadence of the line and the meaning of the line.
That's where the real art comes in. Naturally you have to have faith in
yourself, but that's not a hard stretch, because as long as you have faith
in your capacity to work, it's going to come together.

*Gardner is known as one of the great creative writing teachers, but there is
that question about whether or not writing can be taught. If creative writing
can't be taught, then what did Gardner give? What can a teacher do for his
or her students?*

He can't teach somebody imagination. I mean, a student's got to bring
that himself. You can teach technique, and Gardner was actually quite
good about that. You know, in *The Art of Fiction*, all of those exercises
in the back? My students have done those since I first started teaching.
Maybe not all of them every quarter but at least two-thirds of them.

The other thing John taught was a passion, and he communicated that almost without even consciously teaching it. You just looked at how this man was working. You looked at his love of literature. He had a self-sacrificial capacity to give everything to the work. And once you got that sense, you could apply it to your own. And it should work this way. Once you're willing to go over something, like Hemingway, twenty times. Twenty times, we're told, he went over that last page in *The Sun Also Rises*. If you're willing to do that, then you can achieve the perfection that you're after. At least to your own satisfaction. It's just a matter of sweat. That's all it is. It doesn't even have to be a matter of brilliance.

The amount of sweat that must go into an eight-year project. I know you've been working on a lot of other things, but you've published a novel every eight years since '74.

Is that right?

Faith and the Good Thing *in '74,* Oxherding Tale *in '82,* Middle Passage *in '90, and* Dreamer *in '98. Of course, I have to stick with the novels. I have to throw out* Sorcerer's Apprentice *in order to make it work.*

The stories in *Sorcerer* were written between '77 and probably '83.

While we're here, have you done much short story writing lately?

I haven't really had a chance, though I would like to put a collection together. I was talking to my agent about that. I've got twelve stories that I wrote in January that'll be in a textbook that evolved from a TV series called "Africans in America." The show will premiere in October of 1998 on PBS. The producer is Orlando Bagwell, a very distinguished man, I think, and the series, in four parts, four one-and-a-half-hour shows, will cover history from the slave trade all the way up to the Civil War.

For myself, to make it an interesting assignment, I wanted each one of those to be in a different form, literary form. I don't recommend anyone writing twelve stories in one month, but I couldn't do them until I got all of this work out of the way for *Dreamer*. Then there are occasional stories, here and there, that I've published in various places. There's enough for a new collection.

Backing up to the novel every eight years and the sweat that goes into it, the time that goes into it and the "totalness" that you mentioned before. What are you like on the day you finish?

Exhausted. Totally exhausted.

It's more of a drained feeling than a celebratory one?

Well, there's a deep satisfaction, a feeling of, okay, that is done, but it's like feeling empty. Somebody once told me that after Ralph Ellison finished *Invisible Man*, which he spent seven years on, he just took to his bed for a couple of weeks, like he'd just given a very difficult birth. And I always think about that at the end of a long piece because, for me, a novel has to be everything. If it isn't everything, then I don't want to read it, let alone write it. There's a real feeling of exhaustion, but it's a good exhaustion, almost like a Zen emptiness, if you will. It's like in that one work is everything I could feel. And it's all externalized.

When I was a kid, the thing that used to fascinate me about drawing, more than anything else, was the way I felt, or thought, which nobody else could see. I could draw, and it was externalized on the page. And once it was externalized, I was free of it in a certain kind of way. I could move on to something else. I feel much the same way about a novel. When I write a novel, I literally have to go dead to the last novel. And when I say dead, I mean dead. It's like I never did it. I forget about it. I don't want to repeat the characters. I don't want to repeat the themes, but nevertheless that stuff still creeps in and you still find overlaps. That'll happen, but I have to say to myself, I've never written a novel before. I'm starting from scratch, and I don't know what a novel is, and that's the way I approach it. Each novel I write has to be aesthetically different. Different in style and form and in its philosophical explanations.

For me, it really isn't a careerist or commercial kind of a thing. I wouldn't write fiction if that's why I had to do it. There's things I want to see in existence, and there are things in me that I want to see externalized, too, but other than that I wouldn't do it.

I don't know of anyone who would accuse you of writing fiction for purely commercial reasons. I would think that the simple fact of only coming out with a novel every eight years is enough to dispel that argument. If you were in it for commercial reasons, then you would've had a book out in '91 or '92, and probably your publisher would've been thrilled to be able to follow up so quickly on Middle Passage *and the National Book Award.*

The question is, What kind of book would it have been?

I make money other ways. I teach, and have for twenty-something years. I don't have to rely on art for money. I think you compromise art when you do that. It happens very, very often. I won't mention any particular names, but I've seen it happen, and that's a sad thing. It's sad for the art and it's sad for the culture in the long run. It isn't a contribution to literature.

I was thinking before when you were talking about reusing characters. You know I just finished interviewing Russell Banks and he's a real threat to get those tie-ins in there, like the twins who miss the bus in The Sweet Here-after *end up living in that same bus in* Rule of the Bone.

Is that right?

And I noticed that Chaym Smith's lineage can be traced back to Baleka from Middle Passage.

It's better than that. You know the apartment where Smith lives? That he sets fire to?

On Indiana Avenue?

Yeah, that's exactly where Bigger Thomas lived in *Native Son*. And Smith's landlady, Vera Thomas? That's Bigger's big sister. She's been living there all these years. She gives him the room. And the optic white? The paint that he uses? You know that, right?

Invisible Man.

Right. Certainly those little things that pop up like that are fun but only for literate people.

The Allmuseri tribe has appeared in all your fiction since Oxherding Tale. *How did they come about?*

Just by chance. I started a story called "The Education of Mingo," published in 1977, and I needed a tribe. I just needed a tribe for this boy from Africa. I read something like eighty books on magic for *Faith and the Good Thing* when I was writing it, and in one of the books it said there was this little place in this African village called an Allmuseri. It was a hut, and magic went on in there. So I just copied that down in my notebook, you know, and I came back to it, and I said, Okay, this guy's got to be from a tribe. I think they're described as being a mystical tribe. And I needed another tribe in another story so I just said, Allmuseri.

The title story in Sorcerer's Apprentice.

Yeah, the first story and the last one. Right. And then, with *Oxherding Tale*, I didn't want to designate a particular tribe, so I used the Allmuseri again. I developed Reb along these very spiritual lines, really Taoist. With him, the Allmuseri became more spiritual in its characteristics. So with *Middle Passage*, one of things I wanted to do was just to develop a tribe, top to bottom. Who's their god? What are their rituals? Where do they live? The whole thing. That was actually one of the fun things to do. It's interesting. People still think they're a real tribe. A guy I met in Memphis asked me if they were still living in Africa.

You could have sold me on it.

I'm glad because I didn't make that stuff up. It's all culled from real so-called Third World peoples—India, China, Africa, too—so none of it's made up, but there was just never a tribe like that. So that's how it evolved over time, and I like to play with them that way, in the story, if it fits. I thought about making King an Allmuseri, but I thought that would be pushing it a little too far.

Let's talk about the Book, the Book with a capital B in "Moving Pictures."

That's actually a story about Buddhist epistemology. No one ever gets that.

That story is probably the least appreciated story of the collection.

I guess so. I guess so. I don't think people get it. They think it's just about a writer looking at the movie he's written, but it's about Buddhist epistemology. Some Buddhist commentators and writers use that screen, the movie screen, to talk about consciousness and the way thoughts and ideas and emotions are projected on it.

Is it ever frustrating to be reviewed by people, who by definition know less about what you're doing than you do? Do you read your reviews?

I do, just to see if you come across somebody who's really smart, and there are some smart people out there. I like to see the elegance of a really good reviewer. The reason I started reviewing is because I thought the state of it was really kind of bad in respect to black American writers.

Did you go into it hesitantly? Did you feel you might be crossing a line?

Not really, because there is a kind of literary review that isn't just a book review. The kind that John Gardner used to do. It's almost like a critique. It's the occasion for a critique, and you get an aesthetic. A theory sort of emerges from the review itself, and that's exciting, to me, as literary journalism. Not just a book review, because that's not interesting. But, for example, when I can do a piece on Albert Murray, who I've admired for years, and they give me his novel and his essay collection, then I get to deal with a contemporary writer who I greatly respect. You know what I'm saying? To try and let other people see what is a very nice work. To show them.

Do you only write about novels or writers that you're fond of?

No, sometimes they'll send me somebody that's a turkey, and at some point you've got to say it's a turkey. You have to look at it in terms of not imposing my own aesthetic on it, but to see what the logic of the book is from the inside, what its goals and ambitions are, and then see if it succeeds or fails on those terms. That's the better way to do it, and to quote liberally from the book so readers can see the real prose and the ideas and come to their own judgment, which might be different from the reviewer's. I think that's very important. You had another question, though, prior to that one.

I want to ask about the Book, with the capital B. Probably it's most specific reference is in "Moving Pictures." As in, "You'd shelved the novel, the Big Book, for bucks monitored by the Writers Guild."

That's just some writer working on a book who decides to go do screenplays and not write fiction anymore.

What about Evelyn Pomeroy, the writer in Oxherding Tale? *She's struggling with her work. The guy in "Moving Pictures" has already lost his battle.*

Yeah, he's not going to make it. Evelyn Pomeroy is working on a novel, fairly imitative, if I'm not mistaken, of Harriet Beecher Stowe.

The Stowe part is interesting but I think, in a way, Evelyn Pomeroy can be taken a bit more universally than possibly you intended. "Every year past the publication date of her first book cemented her silence, confirmed the suspicions of critics—and Evelyn Pomeroy herself—that the magic had been a mistake that first time. A fluke." I think that applies to a lot of writers, though you also write, "none of this candies over the fact that Evelyn Pomeroy was crazy."

Eighty percent of first novelists never publish their second. That's a Gardner quote. Eighty percent of first novelists do not publish a second novel. Everybody thinks their first novel is the really important one to do, but it's really the second novel.

Is it telling that Charles Johnson is writing about a woman's difficulties writing her second novel within his second novel?

Yeah, those are thoughts that you have. As a matter of fact, that's probably why I decided this second novel had to be something I truly believed in. It's not just a second novel. This says, This is who you are. You have an aesthetic. There's something you do that nobody else does. And that's very important, I think, for a writer to realize, but still, the point of the matter is, the second novel is more important than the first in an artist's career. The first one could be a fluke. There are a lot of first novelists who do not publish second novels.

Even though Evelyn is a comic character, even though she's crazy, I take her and her problem imitating Harriet Beecher Stowe seriously. I understand what she's going through. She has to have a love-hate relationship with Stowe. Something along the lines of, Look what you've done to my work.

Well, if you'd like, it's a Cain-Abel relationship. I hadn't thought about that in terms of Harriet because I haven't thought about *Oxherding Tale* in a long time, but there is that with Chaym and King. He can't do what King does, and I kind of tell you why that is in that novel. A lot of it has to do with faith and so forth, but this is different. This is art. But that's a Cain-Abel relationship, clearly, even though it's between two women.

Writers need good models. Everybody needs good models. They should have the best models. But more important than that is individual vision. More important than that is how you find individual vision within a tradition.

Isn't that tough for a young writer to find?

I think it's enormously tough, because vision comes with experience. It sounds like a cliché. The point of the matter is, that is what's hard to teach. You tell your students, You must find your own individual voice and vision. That's what you have to do. And finding that, sustaining that, breaking away from the models, which by virtue, actually, of finding your own voice, you might honor in terms of their influence on you. As a matter of fact, I'm thinking of King and there's a connection. I'm thinking of the sources for King, and where they were pulled from. Other ministers and stuff. Everything comes from the world in one way or another. It can be argued even that no one's work arises *ex nihilo*, from the egg, original, but it's how you bring all these things together and interpret them. And then you find the instrument for the expression of that vision. And that's why I think it's interesting to go from genre to genre in literary forms. Because each one can be a different vehicle for a vision, for modulating your vision in different ways. Read my book *Being & Race*, the part on phenomenological aesthetics. You go from screenplays to essays to fiction, and each one, again, is a different vehicle that bodies forth the vision in an entirely different form. And that's discovery and the efflorescence of meaning. But you cannot think in commercial terms to do that, because commercial terms are always, What was successful yesterday? That's what we want today.

Your admiration for Toomer, Wright, and Ellison have been duly noted. Did your admiration, when you were a younger writer, cost you anything?

Well, like I said, I wrote six books before *Faith and the Good Thing*. I had models in my mind. It wasn't so much Toomer then as the naturalistic writers, because my early novels were very naturalistic books. I felt there were dimensions of human experience I couldn't get to through naturalism. When I got to *Faith*, that's when I began to feel at least comfortable with the experiential possibilities of the characters in the novel, because, you know, it's magic, it's spiritual stuff, it's philosophy, it's folklore. All the kinds of things that I really delight in. The tale. I like the tale as a literary form because I heard them as a kid. There, for me, is when I began to get a handle on, at least for myself, what my individual aesthetic/philosophical vision was, a blend of East and West, phenomenology and Buddhism. But that still had to be improved and refined over time. When I wrote that book, it wasn't refined.

My kids have had a big impact on the way I think about, and look at, the world. I think, probably, how I feel about my kids and so forth is what I invested King with, when he's talking about Dexter and little Marty. It's just the way a father feels. So, as you go along, what you see and what you feel deepens. It's a funny thing. We talk about individual vision, but the truth belongs to everybody finally. It's not like this is your truth. It belongs to all of us.